Paris 2008

WHAT'S NEW | WHAT'S ON | WHAT'S BEST

www.timeout.com/paris

Contents

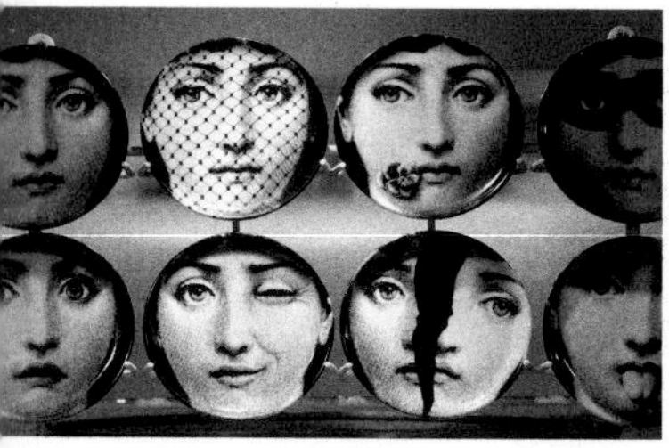

Don't Miss: 2008

Itineraries

Paris by Area

Essentials

Published by Time Out Guides Ltd
Universal House
251 Tottenham Court Road
London W1T 7AB
Tel: + 44 (0)20 7813 3000
Fax: + 44 (0)20 7813 6001
Email: guides@timeout.com
www.timeout.com

Managing Director Peter Fiennes
Editorial Director Ruth Jarvis
Deputy Series Editor Dominic Earle
Business Manager Gareth Garner
Editorial Manager Holly Pick
Accountant Ija Krasnikova

Time Out Guides is a wholly owned subsidiary of Time Out Group Ltd.

Chairman Tony Elliott
Financial Director Richard Waterlow
Time Out Magazine Ltd MD David Pepper
Group General Manager/Director Nichola Coulthard
Managing Director, Time Out International Cathy Runciman
Time Out Communications Ltd MD David Pepper
Production Director Mark Lamond
Group Marketing Director John Luck
Group Art Director John Oakey
Group IT Director Simon Chappell

Time Out and the Time Out logo are trademarks of Time Out Group Ltd.

This edition first published in Great Britain in 2007 by Ebury Publishing
A Random House Group Company
Company information can be found on www.randomhouse.co.uk
10 9 8 7 6 5 4 3 2 1

For further distribution details, see www.timeout.com

ISBN 13: 978184670 0262
ISBN 10: 1-84670-026-4

A CIP catalogue record for this book is available from the British Library

Printed and bound by Firmengruppe APPL, aprinta druck, Wemding, Germany

The Random House Group Limited makes every effort to ensure that the papers used in our books are made from trees that have been legally sourced from well-managed and credibly certified forests. Our paper procurement policy can be found on www.randomhouse.co.uk

Paris Shortlist

The **Time Out Paris Shortlist 2008** is one of a new series of annual guides that draws on Time Out's background as a magazine publisher to keep you current with what's going on in town. As well as Paris's key sights and the best of its eating, drinking and leisure options, it picks out the most exciting venues to have opened in the last year and gives a full calendar of events from September 2007 to December 2008. It also includes features on the important news, trends and openings, all compiled by locally based editors and writers. Whether you're visiting for the first time in your life or the first time this year, you'll find the *Time Out Paris Shortlist 2008* contains all you need to know, in a portable and easy-to-use format.

The guide divides central Paris into ten areas, each containing listings for Sights & Museums, Eating & Drinking, Shopping, Nightlife and Arts & Leisure, and maps pinpointing their locations. At the front of the book are chapters rounding up these scenes city-wide, and giving a shortlist of our overall picks for 2008. We include itineraries for days out, plus essentials such as transport information and hotels.

Our listings give phone numbers as dialled within France. From abroad, use your country's exit code followed by 33 (the country code for France) and the number given, dropping the initial 0.

We have noted price categories by using one to four euro signs (€-€€€€), representing budget, moderate, expensive and luxury options. Major credit cards are accepted unless otherwise stated. We also indicate when a venue is NEW, and give **Event highlights**.

All our listings are double-checked, but places do sometimes close or change their hours or prices, so it's a good idea to call a venue before visiting. While every effort has been made to ensure accuracy, the publishers cannot accept responsibility for any errors that this guide may contain.

Venues are marked on the maps using symbols numbered according to their order within the chapter and colour-coded as follows:

- ❶ Sights & Museums
- ❶ Eating & Drinking
- ❶ Shopping
- ❶ Nightlife
- ❶ Arts & Leisure

Map key

- **Major sight or landmark**
- **Hospital or college**
- **Railway station**
- **Park**
- **River**
- **Autoroute**
- **Main road**
- **Main road tunnel**
- **Pedestrian road**
- **Arrondissement boundary**
- **Airport**
- **Church**
- **Métro station** Ⓜ
- **RER station**
- **Area name** LES HALLES

Time Out Paris Shortlist 2008

EDITORIAL
Editor Simon Cropper
Copy Editor Emma Howarth
Proofreader Gill Harvey

DESIGN
Art Director Scott Moore
Art Editor Pinelope Kourmouzoglou
Senior Designer Henry Elphick
Graphic Designer Gemma Doyle
Junior Graphic Designer Kei Ishimaru
Digital Imaging Simon Foster, Tessa Kar
Ad Make-up Jodi Sher
Picture Editor Jael Marschner
Deputy Picture Editor Tracey Kerrigan
Picture Researcher Helen McFarland

ADVERTISING
Sales Director/Sponsorship Mark Phillips
International Sales Manager Fred Durman
International Sales Consultant Ross Canadé
International Sales Executive Charlie Sokol
Advertising Assistant Kate Staddon

MARKETING
Marketing Manager Yvonne Poon
Sales & Marketing Director, North America Lisa Levinson
Marketing Designer Anthony Huggins

PRODUCTION
Production Manager Brendan McKeown
Production Co-ordinator Caroline Bradford
Production Controller Susan Whittaker

CONTRIBUTORS
This guide was researched and written by Peterjon Cresswell, Alison Culliford, Natasha Edwards, Tina Isaac, Rosa Jackson, David McKenna, Ron Pasas and the writers of *Time Out Paris*.

PHOTOGRAPHY
All photography by Jean-Christophe Godet, except: pages 7, 8, 11, 13, 17, 18, 23, 24, 25, 27, 53, 73, 93, 114, 124, 126, 136, 141, 157, 158 Karl Blackwell; pages 12, 29, 80, 84, 88, 102, 103, 107, 109, 110, 134, 147, 148, 149 Oliver Knight; pages 33, 41, 45, 47, 83, 90, 114, 116, 129, 137 Heloise Bergman; page 39 Laurent Zylbermann; page 46 Eric Laignel; page 120 Britta Jaschinski; page 160 Larrayadieu Eric/CRT IDF.

The following images were provided by the featured establishments/artists: pages 50, 79, 89, 105, 151, 162, 163, 164, 169, 179.

Cover photograph: Métro, Paris. Credit: Photolibrary.com

MAPS
JS Graphics (john@jsgraphics.co.uk).

Thanks to Yuko Aso, Simon Coppock.

About Time Out

Founded in 1968, Time Out has expanded from humble London beginnings into the leading resource for those wanting to know what's happening in the world's greatest cities. As well as our influential what's-on weeklies in London, New York and Chicago, we publish more than a dozen other listings magazines in cities as varied as Beijing and Mumbai. The magazines established Time Out's trademark style: sharp writing, informed reviewing and bang up-to-date inside knowledge of every scene.

Time Out made the natural leap into travel guides in the 1980s with the City Guide series, which now extends to over 50 destinations around the world. Written and researched by expert local writers and generously illustrated with original photography, the full-size guides cover a larger area than our Shortlist guides and include many more venue reviews, along with additional background features and a full set of maps.

Throughout this rapid growth, the company has remained proudly independent, still owned by Tony Elliott nearly four decades after he started Time Out London as a single fold-out sheet of A5 paper. This independence extends to the editorial content of all our publications, this Shortlist included. No establishment has been featured because it has advertised, and no payment has influenced any of our reviews. And, for our critics, there's definitely no such thing as a free lunch: all restaurants and bars are visited and reviewed anonymously, and Time Out always picks up the bill. For more about the company, see www.timeout.com.

Don't Miss 2008

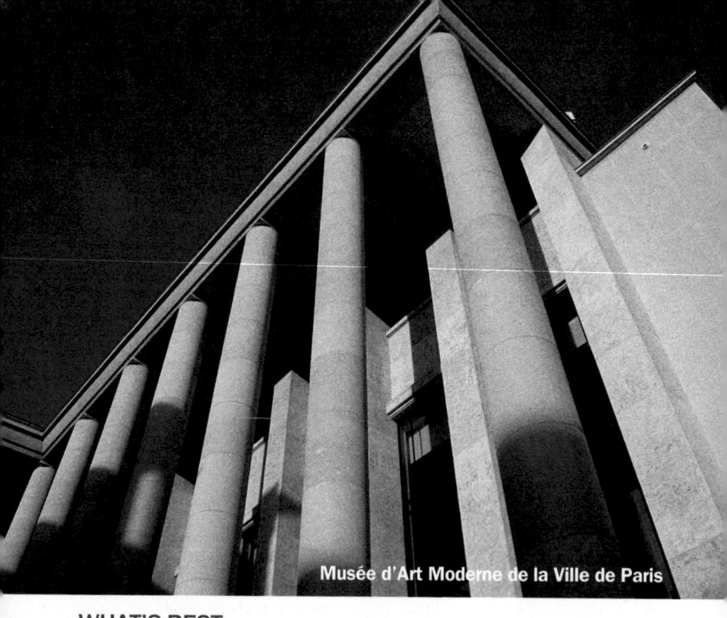
Musée d'Art Moderne de la Ville de Paris

WHAT'S BEST

Sights & Museums

Nicolas Sarkozy's decisive win in the presidential elections of May 2007 has given French pundits no end of opportunity to trumpet 'a new era', though estimates of the social cost of his promised barrage of reform vary wildly. He seems to have a firm grasp of the economy brief, but with matters cultural it's quite the reverse: even during his campaign, commentators wondered where the arts fitted into his vision of a reinvigorated France. It's now widely assumed that the dynamic politico many are comparing to Napoleon has none of that great reformer's appetite for grand cultural gestures (or, indeed, culture); he'll put no Mitterrand-style imprimatur to spectacular *grands projets*.

As it turns out, Paris's most recent *grand projet* was due not to Mitterrand but to his successor Jacques Chirac. Launched in summer 2006, the Musée du Quai Branly (p125) is a museum of non-Western arts in specially built premises by Jean Nouvel near the Eiffel Tower. The museum amalgamates the defunct Musée des Arts d'Afrique et d'Océanie and the ethnology collections of the Musée de l'Homme, and its impressively wide reach takes in Dogon and Gabonese sculpture, Vietnamese and Peruvian costumes, masks from Cameroon and a great deal more.

The Musée de l'Homme has stayed put in the Palais de Chaillot, but got two new neighbours in

2006 and 2007: the first, CinéAqua (p55), is a slick, modern aquarium and three-screen cinema, and the newer arrival, the long-awaited Cité de l'Architecture et du Patrimoine (p5), occupies a vast space in the eastern wing and abounds in fascinating architectural models, some at life size.

If high-profile newcomers like these are rare in Paris (and, under Sarkozy, likely to stay that way), the last couple of years have brought a stream of renovations at several major museums: the Musée des Arts Décoratifs (p67), Musée de l'Orangerie (p67), Musée d'Art Moderne de la Ville de Paris (p59) and Musée du Petit Palais (p59). Just across the road from the latter, the Grand Palais (p59) has also emerged from a period of extensive renovation looking absolutely magnificent.

Still, the new and revamped are just a fraction of what Paris has to offer: this is, after all, the home of the Louvre (p67), alone worth several museums elsewhere. The Louvre, too, like a colossal work in progress, has been progressively finessed in recent years, most notably with the opening in 2005 of a new gallery for the Mona Lisa.

In other parts of Paris, the sightseeing list is almost endless – from defining monuments like the Eiffel Tower (p122) to lesser-known but entirely cherishable museums like the Musée de la Vie Romantique (p84). Even the city's largest attraction, the Seine, is enjoying something of a renaissance lately, with the annual Paris Plage jamboree now taking place on both banks, a new floating swimming pool (p163) and regular cycle- and rollerskate-only days along the riverside roads in the city centre. All this, and far more that we haven't yet mentioned, can be enjoyed in a

SHORTLIST

Best new
- CinéAqua (p55)
- Cité de l'Architecture et du Patrimoine (p55)

Best revamped
- Galeries Nationales du Grand Palais (p59)
- Musée d'Art Moderne de la Ville de Paris (p59)
- Musée de la Chasse (p101)
- Musée de l'Orangerie (p67)

Best secret
- Les Egouts de Paris (p122)
- Musée de la Vie Romantique (p84)
- Promenade Plantée (p101)

Best art
- Centre Pompidou (p97)
- Musée Carnavalet (p100)
- Musée du Louvre (p67)
- Musée d'Orsay (p134)
- Musée National Picasso (p101)

Best dead
- Cimetière du Montparnasse (p155)
- Cimetière du Père-Lachaise (p97)

Best tours
- Bateaux-Mouches (p55)
- Canauxrama (p90)
- Vedettes du Pont-Neuf (p114)

Best outdoors
- Jardin du Luxembourg (p132)
- Jardin des Tuileries (p67)
- Palais-Royal (p70)

Best views
- Arc de Triomphe (p54)
- Eiffel Tower (p122)
- Notre-Dame de Paris (p117)
- Parc des Buttes Chaumont (p92)
- Sacré-Coeur (p84)
- Tour Montparnasse (p156)

city that's of manageable size and, into the bargain, blessed with one of the finest transport networks anywhere in the world.

Neighbourhoods

Paris residents think of their city in terms of two systems: the named districts – the Marais, the Latin Quarter, Beaubourg and so on – and the arrondissements. The former tend to have uncertain boundaries. The latter, numbering 20, are fixed administrative districts that spiral out, clockwise and in ascending order, from the Louvre. Together, they make a jigsaw puzzle compared by novelist Julien Green to medical models of the human brain, and each piece has its connotations. 5th: intellectual. 6th: chic. 16th: affluent and stuffy. 18th, 19th, 20th: lively and multicultural. Rightly or wrongly, residents are often assessed, at least on first meeting, by their postcodes – and many say that Paris is not a city but a coagulation of villages.

We've divided this book up into areas – not necessarily in the shapes that a resident would think of, but a visitor-friendly collections of shops, sights, restaurants and bars. The Champs-Elysées & Western Paris section has as its spine the famous avenue, lined with shops and concept stores; it also includes fashion's glammest thoroughfare, avenue Montaigne, and its second glammest, rue du Faubourg-Saint-Honoré. Montmartre & Pigalle has, at its northern end, picturesque Montmartre with its steep flights of steps, narrow windy streets and iconic Sacré-Coeur; and, to the south, Pigalle, famous for the Moulin Rouge, strip clubs and scuzzy bars, though now a far cleaner act than it was, say, 20 years ago. Opéra to Les Halles

Musée du Petit Palais p9

covers much of the city's shopping heartland, as well as its biggest cultural hitter, the Louvre – ably supported by the Palais Garnier (p82) and the Musée de l'Orangerie (p67). There's no shortage of history, either: take a stroll around the pretty and newly fashionable Palais-Royal (p70) to see what we're referring to.

North-eastern Paris is the part of the city visitors from the UK are likely to see first: here, at the Gare du Nord, is where Eurostar trains terminate. The area is bisected by the charming Canal St-Martin, the length of which is a steadily up-and-coming stretch of hip little cafés and fashion boutiques; further east is the Parc des Buttes Chaumont (p92), with its grottoes and romantic bridge. Marais, Bastille & Eastern Paris is barfly territory, especially along rue Oberkampf and rue Jean-Pierre-Timbaud. The

Marais itself is the city's gay heartland, but is also terminally trendy, seething with art galleries and dinky little purveyors of foodstuffs and accessories.

The Islands – Ile de la Cité, oldest part of the city, home to Notre-Dame cathedral, and the quieter Ile St-Louis, home to shops and restaurants – are unlike any other parts of the city, and should not be overlooked.

The star attraction of the affluent 7th & Western Paris area is the Eiffel Tower (p122), the monument most people think of when they hear the word Paris. Always elegant, it's prettiest after dark, when the tens of thousands of flashbulbs attached to it give the effect of a shimmering sequinned dress. Night is also the best time to ascend the Tower, when queues are at their shortest. St-Germain-des-Prés is, in popular mythology, the intellectual bit of the city, famous for Sartre and co. These days it's more a pillar of fashion, and the cafés are expensive. But the city's loveliest park, the Jardin du Luxembourg (p132) is here, and it costs nothing; and the Musée d'Orsay (p134), though not free, is still terrific value. To the east, the Latin Quarter is where several of the city's academic institutions are based – and, in pleasing contrast, home to some of its jazz institutions. South of here is Montparnasse, no longer the artistic stronghold of the 1920s, but good for cafés and the dead – the Cimetière Montparnasse is home to some of France's most illustrious deceased.

Musée des Arts Décoratifs p9

Making the most of it

Invest in a Mobilis travel pass (p183) and travel cash-free through the city by bus and métro. The Paris métro is a world champion among public transport networks and merits a ride in its own right (especially on the driverless line 14); the local buses are clean, frequent and cheap. Some good bus routes to try just for their sightseeing opportunies are 24, which takes you through St-Germain-des-Prés and the Latin Quarter; 29, which goes through the Marais; and 73, which runs up the Champs-Elysées and beyond to the concrete jungle of La Défense.

But in the main, you just can't beat walking. Your best chance of hearing this city's heartbeat lies in putting one foot in front of the other, above ground, among the people who live and work here; only then will you be able to see the 'museum city' clichés for what they are. Paris is alive, thriving: joyous proof that a city can love the trappings of the contemporary world without forgetting – or fossilising – its past.

L'Ami Jean

WHAT'S BEST

Eating & Drinking

Paris might take some flak for having a less dynamic dining scene than other world capitals, but in this city, dynamic is not really the point. Change occurs slowly and thoughtfully, and the current buzzword, *bistronomique* (a meld of *bistro* and *gastronomique*), describes a ten-year-old trend. And what does that matter, if there's still great food to be had? There are still plenty of chefs who take real pride in their work – though the chances of finding them by accident seem to be dwindling, as more and more cooks rely on such shortcuts as pre-prepared sauces and desserts.

Among the best *bistronomiques*, which put a modern spin on French classics, are Le Temps au Temps (p108) and La Cerisaie (p135), and the well-established Le Pré Verre (p150), Chez Michel (p92) and L'Ami Jean (p126); newcomer Le Chateaubriand (p104) pushes the boundaries of French bistro cooking in a buzzy setting. Another rapidly emerging trend is the Anglo-style snack shop, such as Cojean (17 bd Haussmann, 9th, 01.47.70.22.65; several branches), which serves sandwiches, soups and salads, and the organic Bioboa (3 rue Danielle-Casanova, 1st, 01.42. 61.17.67). The Anglo-French Rose Bakery (46 rue des Martyrs, 9th, 01.42.82.12.80) has shown Parisians that the British know a thing or two about food, and the chic bakery-deli Bread & Roses (p135) is run by a Frenchman with a passion for the best of British nosh.

Paris's ongoing gentrification means that the previously sleepy 9th arrondissement is booming with new restaurants that are opening up to feed the young professionals settling here. One of the best is Spring (p87), run by American chef Daniel Rose, who cooks a single, no-choice menu every night. Meanwhile, the 10th and 11th continue to be the most happening areas for bars. Nothing has yet managed to surpass the Café Charbon (p103) or the nearby bars that have since set up around it – Au P'tit Garage (p103), La Mercerie (p107), L'Alimentation Générale (p102) – for excitement. Yet the burgeoning hub north-west of the Marais boasts De La Ville Café (p72) – from the same stable as Charbon – and Pigalle now has the stylish Hôtel Amour (p173) all-night bar. The rough and ready La Chapelle area, meanwhile, is home to the city's only ice bar, in the Kube hotel (p173).

For those with deep pockets, the city's other thumping party precinct is on the Champs-Elysées and surrounding streets. Written off as the height of naff less than a decade ago, today the area draws in the city's designer-clad youth, aristos, socialites and young execs. If you're curious, see what's happening at the surprisingly smart Culture Bière (p62), a new venture from Heineken.

Then there are the old-school pleasures. The city's gorgeous Belle Epoque brasseries, including Bofinger (p103) in the Bastille, pull multi-generational families, hand-holding couples and tourists looking for a taste of history. The Flo chain serves reliable (if not outstanding) food, whereas standards are variable at other brasseries – if in doubt, stick to the seafood and simple dishes. Another gift from the Belle Epoque is the haute cuisine tradition, which

SHORTLIST

Best new
- Le Brébant (p86)
- La Cerisaie (p156)
- Le Chateaubriand (p104)
- Les Ombres (p130)
- Le Petit Pamphlet (p107)
- Spring (p87)
- Le Temps au Temps (p108)

Best value
- Le Baron Rouge (p103)
- Chez Jean (p86)
- Crêperie Bretonne Fleurie (p104)
- L'Encrier (p105)

Most glamorous
- Alain Ducasse au Plaza Athénée (p60)
- L'Atelier de Joël Robuchon (p135)
- Café de la Paix (p72)
- La Coupole (p156)
- Lapérouse (p149)
- Senderens (p75)
- Taillevent (p63)

Bars with character
- Le Bar Dix (p135)
- Café Charbon (p103)
- Le Piano Vache (p150)

Cocktail hour
- Alcazar (p135)
- China Club (p104)
- Le Fumoir (p72)

Nighthawk territory
- La Perle (p107)
- Au P'tit Garage (p103)
- Le Sancerre (p87)
- Le Tambour (p76)

Regional cuisine
- L'Ambassade d'Auvergne (p102)
- L'Ami Jean (p126)
- Aux Lyonnais (p71)
- Au Pied de Cochon (p71)
- Chez Michel (p92)
- D'Chez Eux (p130)
- Granterroirs (p62)

Le Chateaubriand p13

blossomed as the city's newly wealthy bourgeoisie thrilled to elaborate meals served in lavish settings. Taillevent (p63) is a perfect example of this tradition in terms of setting, service and impeccable haute cuisine cooking.

Still, before you spend a week's salary at a high-end restaurant, consider what's important to you. Some of the best bistros and contemporary restaurants serve cooking of comparable skill and quality, albeit using fewer costly ingredients. Unless you're looking for an all-out luxe experience – where you're made to feel like royalty for a few hours – a visit to an haute cuisine restaurant might not be so vital. Remember, too, that most of these restaurants offer more affordable lunch menus (though keep an eye on the cost of extras like aperitifs, wine and coffee). If haute cuisine does appeal (and it's worth having at least once in a lifetime), L'Astrance (4 rue Beethoven, 16th, 01.40.50.84.40) and Le Meurice (p75) are two sure bets at the moment, while Pierre Gagnaire (p136) caters to cutting-edge tastes.

Bear in mind that even haute cuisine regulars enjoy the convivial bistro experience. However, classic examples serving hearty French grub are now rather thin on the ground, as more chefs trade in butter for olive oil – but you can count on Chez Dumonet Joséphine (117 rue du Cherche-Midi, 6th, 01.45.48.52.40) or Chez La Vieille (37 rue de l'Arbre-Sec, 1st, 01.42.60.15.78) to dish up giant helpings of boeuf bourguignon and veal rib steak, followed by huge desserts.

All in all, though it's easy to grumble about mean salads and indifferent croque-monsieurs served in touristy cafés, this is still a city that worships food – as proved by its 90 or so markets and hundreds of specialist food shops. The new generation of bistro chefs has been making the most of this plethora of ingredients, offering regularly changing, market-inspired menus at reasonable prices. Many of the best are listed in this guide and, while it can be hard to secure a last-minute reservation for dinner, they're usually quieter at lunch.

For all the ups and downs, something about the world's original gastronomic capital keeps people coming back in search of the bistro that hasn't changed its menu in decades, the brasserie where oyster-slurping is really just an excuse to people-watch, and the haute cuisine temple where food becomes art. Thankfully, only the most unprepared visitors leave without having experienced a meal that justifies the city's reputation.

Making a meal

Parisian restaurants rarely feel overtly commercial, though some of the most popular bistros do have up to three sittings and insist that you arrive at a certain time. Apéritifs are not aggressively pushed and you're free to linger as long as you like, even if there are people waiting. In fact, it's considered the height of rudeness for a waiter to bring your bill before you've asked for it. Do expect the waiter to look surprised if you refuse wine, which is considered as essential to a French meal as a basket of fresh baguette.

As a general rule, the better the view, the worse your chances are of eating very well; but there are a few exceptions, such as Au Bon Accueil (p126), which has an Eiffel Tower view from its little pavement terrace, and the recently opened Les Ombres (p130) at the top of the new Musée Branly. The glassed-in dining room offers a full-on view of the Eiffel Tower, resplendent of an evening in its sparkling flashbulb dress, and the food is prepared with unusual care for a museum restaurant.

Avoid eating in cafés if the quality of food is a priority. The exceptions are easy to spot: they're filled with happy locals tucking into duck confit with sautéed potatoes or delicious-looking steak tartare. The hundreds of Asian *traiteurs* that have popped up in recent years are almost uniformly mediocre, too, reheating pre-made dishes in a microwave before your eyes. It would be wiser to eat a sandwich in a park at lunch and save your money for a memorable dinner (expect to spend €80 or more per couple for a meal with drinks). Fast-food aside, non-French options are multiplying by the minute as Parisians grow more open to global flavours: Moroccan, South Indian, Chinese, Laotian, Italian and Jewish cuisines are all represented, if you know where to look. Unico (15 rue Paul Bert, 11th, 01.43.67.68.08) is a fine example of quality Argentine cuisine, for example.

Finally, note that the scribbled blackboard menus typical of these bistros rarely come with English translations, unless you're lucky enough to be served by a bilingual waiter. Top-notch establishments require bookings weeks in advance and confirmation the day before.

Palais Royal p21

WHAT'S BEST

Shopping

The Paris consumer has never had it so good. Every week, new shops open in high-profile locations, with cutting-edge stock, and at lofty levels of chic. Make no mistake, Paris is inching inexorably upmarket.

That said, this isn't a city that's unduly swayed by the short-lived fads of the marketplace. Though the pressures on family-run and specialist shops are the same here as in any major western city, Paris still has a heart-lifting profusion of outlets that have been in business for generations, or stick doggedly to one particular product – cheeses, say, or watchbands. In this city, almost everything, from a vintage armagnac to a single praline chocolate, is lovingly served and wrapped, whatever the shop.

Famously fashionable

Paris has been the world capital of fashion since at least the reign of Louis XIV, when the Sun King sent ambassadors bearing dolls dressed in the latest looks to neighbouring European courts. In 2008, the Paris fashion scene is booming. The Golden Triangle around the Champs-Elysées, anchored by Louis Vuitton's new global concept store with a trickle-down along avenue Montaigne, has taken a youthful direction with the arrival of hip labels like Zadig & Voltaire (p113) and Paul & Joe (p142). But Paris is no longer a city with one golden triangle; there are several. The one on the Left Bank has chic department store Le Bon Marché (p138) as its apex; and the trendiest

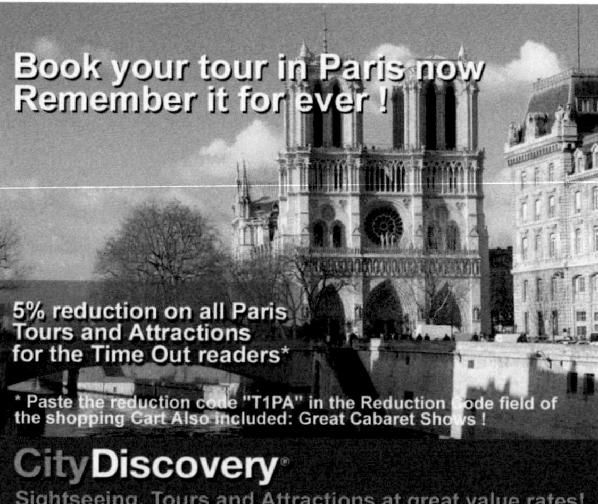
Book your tour in Paris now
Remember it for ever !
5% reduction on all Paris
Tours and Attractions
for the Time Out readers*
* Paste the reduction code "T1PA" in the Reduction Code field of
the shopping Cart Also included: Great Cabaret Shows !
CityDiscovery®
Sightseeing, Tours and Attractions at great value rates!
www.city-discovery.com

BERCY
VILLAGE

continues to blossom along rue Charlot and rue Vieille-du-Temple in the 3rd arrondissement.

Extensive renovations along rue St-Honoré between place Vendôme and the Palais Royal – and especially rue du Mont-Thabor, near landmark concept store Colette (p76) have made this an attractive area for new designer shops, from arrivals such as Diane von Furstenberg (14 rue d'Alger, 1st, 01.42.60.22.22) and Roberto Cavalli – whose flagship (68 rue du Fbg-St-Honoré, 8th, 01.44.94.04.15) opened in 2007 – to small fashionable boutiques such as Jay Ahr (2 rue du 29 Juillet, 1st, 01.42.96.95.23). L'Eclaireur (p111) has a new branch in these parts, too (8 rue Boissy d'Anglas, 8th, 01.53. 43.03.07). Back at the Palais Royal, the 2006 inauguration of Marc Jacobs's first European flagship (p80) has made the neighbourhood a magnet for fashionistas. As this particularly high-profile example confirms, Paris is still a rite of passage for any fashion designer worth his or her sketchbook.

The iconic couture houses are also alive and well, thanks to the talents of Karl Lagerfeld at Chanel, John Galliano at Dior and Nicholas Ghesquiere at Balenciaga. More recently, the fortunes of Rochas have been revived by Belgian designer Olivier Theyskens, those of Azzaro by English designer Vanessa Seward, and Lanvin's return to the limelight is down to Israeli-born designer Alber Elbaz. At Yves Saint Laurent, Stefano Pilati is approved by the master himself and, after an identity crisis that lasted close to a decade, the house that Hubert de Givenchy built may blossom thanks to newcomer Riccardo Tisci.

Meanwhile, semi-couture (aka luxury ready-to-wear) and unique pieces are all the rage, a trend that is bringing in new designers like Martin Grant and Andrew Gn.

SHORTLIST

Best new
- Marc Jacobs (p80)

Best boutiques
- Agnès b (p76)
- APC (p138)
- Boutique M Dia (p76)
- Jean-Paul Gaultier (p79)

Best bargains
- Le Mouton à Cinq Pattes (p140)
- Paris-Musées (p112)
- Tati (p87)

Best possible taste
- Arnaud Delmontel (p87)
- Culture Bière (p62)
- Marie-Anne Cantin (p130)
- Julien, Caviste (p111)
- Legrand Filles & Fils (p80)
- Mariage Frères (p112)
- Poilâne (p142)

Best accessories
- Alice Cadolle (p76)
- L'Artisan Parfumeur (p138)
- Erès (p78)

High concept
- Colette (p76)
- Ekivok (p78)
- Lancel (p63)

The classics
- Le Bon Marché (p138)
- Chanel (p76)
- Christian Dior (p63)
- Galeries Lafayette (p78)
- Mariage Frères (p112)
- Printemps (p81)
- Yves Saint Laurent (p143)

Vintage condition
- Come On Eileen (p110)
- Didier Ludot (p78)
- Wochdom (p87)

Literary leanings
- Bouquinistes (p152)
- La Hune (p140)
- Red Wheelbarrow (p112)
- Shakespeare & Co (p153)

Paul & Joe p19

Grant is known for sharply cut trenches and modern, Kennedy-esque separates; Gn for exquisitely embellished coats and high-luxe ensembles. Rather than rush into opening signature boutiques, such designers continue to serve private customers from their *ateliers*, relying on influential fashion mags and stores like Le Bon Marché to bring their work to wider attention.

Arts in the right place

Highbrow second-hand bookshops are scattered throughout the city, and there's a cluster around the Sorbonne; bookworms should also browse the famous *bouquinistes* (p151) along the banks of the river. Likewise, if you prefer to avoid the giant chain stores such as Virgin Megastore (p64) on the Champs-Elysées or the national chain Fnac (p63) – though these all have their advantages – you'll find a good selection of new and used books, CDs and DVDs at the bookshops on boulevard St Michel. On the right bank, explore the warren of pedestrian streets around Châtelet, expecially for DVDs and old vinyl.

Market forces

No trip to Paris would be complete without a wander through its many markets. Each arrondissement has a produce market, and the larger ones have several. The foodie's favourite is the Marché d'Aligre, which is comprised of an old-fashioned food hall as well as the streets around it; bibliophiles will while away many an hour at the Marché aux Livres Anciens in the parc Georges Brassens. For addresses and opening times of all the city's markets, large and small, log on to www.paris.fr.

Neighbourhood watch

The two department store giants are on boulevard Haussmann. Galeries Lafayette (p78) and Printemps (p81) have both been renovated in recent years. They offer fashion, accessories

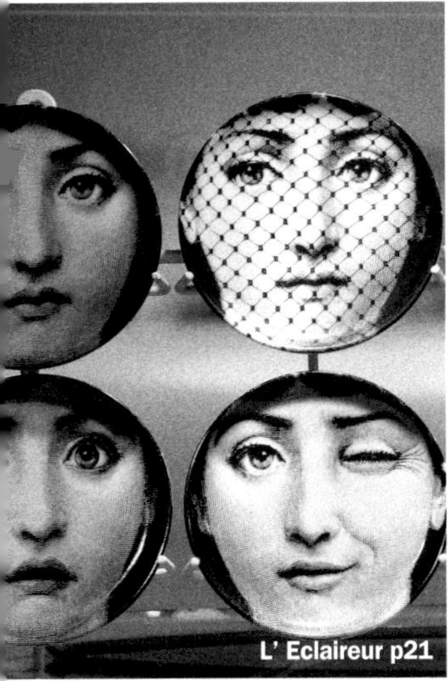

L' Eclaireur p21

and large beauty and shoe departments. Not to be outdone, Le Bon Marché, the Left Bank's only department store, has recently unveiled its L'Appartement de la Mode, which presents edited fashion (next door you'll find the chicest gourmet *epicerie* in the capital).

Meanwhile, each neighbourhood has its shopping axis. If, like the locals, you find that rue des Francs-Bourgeois has become too saturated with tourist traffic, venture a few blocks north on the rue Vieille-du-Temple to explore the 3rd, fast becoming the Soho of Paris. The neighbourhood, once a working-class area filled with family-run shops, has blossomed with *ateliers*, designer boutiques, vintage troves, hot art galleries and restaurants. And, despite its newfound hipness, it still feels like old Paris.

In addition to harbouring the world's biggest fashion names, the avenue Montaigne is shaking off its bourgeois image with the arrival of hip young stores like LA-based jewellery brand Chrome Hearts (No.18, 8th, 01.40.70.17.35), plus the Montaigne Market (No.57, 8th, 01.42. 56.58.58), the avenue's lone multi-brand boutique. Meanwhile, if you wander around the edgier rue Keller (10th) and rue Oberkampf (11th), you'll find plenty of *atelier* boutiques.

Shopping talk

VAT of 19.6 per cent is included in the price of most items. If you're visiting from outside the EU, most major retailers will give you a tax refund receipt that you can have stamped and drop off at the airport on your way out of the EU.

Opening hours vary: the big department stores open until 9.30pm once a week; smaller shops may close at lunch time (between noon and 2pm); and many family-owned businesses close for much of August. On Sundays, shopping is confined to major tourist areas and the Champs-Elysées (plus flea markets).

Le Showcase

WHAT'S BEST
Nightlife

Paris no longer has a reputation as a top nightlife city, but beneath the apparently uneventful surface there's a vibrant assortment of venues throbbing to a rich mix of sounds. Look in the right places and you'll find sweaty dancefloors, dive bars hosting celebrity DJs, boats rocking (literally) from dusk till dawn and some of the most stylish clubs in the world. What's more, the locals are good fun once they let their hair down and stop playing it cool. And when it comes to music – especially jazz, blues and chanson – you'll find more than enough going on to keep your feet tapping.

Nightclubs

Since 2005 the Paris clubbing scene has been enjoying a renaissance. Among the new wave of clubs, the most exciting are Le Showcase (p64), housed in a cavernous, stone-vaulted former warehouse directly underneath the Pont Alexandre III, and Paris Paris (p81), a cosy basement venue that was the talk of the town in 2006. Provided you can get in to either, you'll be rubbing shoulders with the likes of Justice, Sebastian, Mr Oizo, Kavinsky, Busy P and other members of the city's cool clubbing community. As well as the all-out newcomers, a couple of old favourites are back on fine form – the revived Bains Douches (p113) and the reincarnated Bus Palladium (p88). Meanwhile, the Rex (p81), already a winner for sound, has just installed one of the best systems in Europe.

The trendy new places tend to produce a constantly changing line-up of electronic music, techno, hip hop, house, disco and even rock –

as epitomised by the fashion for 'selectors' rather than mix DJs. Look out for one-offs by such hip new labels as Ed Banger, Kitsune Midnight and Record Makers, as well as by veterans Versatile, F Communications, UWE and Yellow.

For the superclub experience, make for Queen (mostly gay, p64) or Club Mix (mostly mixed, p158). Smaller but well worth checking out, especially for 'after' parties, are the floating Batofar (opposite 11 quai François-Mauriac, 13th, 01.53.60.17.30) and Bateau Concorde Atlantique (Porte de Solférino, 25 quai Anatole-France, 7th, 01.47. 05.71.03), and the Nouveau Casino (p113). In fact, it's with the 'afters' that things really get going in Paris: there are as many early Sunday morning events here as there are Saturday-nighters.

For standard house there are Folies Pigalle (p88) and Redlight (p158), among others; for deep, progressive or minimal sounds, make tracks for Nouveau Casino. Straightforward hip hop nights are

SHORTLIST

Best newborn and reborn
- Les Bains Douches (p113)
- Le Bus Palladium (p88)
- Le Showcase (p64)

Best bands
- Le Bataclan (p113)
- Café de la Danse (p113)
- La Cigale/La Boule Noire (p88)
- Olympia (p81)
- Le Triptyque (p82)

Best sound systems
- Rex (p81)

Best all-nighters
- Nouveau Casino (p113)

Best Sunday sessions
- Wagg (p143)

Best for sunny days
- Point Ephémère (p95)
- Le Redlight (p158)

Best for posing
- Le Baron (p64)

Best for megastar DJs
- Rex (p81)

Best for food with grooves
- Café Charbon (p103)
- Le Sabot (p143)

Best gay clubs
- Pulp (p81)
- Queen (p64)

Best jazz nights
- Caveau de la Huchette (p153)
- New Morning (p95)
- Petit Journal Montparnasse (p158)
- Sunset/Sunside (p81)
- Théâtre du Châtelet (p82)

Best cocktails
- Alcazar (p134)

Best cabarets
- Le Lido (p64)
- Moulin Rouge (p88)

held at Triptyque (p82); R&B is played on Wednesdays at Queen's Break'n. For drum 'n' bass the main nights are monthly Massive at Rex and I Love Jungle at a succession of hired venues. Trance and hardcore tend to stay outside Paris, with outdoor events organised by local collectives and sound systems, though a few crop up indoors. Dance music of every stripe gets an outing at the Paris version of Berlin's Love Parade, the Techno Parade (p33), which takes place in the middle of September and draws thousands.

If you like your clubbing cosy, there are hip bars around Bastille, the Marais, Oberkampf and the Grands Boulevards happy to oblige. Traditionalists can find plenty to keep them happy, too; swing, be-bop and rock 'n' roll after the jazz concerts at Le Slow Club (p81), and a stream of school-disco-type nights where the DJ is no superstar: check out the monthly Bal at Elysée Montmartre (p88) and Le Gala des Ringards at Le Divan du Monde (p88). Salsa and world music events are plentiful, with regular nights at Le Divan.

Paris clubs don't really get going until 2am, and people often hit a DJ bar beforehand. Many clubbers visit several venues in one night and finish their evening at an 'after' on Sunday morning. This can be costly, but there's also quality DJing at free nights in some clubs during the week. Free passes can be found on various flyers; flyer information is available at www.flyersweb.com. Other good sites are www.radiofg.com, www.novaplanet.com and www.lemonsound.com.

Note that the last métro leaves at around 12.45am, and the first only gets rolling at 5.45am; in between those times you'll have to get home by night bus or taxi.

La Bellevilloise p28

Rock, roots & jazz

If you'd set your heart on a late-night gig, think again. Trendsetters may flock to Paris to meet, plan and jam, but many punters complain that the powers-that-be – the people who dreamed up the *lutte contre le bruit*, or noise clampdown – are spoiling the party. Live music often winds up at 10.30pm (sometimes earlier). Venues like Triptyque, Nouveau Casino and Point Ephemère (p95), all with a varied showcase of contemporary sounds, are fighting an ongoing battle to persuade the authorities that increased sound levels will not bring social meltdown.

Still, the *banlieue* raps on, currently to the strains of TTC, La Rumeur and Le Remède; and should you like your Francophonia delivered by husky-voiced ladies in smoky bars, you'll be glad to know *la chanson française* continues to thrive – in places like newcomer La Bellevilloise (19 rue Boyer, 20th, 01.53.27.35.77), founded in 1877 as a socialist cooperative and now a multi-purpose exhibition and concert venue. On similarly solid foundations is the city's rep as an international hotspot for jazz and blues. Established venues like New Morning (p95), Sunset (p81) and Caveau de la Huchette (p153) have been hosting big names for years, and few arrondissements are without a similar cellar. The multi-disciplinary Théâtre du Châtelet (p82) is also a prime purveyor of big-name jazz with its annual Bleu sur Scène festival. And Paris has a lively world music scene – often Arabic and African – at places like Le Bataclan (p113). US and UK indie acts and rocktagenarians drop by on tour to places like Olympia (p81) and La Cigale (p88).

Listings can be found in the weekly *Les Inrockuptibles*, whose database at www.lesinrocks.com has all that's hot in town. Bi-monthly *Lylo* is distributed free at Fnac (p63) and in bars such as La Fourmi (p86). Virgin Megastore (p64) and Fnac have their own ticket offices. Get to a gig at the time given on the ticket; concerts usually start on time.

Cabaret

A century and a half after cancan was born, dancers are still slinking across Parisian cabaret stages. The Moulin Rouge (p88) popularised the skirt-raising concept in the late 19th century, and since then venues like Le Lido (p64) have institutionalised garter-pinging forever.

These days a cabaret is an all-evening, €100, smart-dress event, served with a pre-show meal and champers. Male dancers, acrobats and magicians complement the foxy foxtrots; dancing is synchronised, costumes are beautiful, and the whole caboodle totally respectable. The Moulin Rouge is the most traditional glamour revue and the only place with cancan. Toulouse-Lautrec posters, glittery lamp-posts and fake trees lend tacky charm, while 60 Doriss dancers cover the stage with faultless synchronisation. Sadly, elbow room is nil, with hundreds of tables and bodies packed in like sardines. But if you can bear intimacy with international businessmen, the Moulin Rouge, the cheapest of the food-serving cabarets, won't disappoint.

For space go to Le Lido. With 1,000 seats, this classy venue is the largest, priciest cabaret of the lot: the art nouveau hall's high-tech touches (descending balcony and disappearing lamps) optimise visibility and star chef Paul Bocuse has revolutionised the menu. The slightly tame show, with 60 Bluebell Girls, has boob-shaking, wacky costumes and numerous oddities: courtesan cats meeting Charlie Chaplin, for example.

Salle Pleyel p31

WHAT'S BEST
Arts & Leisure

Paris and the high arts go way back. The city invented the public film screening; classical music and opera have been a vital part of its cultural life since the Middle Ages; its theatrical heritage is world-class; and it has been fertile ground for contemporary dance for decades. What's especially good about the arts here is their accessibility: there are any number of festivals and discount promotions throughout the year, many organised by the city council, that bring what Anglo-Saxons often consider to be 'elitist' art forms within the reach and appreciation of the general public. The result is that Parisians are more curious and catholic in their tastes than perhaps any other city community – and even the fleeting visitor can reap the benefits.

Film

Cinema-going is a serious pastime in Paris. More tickets per head are bought here than anywhere else in Europe, and in any given week there's a choice of around 230 movies – not counting festivals (p33). There are nearly 90 cinemas and almost 400 screens, 150 of them independently owned – and of those, 89 show nothing but arthouse. You like cinema? You'll love Paris.

Even if you're only in town for a couple of days, it would be a shame not to visit at least one of the city's many and varied picture palaces – the glorious faux-oriental Pagode (p130) and kitsch excesses of the Grand Rex (p82), for example, or the active and innovative Forum des Images (p82), which reopened in February 2007 after a major

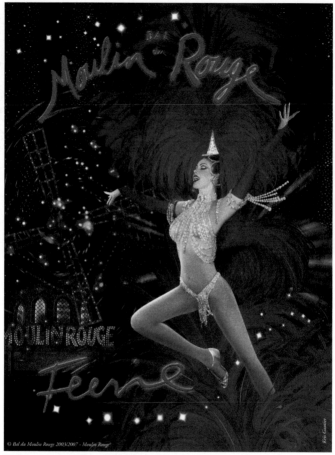

facelift. In addition to the multitude of retrospectives and discount deals, there are many Q&A sessions with directors and actors.

New releases, sometimes as many as 15, hit the screens on Wednesdays. Hollywood is well represented, but Paris audiences still have an insatiable appetite for international product and non-standard formats like shorts or documentaries.

Opera and classical

The recent reopening of the capital's only large concert hall, the Salle Pleyel (p65), has shifted attention briefly away from Gérard Mortier, director of the Opéra National de Paris. Some see his strong modernist theatrical convictions as part of an exciting musical adventure, while others find the repertoire, production values and musical performances to be a betrayal of all they hold dear. At least his efforts to introduce the public to unfamiliar work have generally made a welcome change from the conservative approach of his predecessor, Hugues Gall. Mortier also takes the trouble to give personal pre-show talks, which appeal to an audience not always entirely free of intellectual pretension. Elsewhere, the recently elected director of the Châtelet (p82), Jean-Luc Choplin, provides a populist antidote to Mortier's elitist sensibilities; and the Opéra Comique (p82), newly promoted to National Theatre status, is flourishing.

Contemporary composition remains a strong suit in Paris's musical makeup, thanks to the work of the IRCAM, the Ensemble Intercontemporain and the active involvement of Pierre Boulez. It's matched only by the early music scene, led by William Christie's Les Arts Florissants, with French conductor Emmanuelle Haïm joining other native specialists such as Christophe Rousset and

SHORTLIST

Most innovative
- Cutting-edge international opera at the Festival d'Automne (p33)

Most star-studded
- Cinema's greats and rising talents at the Festival Paris Ile-de-France (p35)
- Classical music luminaries at the Festival de St-Denis (p35)

Most romantic
- Candlelit recitals for the Festival Chopin (p38)

Best bargains
- Film tickets at just €3.50 during Printemps du Cinéma (p37)
- Free concerts and gigs at Fête de la Musique (p38)

Best open air
- Cinéma en Plein Air (p38)
- Festival Classique au Vert (p33)

Best film venues
- Forum des Images (p82)
- MK2 (p95)
- La Pagode (p130)

Best classical venues
- Salle Pleyel (p65)
- Théâtre des Champs-Elysées (p65)
- Théâtre de la Ville (p82)

Best opera venues
- Opéra Comique (p82)
- Palais Garnier (p82)

Best churches for music
- Eglise St-Germain-des-Prés (p132)
- Sainte-Chapelle (p119)

Best museums for music
- Centre Pompidou (p97)
- Musée du Louvre (p67)
- Musée de la Musique (p161)
- Musée d'Orsay (p134)

Jean-Claude Malgoire. There's plenty going on in churches and other venues, too. The Festival d'Art Sacré (01.44.70.64.10, www.festivaldartsacre.new.fr) presents church music in authentic settings in the run-up to Christmas; Les Grands Concerts Sacrés (01.48.24.16.97) and Musique et Patrimoine (01.42.50.96.18) also offer concerts at various churches, while music in Notre-Dame cathedral is taken care of by Musique Sacrée Notre-Dame (01.44.41.49.99, tickets 01.42.34.56.10). The main music in summer is the Paris Quartier d'Eté festival (p38), with concerts in gardens.

Many venues and orchestras offer cut-rate tickets to students (under 26) an hour before curtain-up – but be suspicious of smooth-talking touts around the Opéra and at big-name concerts. On La Fête de la Musique (21 June), all events are free, and year-round freebies crop up at the Maison de Radio France and the Conservatoire de Paris, as well as at certain churches.

Dance

Although the sumptuous ballet productions at the Opéra Garnier (p82) and international companies at Châtelet (p82) will always delight audiences, it's in the sphere of contemporary dance that Paris currently shines brightest. Opened in 2004, the prestigious Centre National de la Danse (1 rue Victor-Hugo, 93507 Pantin, 01.41.83.27.27), just outside the city centre, has given France an impressive HQ for its 600-plus regional dance companies, and welcomes international stars – with emphasis on new creation. Superstars Pina Bausch and William Forsythe come to Paris regularly, drawing healthy crowds.

For would-be performers, there are masses of dance classes – ballet and hip hop being the most popular. And every season sees some kind of contemporary dance festival in or near Paris; Paris Quartier d'Eté and the Festival d'Automne (p33) are just two of the biggest.

Theatre

From the premonitory plays of the medieval era to the revolutionary street theatre of 1968, French drama has always mirrored, shaped and commented on French society. Paris has led the pack in the development of new acting styles, dramatic movements and landmark theatre buildings. But for the outsider, especially the outsider whose French isn't fluent, the options are limited: none of the iconic theatrical venues subtitles performances. Meanwhile, a couple of troupes cater to the English-speaking crowd. Dear Conjunction Theatre Company (6 rue Arthur-Rozier, 19th, 01.42.41.69.65) is the main source of English-language theatre, in various venues. And Shakespeare in English is performed at the Bois de Boulogne's Théâtre de Verdure du Jardin Shakespeare (08.20.00.75.75) by London's Tower Theatre Company (www.towertheatre.org.uk).

What's on

For listings, see the weekly *L'Officiel des Spectacles* or *Pariscope*. When it comes to films, take note of the two letters printed somewhere near the title: VO (*version originale*) means a screening in the original language with French subtitles; VF (*version française*) means that it's dubbed into French. Matters musical are covered by monthly mags *Le Monde de la Musique* and *Diapason*, which list classical concerts; *Opéra International* has good coverage of all things vocal. *Cadences* and *La Terrasse*, two free monthlies, are distributed outside concert venues. Another useful source of information is website www.concertclassic.com.

Calendar

Tour de France p38

This is the pick of events that had been announced as we went to press. On public holidays, or *jours feriés*, banks, many museums, most businesses and a number of restaurants close; public transport runs a Sunday service. New Year's Day, May Day, Bastille Day and Christmas Day are the most piously observed holidays. Dates highlighted in **bold** indicate public holidays.

September 2007

1-9 **Jazz à la Villette**
Parc de la Villette
www.jazzalavillette.com
One of the best local jazz fests.

1-23 **Festival Classique au Vert**
Parc Floral de Paris
www.classiqueauvert2007.com
Free classical recitals in a park setting.

15 **Techno Parade**
www.technopol.net
This parade (finishing at Bastille) marks the start of electronic music festival Rendez-vous Electroniques.

15 16 **Journées du Patrimoine**
Various venues
www.journeesdupatrimoine.culture.fr
Embassies, ministries and scientific establishments open their doors.

Mid Sept-end Dec **Festival d'Automne**
Various venues.
www.festival-automne.com
Major annual festival of challenging theatre, dance and modern opera.

October 2007

Ongoing Festival d'Automne

Paris-Plage p38

6 **Nuit Blanche**
Various venues
www.nuitblanche.paris.fr
For one night, galleries, museums, swimming pools, bars and clubs stay open till very late.

6, 7 Oct **Prix de l'Arc de Triomphe**
Hippodrome de Longchamp
www.france-galop.com
France's richest flat race attracts the elite of horse racing.

13, 14 **Fête des Vendanges de Montmartre**
Various venues
www.fetedesvendangesdemontmartre.com
Folk music and a parade celebrate the 800-bottle Montmartre grape harvest.

18-22 **FIAC**
Paris-Expo
www.fiacpais.com
Respected international art fair.

30-4 Nov **Grand Marché d'Art Contemporain**
Place de la Bastille
www.organisation-joel-garcia.fr
Contemporary artists display and sell their work at this annual arts fair.

November 2007

Ongoing Festival d'Automne, Grand Marché d'Art Contemporain

4-8 **Festival Inrockuptibles**
Various venues
www.lesinrocks.com
Rock, pop and trance festival curated by the popular rock magazine *Les Inrockuptibles.*

11 L'Armistice (Armistice Day)
Arc de Triomphe
The President lays wreaths to honour French combattants who died in the World Wars.

16 **Fête du Beaujolais Nouveau**
Various venues
www.beaujolaisgourmand.com
The new vintage is launched to packed cafés and wine bars.

24-23 Dec **Africolor**
Various venues in St-Denis
www.africolor.com
African music festival with a spirited wrap party.

December 2007

Ongoing Africolor, Festival d'Automne

Dec-Mar **Paris sur Glace**
Various venues
www.paris.fr
Three free outdoor ice rinks.

Mid Dec-late Jan **Patinoire de Noël**
Eiffel Tower
www.tour-eiffel.fr
Hire a pair of free skates at the ice rink on the first floor of the glittering tower.

24-**25 Noël (Christmas)**

31 **New Year's Eve**
Huge crowds on the Champs-Elysées.

January 2008

Ongoing Paris sur Glace, Patinoire de Noël

1 Jour de l'An (New Year's Day)
The Grande Parade de Paris brings floats, bands and dancers.

6 **Fête des Rois (Epiphany)**
Pâtisseries sell *galettes des rois*, frangipan-filled cakes in which a *fêve*, or tiny charm, is hidden.

20 **Mass for Louis XVI**
Chapelle Expiatoire
Royalists and right-wing crackpots mourn the end of the monarchy.

February 2008

Ongoing Paris sur Glace

2-15 Mar **Six Nations**
Stade de France
www.rbs6nations.com
Paris is invaded by Brits and Celts for five big weekends of rugby.

7 **Nouvel An Chinois**
Various venues
Dragon dances and martial arts demos celebrate the Chinese new year.

March 2008

Ongoing Paris sur Glace, Six Nations

Early Mar-Apr **Banlieues Bleues**
Various venues in Seine St-Denis

www.banlieuesbleues.org
Five weeks of quality French and international jazz, blues, R&B and soul.

Mid Mar **Printemps du Cinéma**
Various venues
www.printempsducinema.com
Film tickets across the city are cut to a bargain €3.50 for three days.

21 Le Chemin de la Croix (Way of the Cross)
Square Willette
Good Friday pilgrimage as crowds follow the Archbishop of Paris from the bottom of Montmartre to Sacré-Coeur.

23 Pâques (Easter Sunday)

April 2008

Ongoing Banlieues Bleues

Early Apr-end May
Foire du Trône
Pelouse de Reuilly
www.foiredutrone.com
France's biggest funfair.

13 Apr **Marathon de Paris**
Av des Champs-Elysées to av Foch
www.parismarathon.com
35,000 runners take in the sights.

Apr **Festival Paris Ile-de-France**
Various venues
www.festivaldeparisidf.com
The capital's own film festival.

29-4 May **Grand Marché d'Art Contemporain**
Place de la Bastille
www.organisation-joel-garcia.fr
Contemporary artists display and sell their work at this annual arts fair.

May 2008

Ongoing Foire du Trône, Grand Marché d'Art Contemporain

1 Fête du Travail (May Day)
Key sights close; unions march in eastern Paris via Bastille.

1 Jour de l'Ascension

Early May **Printemps des Musées**
Various venues
www.printempsdesmusees.culture.fr
For one Sunday in May, selected museums open for free.

Early-mid May **Foire de Paris**
Paris Expo
www.foiredeparis.fr
Enormous lifestyle salon, full of craft and food stores, plus health exhibits.

Early May-June **La Fête des Enfants du Monde**
Various venues
www.koinobori.org
A Franco-Japanese festival with shows, exhibitions and concerts.

8 Victoire 1945 (VE Day)

12 Lundi de Pentecôte (Whit Monday)

Mid May **La Nuit des Musées**
Various venues
www.nuitdesmusees.culture.fr
For one night, the landmark museums across Paris stay open late and put on special events.

Mid May **Festival Jazz à Saint-Germain-des-Prés**
St-Germain-des-Prés, various venues
www.espritjazz.com
A ten-day celebration of jazz and blues.

Mid May-early June **Quinzaine des Réalisateurs**
Forum des Images
www.quinzaine-realisateurs.com
The Cannes Directors' Fortnight programme comes to Paris.

End May-end June **Festival de St-Denis**
Various venues in St-Denis
www.festival-saint-denis.fr
Four weeks of concerts showcasing top-quality classical music.

End May **Le Printemps des Rues**
Various venues
www.leprintempsdesrues.com
Annual street-theatre festival.

End May-early June
French Tennis Open
Stade Roland Garros
www.rolandgarros.com
Glitzy Grand Slam tennis tournament.

June 2008

Ongoing Festival de St-Denis, Quinzaine des Réalisateurs, French Tennis Open

Early June **Tous à Vélo**
Across Paris
www.tousavelo.com
Cycling tours and activities as Paris's two-wheelers take to the streets.

Early June-July **Foire St-Germain**
Various venues
www.foiresaintgermain.org
Concerts, theatre and workshops.

June-July **Paris Jazz Festival**
Parc Floral de Paris
www.parcfloraldeparis.com/ www.paris.fr
Free jazz at the lovely Parc Floral.

June-July **Festival Chopin à Paris**
Orangerie de Bagatelle
www.frederic-chopin.com
Romantic candlelit piano recitals in the Bois de Boulogne.

21 **Fête de la Musique**
Various venues
www.fetedelamusique.fr
Free gigs (encompassing all musical genres) take place across the city.

Late June **Gay Pride March**
www.fiertes-lgbt.org
Outrageous floats and costumes parade towards Bastille, followed by an official party and various club events throughout the city.

Late June-early July **La Goutte d'Or en Fête**
square Léon
www.gouttedorenfete.org
Raï, rap and reggae.

Late June-early July **Paris Cinéma**
Various venues
www.pariscinema.org
Premieres, tributes and restored films at the city's excellent summer filmgoing initiative.

July 2008

Ongoing Foire St-Germain, Paris Jazz Festival, Festival Chopin à Paris, La Goutte d'Or en Fête, Paris Cinéma

Early July **Solidays**
Hippodrome de Longchamp
www.solidays.com
A three-day music bash for AIDS charities, featuring French, world and new talent.

Early-late July **Etés de la Danse**
Centre Historique des Archives Nationales
www.lesetesdeladanse.com
International classical and contemporary dance festival.

July **Tour de France**
Av des Champs-Elysées
www.letour.fr
The ultimate cycle endurance test climaxes on the Champs-Elysées.

July-Aug **Cinéma en Plein Air**
Parc de La Villette
www.villette.com
A summer fixture: a themed season of free films screened under the stars.

14 Quatorze Juillet (Bastille Day)
Various venues
France's national holiday commemorates 1789. On the 13th, Parisians dance at place de la Bastille. At 10am on the 14th, crowds line the Champs-Elysées as the President reviews a military parade. By night, the Champ de Mars fills for a huge and spectacular firework display.

Mid July-mid Aug
Paris, Quartier d'Eté
Various venues
www.quartierdete.com
Classical and jazz concerts, plus dance and theatre, in outdoor venues.

Mid July-mid Aug **Paris-Plage**
Pont des Arts to Pont de Sully
www.paris.fr
Palm trees, huts, hammocks and around 2,000 tonnes of fine sand on both banks of the Seine bring a proper seaside vibe to the city. Not only this, there's a floating pool and a lending library too.

August 2008

Ongoing Cinéma en Plein Air; Paris, Quartier d'Eté; Paris-Plage

15 Fête de l'Assomption (Assumption Day)
Cathédrale Notre-Dame de Paris
Notre-Dame again becomes a place of religious pilgrimage.

End Aug **Rock en Seine**
Domaine National de St-Cloud
www.rockenseine.com

Sounds of the suburbs

Banlieues Bleues

Paris's *banlieues* (housing estates outside the ring road) are as newsworthy as ever in France – and often for negative reasons. To many English speakers, suburbia means middle-class content, but to the French, the capital's outer reaches are more commonly associated with high-density social housing and race issues. That said, there's a rich cultural life beyond the confines of Paris's historical centre – and there's no better counter to *La Haine*-style perceptions than the Banlieues Bleues festival, which celebrates its 25th anniversary in 2008.

The 'bleues' in the name is misleading: this is far from being an event for 12-bar purists. The festival was founded in 1984 by Bernard Vergnaud and Jacques Pornon with the aim of promoting talent from around the world. Aside from the fact that most nominally 'jazz' and 'blues' festivals are broad churches these days, 'bleues' here has several connotations. Foremost is the fact that blues begat jazz, and many of the other musical forms which find a place at the festival (soul, hip hop, reggae); but the name is also a play on 'banlieue rouge', a term used to describe communist-leaning suburbs that were bastions of working-class culture.

The roll-call of artists the festival has attracted over its quarter-century is remarkable: Miles Davis, Dizzy Gillespie, Sly and Robbie, and Solomon Burke, to name a few. Highlights in 2007, which emphasised musical fusion and hybrid forms, included the likes of Allen Toussaint, Roy Ayers and Pharoah Sanders, alongside Lebanese oud-player Rabih Abou-Khalil and drum 'n' bass visionaries Spring Heel Jack.

Crucially, though, Banlieue Bleues is about more than just the performances. Visiting artists are enouraged to get involved in local projects and workshops in schools and community centres.

Two days, two stages, one world-class rock line-up.

September 2008

Early Sept **Jazz à la Villette**
Parc de la Villette
www.jazzalavillette.com
One of the best local jazz festivals in the city.

Sept **Festival Classique Au Vert**
Parc Floral du Paris
www.paris.fr
Free classical recitals in a park setting.

Mid Sept **Techno Parade**
Various venues
www.technopol.net
This parade (finishing at Bastille) marks the start of electronic music festival Rendez-vous Electroniques.

Mid Sept **Journées du Patrimoine**
Various venues
www.jp.culture.fr
Embassies, ministries and scientific establishments open their doors. Get Le Parisien for a full programme of scheduled events.

Mid Sept-mid Dec **Festival d'Automne**
Various venues
www.festival-automne.com
Major annual festival for all kinds of challenging theatre, dance and modern opera performances.

October 2008

Ongoing Festival d'Automne

Early Oct **Prix de l'Arc de Triomphe**
Hippodrome de Longchamp
www.france-galop.com
France's richest flat race attracts the elite of horse racing.

Early Oct **Nuit Blanche**
Various venues
www.nuitblanche.paris.fr
For one atmospheric night, a selection of galleries, museums, swimming pools, bars and clubs across Paris stay open until very late.

Mid Oct **Fête des Vendanges à Montmartre**
Various venues
www.fetedesvendangesdemontmartre.com
Folk music and a parade to celebrate the Montmartre grape harvest.

End Oct **FIAC**
Paris-Expo
www.fiacparis.com
Respected international art fair.

End Oct **Grand Marché d'Art Contemporain**
Place de la Bastille
www.organisation-joel-garcia.fr
Contemporary artists display and sell their work at this annual arts fair.

November 2008

Ongoing Festival d'Automne

1 Toussaint (All Saints' Day)

Early Nov **Festival Inrockuptibles**
Various venues
www.lesinrocks.com
A rock, pop and trance festival curated by rock magazine *Les Inrockuptibles.*

11 L'Armistice (Armistice Day)
Arc de Triomphe
The President lays wreaths to honour French dead of both World Wars.

Mid Nov **Fête du Beaujolais Nouveau**
Various venues
www.beaujolaisgourmand.com
The new vintage is launched to packed cafés and wine bars.

December 2008

Ongoing Festival d'Automne

Dec-Mar **Paris sur Glace**
Various venues
www.paris.fr

Mid Dec **Africolor**
Various venues in St-Denis
www.africolor.com
African music festival.

Mid Dec-late Jan **Patinoire de Noël**
Eiffel Tower
www.tour-eiffel.fr
Check out the ice rink on the first floor of the glittering tower.

24-**25 Noël (Christmas)**

31 **New Year's Eve**

Itineraries

Musée de Montmartre p44

Montmartre by Night

Changing from impossibly romantic to horribly tacky in the blink of an eye, the Butte Montmartre has an amazingly schizophrenic personality. While souvenir shops selling Chat Noir fridge magnets draw tourists like iron filings, neighbouring streets can be like silent film sets. This walk gives you the choice of avoiding the tourist madness or taking the road more travelled. Either way, the Butte is a wonderful place for a moonwalk, and one of the safer areas of Paris to wander at night. For once, trainers are a good idea.

START: M° Anvers.

Your route starts with a steep climb up rue de Steinkerque, where, by night, the fabric shops of the Marché St Pierre metamorphose into sellers of Eiffel Tower T-shirts. Gangs of American high-school pupils will be heading down as you go up, but bear with us. At the top you get your first view of the magnificent **Sacré-Coeur** (p84), all lit up and slightly unreal. Turn right and skirt round the basilica's park via rue Ronsard. Suddenly the crowds are gone, and all you can hear is the distant beating of tribal drums from somewhere inside the closed park gates.

Coloured lights beckon at the top of the steps on rue Paul Albert (only in Montmartre can a street actually be a staircase) and you come out on the delightful place Maurice Utrillo with three lovely dining terraces: those of restaurant L'Eté en Pente Douce, and of cafés

Sacré-Coeur

Le Sancerre

Botak and Au Soleil de la Butte. The latter has a free, cheesy nightclub down below, but press on, there's more enchantment to come. Continuing up steep rue Paul Albert, now silent as a winter night, you'll come to the steps of rue du Chevalier de la Barre, flanked by earthbound constellations of fibre-optic stars leading you, as if in a Disney fantasy, towards the ghostly basilica. At the top, turn around and savour the sea of twinkling lights before you: Paris!

Carry on walking, keeping the basilica on your left, and eventually you come down to the parvis with its fabulous view of the whole illuminated city. Unfortunately, everyone knows about this view, and it's thronging with people, bad guitar strummers and randomly strewn bottles, so don't attempt to descend the steps, but go back the way you came (rue du Cardinal Guibert) to join rue du Chevalier de la Barre. Up to the left, past the Irish pub **Corcoran's** (51 rue du Chevalier de la Barre, 18th, 01.42.52.10.57) and huge white water tower, another sparkling view spreads out before you, this time to the north, at the bottom of the hundreds of steps of rue du Mont Cenlis.

Now you have a choice: if you want to avoid the Montmartre theme park of the place du Tertre, take silent rue Cortot to the left, past the **Musée de Montmartre** (p84), then left up rue des Saules and right to place Jean-Baptiste Clement, before bearing left down steep cobbles to rue Ravignan and rue Gabrielle. This is a bit of a slog, however. The alternative is to cross place du Tertre with its picket-fence terraces and portrait painters, brave rue Norvins, then go down rue Poulbot, which is a pretty enclave with classier restaurants and a good view of the **Eiffel Tower** (which you can't see from the parvis) on place du Calvaire. The steps of rue du Calvaire take you straight down to one of our favourite bars, **Le Rendezvous des Amis** (23 rue Gabrielle, 18th, 01.46.06.01.60), whose streetside terrace is a lovely place for a cheap drink in the heights of Montmartre.

Descend the steps at the corner of the bar, then turn right and go up rue Berthe till you descend more steps at rue Androuet and rue des Abbesses, taking you down to place des Abbesses, with its bars that feel a world away from the heights you've just come from.

The walk sounds short, but it's the night-time equivalent of a step class. You'll need a beer: go to **Le Sancerre** (35 rue des Abbesses, 18th, 01.42.58.08.20), where you might even catch some live music and certainly some lively company at the bar – and not a Chat Noir T-shirt in sight.

Canal St Martin

The Water Way

Now one of Paris's hippest quarters, the Canal St-Martin narrowly escaped being paved over in the 1960s when its original function of transporting cargo dwindled. Happily, *les riverains* (the locals) saved it. Echoes of the days when sweaty bargemen stopped off for pots of red wine are found only in the names of some of the establishments – La Marine restaurant, for instance – but the cobblestones, arched bridges and locks nestling in tree-lined enclaves retain the *pittoresque* charm that was immortalised in Marcel Carné's film *Hôtel du Nord*. This half-day walk takes you along the canal's banks and bridges, suggesting plenty of refreshment and shopping stops along the way.

START: M° Jacques Bonsergent.

Take rue de Lancry and turn right into rue Yves Toudic. On the corner with rue de Marseille is one of Paris's most atmospheric bakeries, **Du Pain et des Idées** (34 rue Yves Toudic, 10th, 01.42. 40.44.52), filled with mirrors and painted panels, where on weekdays only you can buy old-fashioned pastries crisped in a wood-fired oven. Continue up rue de Marseille which comes out at the canal on the junction with rue Beaurepaire. Here the café that started the area's renaissance, **Chez Prune** (36 rue Beaurepaire, 10th, 01.42.41.30.47), spreads its terrace and offers tasty lunch dishes and coffee with attitude. Rue Beaurepaire is a great shopping street for those in search of boho clobber, with young designers' clothes and kitsch trinkets at **Ginger Lyly** (33 rue Beaurepaire, 10th, 01.42.06.07.73) and bargain jeans, Lolipop bags, jewellery and vintage at **Seven Seventies** (29 rue Beaurepaire, 10th, 01.42.02.07.88). On the opposite

Maison de l'Architecture

side of the street, the *dépôt vente* **Frivoli** (26 rue Beaurepaire, 10th, 01.42.38.21.20) has colour-coded second-hand clothes, while **Potemkine** (30 rue Beaurepaire, 10th, 01.40.18.01.81/www.potemkine.fr) is a movie buff's paradise, great for rare art films.

From here you'll get your first sight of the attractive wrought-iron bridges that were made much of in the film *Amélie*, and maybe, if a péniche is passing, the swing bridge down to the right opening to let it make its stately progress through. **La Marine** (55bis quai de Valmy, 10th, 01.42.39.69.81), opposite the swing bridge, is another cosy café-restaurant, decorated with old barge memorabilia.

Stay on this side of the road and walk up with the canal on your right. Past the Columbian restaurant **Mukura** (70 quai de Valmy, 10th, 01.42.01.18.67), which will serve you a delicious, bitter hot chocolate, you'll find **Artazart** (83 quai de Valmy, 10th, 01.40.40.24.00/www.artazart.com), an unabashedly pretentious bookstore with a stock of architecture tomes, Japanese manga, art books and handbags made from old 78 records. Free photography and fashion exhibitions are held in the room next door. Then there's the Brazilian boutique **Oba** (83 quai de Valmy, 10th, 01.42.40.39.91/www.obamerca dogeneral.com), stocking one-off but pricey clothing (tracky bottoms for €60?) and all manner of stuff with the inimitable stamp of Brazilian cool. Just round the corner on rue de Lancry, **Le Verre Volé** (67 rue de Lancry, 10th, 01.48.03.17.34) is a wine merchant with a couple of little tables for tastings and food.

Just to the left of the traffic bridge, you cross the pretty arched turquoise bridge, from which you can watch the lock fill up under overarching trees. You'll arrive on the other bank almost opposite the **Hôtel du Nord**. This Paris icon is famous for the 1938 film by Marcel Carné, with Arletty and Jouvet as the prostitute and small-time crook who get mixed up with a suicidal couple. *Pas si gai*, as the French say, but the nostalgic '30s atmosphere of the film, with a little extra glamour, has been restored to the place in its latest incarnation as a restaurant (102 quai de Jemmapes, 10th, 01.40. 40.78.78/www.hoteldunord.org). Pop your head inside the door and you'll undoubtedly want to stay for dinner – though you may have to come back, as it normally requires booking in advance. The interesting thing about the hotel is that although the whole set for the film was built in a studio, the author of the novel that gave rise to the film, Eugène Dabit, did actually live here when the place was run by his parents; he dreamed up the story while working the night shift.

A little further up is a delightfully ramshackle *brocante*, **Loulou Les Ames Arts** (104 quai de Jemmapes, 10th, 01.42.00.91.39), full of a jumble of lights, games and unusual bits of unrestored furniture. Double back to go up rue de la Grange aux Belles, which has some more little boutiques; Italian designer **Carmen Ragosta** (Napoliparis, 8 rue de la Grange aux Belles, 10th, 01.42.49.00.71/www. carmenragosta.com) has just opened a vegetarian Italian restaurant beneath her showroom. It also does takeaway, which is perfect for a picnic on the canal. Next along is a more minimal *brocante*, **Belles & Loups** (10 rue de la Grange aux Belles, 10th, 06 61 44 02 53), and the gorgeous little florist **Bleuet Coquelicot** (10 rue de la Grange aux Belles, 10th, 01.42.41.21.35). Further up the road on the left (if you're prepared to climb the hill) is the contemporary jeweller **Viveka Bergström** (23 rue de la Grange aux Belles, 10th, 01.40.03.04.92/ www.viveka-bergstrom.com).

Cut down rue Bichat, past the wine merchant La Cantine de Quentin, and you can cross another bridge to boho boutiques **Stella Cadente** (21 rue Beaurepaire, 10th, 01.40.40.95.47) and **Antoine et Lili** (p94), and cafés **Le Sporting** (3 rue des Récollets, 10th, 01.46. 07.02.00) and **L'Atmosphère** (p92). From here you can walk through the Jardin Villemin to the Couvent des Récollets, a 17th-century monastery that once housed 200 monks and later became a military hospital. Since 2003, it's been home to the **Maison de l'Architecture** (148 rue du Fbg-St-Martin, 10th, 01.53. 26.10.85/www.maisonarchitecture-idf.org), with exhibitions and talks in the impressive vaulted chapel and a café with a garden. From here's it's only a short walk to Gare de l'Est Métro.

George V p50

Lap of Luxury

The 'golden triangle' of Paris luxury, between avenues George V, Montaigne and the Champs Elysées, did not come about by accident. Developed in the 19th century as a bourgeois residential neighbourhood, the area was commandeered in the 1930s by Louis Vuitton and friends, who formed the Société des Amis des Champs-Elysées to protect their exclusive labels from the march of gaudy commerce on the iconic avenue. Oddly enough, both the masonic compass and square and the letters LV seem to be formed by the conjunction of streets. We leave you to speculate, Dan Brown-like, as you take a leisurely afternoon stroll through the area and window-shop the city's most famous luxury brands.

START: M° Kléber or Etoile.

March down the grand avenue Kléber until you reach rue de Belloy on the left. This comes out on the place des Etats-Unis, an oasis in a desert of Paris stone, with its chestnut-shaded lawns, two playgrounds and a little *boulodrome* where a group of contented players (chauffeurs and off-duty concierges, we imagine) pitch their metal balls across the sand. The large statue commemorates the collaboration of the French general Lafayette and George Washington in 'the American people's fight for independence and liberty'. At the other end of the square is a memorial to Americans who died for France in the Second World War.

The square is bordered by the embassies of various central American countries. On the right, the striking lips and eyes framed by mirrors proclaim the **Maison Baccarat** (11 pl des Etats Unis, 16th, 01.40.22.11.22/www.baccarat.fr), where Philippe Starck has designed an imaginative museum for the crystal company in the former mansion of the art patron and good-time girl the Vicomtesse de Noailles. As you approach, cop a look at the **Eiffel Tower** (p122) down rue de l'Amiral d'Estaing. The museum is well worth a visit, as much for Starck's mirrored decor as the crystal itself. Afterwards, continue to the end of the park, cross the road and walk down rue Freycinet, where a tiny square has a statue of the **Comte de Rochambeau**, another friend of Washington. Opposite is the back entrance of the **Galliera** fashion museum (10 av Pierre-1er-de-Serbie, 16th, 01.56.52.86.00) in the 19th-century palace of the Duchess of Galliera. Carry on down rue Freycinet and take a left into rue Léonce-Reynaud. While we walked down this road, a man with a red rose appeared on a balcony and proclaimed: 'Je vous aime! Je vous ai toujours aimé!' Our guess is that this romantic figure worked for the **Fondation Yves Saint Laurent** (3 rue Léonce-Reynaud, 16th, 01.44.31.64.31/www.ysl-hautecouture.com), which shows exhibitions of the retired couturier's work and inspirations. Next to the public entrance is th e door that was used by Saint Laurent's aristocratic clients as they called for appointments with the haute couture master.

You've arrived at place de l'Alma, where café terraces attempt to trap you into buying the most expensive coffees in all

Maison Baccarat p49

Paris. Shun them, and walk up avenue George V. The presence of Givenchy and YSL boutiques herald your arrival in the golden triangle, while opposite is the strange anomaly of saucy Paris cabaret **Crazy Horse** (12 av George V, 8th, 01.47.23.32.32/ www.lecrazyhorseparis.com). But what's this on the left, with the big red lantern and security gates all round? It's the Chinese embassy, well placed considering China's burgeoning luxury consumption, but still sporting an old-fashioned air of espionage, and definitely in need of a facelift.

Unless you want to do some celebrity spotting in the lobby of the **George V** hotel further up the avenue (31 av George V, 8th, 01.49.52.70.00/www.fourseasons.com), where actor Olivier Martinez was first clocked in an assignation with Penelope Cruz, cross over and take rue de La Trémoille. The centre of the triangle is not particularly interesting, but reveals that even in this deluxe neighbourhood, there are supermarkets, dry cleaners and – get this – launderettes. Turn right down rue Boccador, where the Carita spa and Valentino shop usher in the primped fashion world of avenue Montaigne. Double back down the avenue to look at Auguste Perret's art deco masterpiece, the **Théâtre des Champs-Elysées** (p65), with its sculptures by Antoine Bourdelle. Though it now hosts respectable classical concerts and recitals, the theatre was the scene of the scandalous premier of Stravinsky's *Rite of Spring* by the Ballets Russes, as well as Josephine Baker's Revues Nègres in 1925. A swish restaurant and bar, the **Maison Blanche** (15 avenue Montaigne, 8th, 01.47.23.55.99), is on the top floor, and no one minded us ascending in the lift just to take a look.

It's easy to imagine la Baker holding forth in the peachy deco surroundings of the Plaza Athénée's **Relais** restaurant (p169, 01.53.67.64.00) just before you reach the main entrance of this sumptuous palace hotel. If you feel you're suitably attired, swish through the revolving doors and have afternoon tea – it won't cost much more than a drink on the place de l'Alma. Cross over to look in the windows of the big fashion brands: **Prada** (p64), **Louis Vuitton** (p64), Dolce & Gabbana and LVMH's headquarters, with its flashy big screen columns; then a whole bank of **Christian Dior** (p63) stores, starting with Baby Dior, where you can see filthy rich toddlers and babes in arms trying to mess up the displays while assistants coochy-coo.

Cut up rue François I, past Dior Homme and eyewear, to check out the elegant fountain square that marked the birth of posh for this area. In a 19th-century property development travesty, the 16th-century mansion François I built for his mistress the Duchess d'Etampes was moved from here to the end of rue Bayard, left to rot, then destroyed in 1956. Returning to avenue Montaigne the way you came, you can join the fashionable crowd on the terrace of **L'Avenue** (41 av Montaigne, 8th, 01.40.70.14.91) – Dior shades obligatory – or covet Gucci bags at the showcase boutique (57 av Montaigne), or join the smart art set at auction house Artcurial in the imposing **Hôtel Dassault** (7 Rond-Pont des Champs-Elysées, 8th, 01.42.99.20.20/www.artcurial.com), before escaping from the luxury triangle and its insidious charms via Métro Franklin D. Roosevelt. Or alternatively, just call for your chauffeur.

Paris by Area

Café de l'Homme p61

Champs-Elysées & Western Paris

You can tell the French are proud of the 'Elysian Fields': every time the avenue is mentioned in the media, it's almost always with the words 'the most beautiful avenue in the world'. It's certainly grand, even when swarming with tourists (which is most of the time); it's also the symbolic gathering place of a nation for sports victories, New Year's Eve and displays of military might on 14 July. In the last ten years, the Champs-Elysées has had a renaissance, thanks initially to a facelift – underground car parks and granite paving. Chi-chi shops and chic hotels have set up in the 'golden triangle' (avenues George V, Montaigne and the Champs); restaurants and nightspots draw an affluent and fashionable pack.

South of the Arc de Triomphe, avenue Kléber leads to monumental buildings with views over the Eiffel Tower across the Seine.

Sights & museums

Arc de Triomphe

pl Charles-de-Gaulle (access via underground passage), 8th (01.55.37. 73.77/www.monuments-nationaux.com). M° Charles de Gaulle Etoile. **Open** *Oct-Mar* 10am-10.30pm daily. *Apr-Sept* 10am-11pm daily. **Admission** €8; free-€5 reductions. **Map** p56 B2 ❶

Napoléon ordered the construction of the arch in 1809 as a monument to the Republican armies, but the empire he'd

built began (almost immediately) to collapse. The arch, 50m high and 45m wide, was finally completed in 1836. It bears the names of Napoléon's victories, and is decorated with a frieze of battle scenes and sculptures. It is also the starting point for the annual Bastille Day military procession.

Bateaux-Mouches

Pont de l'Alma, 8th (01.40.76.99.99/ www.bateaux-mouches.fr). M° Alma Marceau. **Departs** *Apr-Sept* every 30mins 10am-11pm daily. *Oct-Mar* every 45mins 11am-9pm daily. **Admission** €8; free-€4 reductions. **Map** p56 C4 ❷

If you're after a quick tour of the sites, this, the oldest cruise operation, is the one to choose.

CinéAqua

NEW *2 av des Nations-Unies, 16th (01.40.69.23.23/www.cineaqua.com). M° Trocadéro.* **Open** 10am-8pm daily. **Admission** €19.50; free-€15 reductions. **Map** p56 B5 ❸

See box p58.

Cité de l'Architecture et du Patrimoine – Palais de la Porte Dorée

NEW *293 av Daumesnil, 12th (01.58.51.52.00/www.citechaillot.fr). M° Trocadéro.* **Open** 10am-5pm Mon, Wed-Sun. **Admission** *Exhibitions* free. *Art deco rooms & aquarium* €5.50; €4 reductions. **Map** p56 A4 ❹

See box p58.

Galerie-Musée Baccarat

11 pl des Etats-Unis, 16th (01.40.22. 11.00/www.baccarat.fr). M° Iéna. **Open** 10am-6pm Mon, Wed-Sat. **Admission** €7; free-€3.50 reductions. **Map** p56 B3 ❺

It didn't take long for this fab showcase – a neo-rococo wonderland in the old Musée Baccarat – to make the itinerary of every fashion victim in town. See items by great designers, services for princes and maharajahs, and ones made for great exhibitions of the 1800s. Its restaurant, Le Cristal Room, has decor by Philippe Starck, a menu by Thierry Burlot – and a two-month waiting list.

A
B
C
1
2
3
4
5
TERNES
CHAILLOT
16
AVENUE DES TERNES
BOULEVARD DE COURCELLES
AVENUE DE WAGRAM
AVENUE DE LA GRANDE ARMEE
AVENUE FOCH
AVENUE VICTOR HUGO
AVENUE KLEBER
AVENUE D'IENA
AVE MARCEAU
AVENUE MARCEAU
AVENUE HOCHE
AVENUE DE FRIEDLAND
AVENUE DES CHAMPS
AVENUE GEORGE V
AVENUE DU PRESIDENT WILSON
AVENUE DE NEW YORK
AV. D'IENA
AV. RAYMOND POINCARE
AV. MAC MAHON
AVENUE CARNOT
PONT DE L'ALMA
QUAI D'ORSAY
QUAI BRANLY
AVENUE RAPP
AVENUE BOSQUET
Seine
Arc de Triomphe
PLACE CHARLES DE GAULLE
Charles de Gaulle-Etoile
Ternes
Argentine
Kléber
Victor Hugo
Boissière
Iéna
Trocadéro
George V
Alma Marceau
Chambre de Commerce
American Cathedral
Palais Galliera
Musée Guimet
Palais de Tokyo
Palais de Chaillot
Musée du Quai Branly
Tour Eiffel
Cimetière de Passy
Porte Maillot
PL. DU TROCADERO ET DU 11 NOVEMBRE
PLACE VICTOR HUGO
PLACE DES ETATS-UNIS
Pont de l'Alma
1 Sights & museums
1 Eating & drinking
1 Shopping
1 Nightlife
1 Arts & leisure

Champs-Elysées & Western Paris

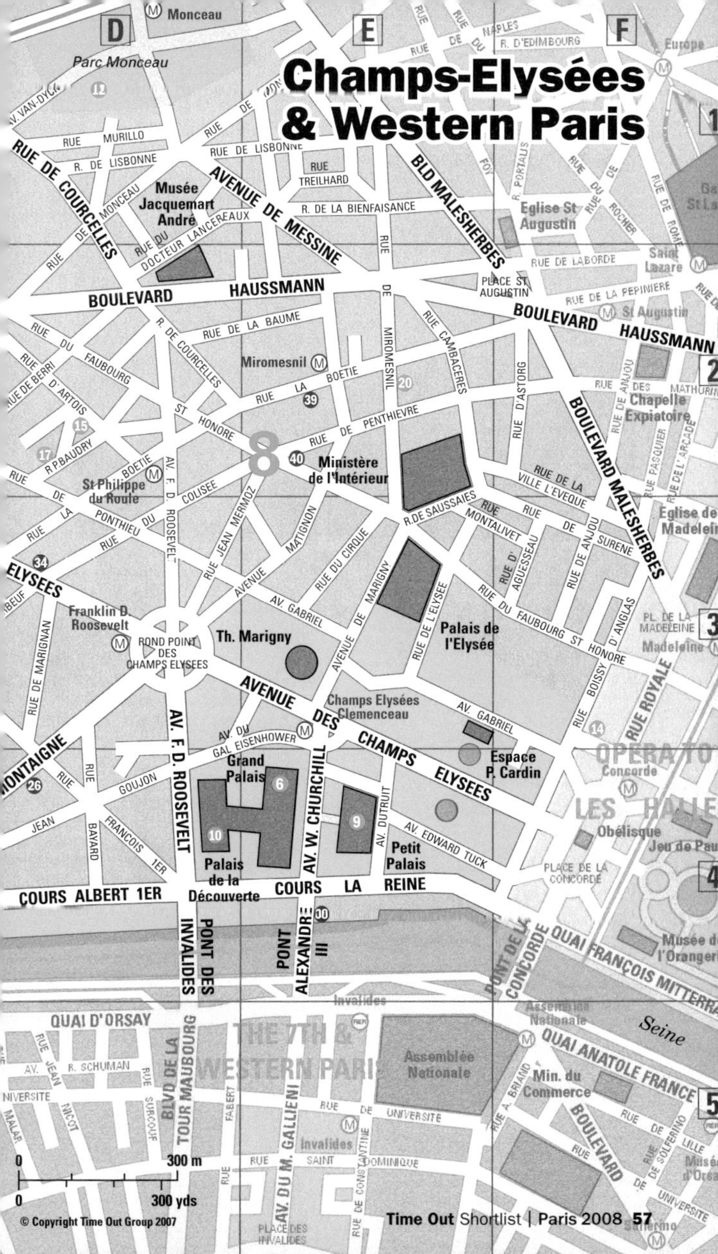

New kids on the Troc

CinéAqua

Hitherto best known for its views of the Eiffel Tower, the Trocadéro quarter is basking in a cultural renaissance having gained two major attractions in the space of a year. First came the aquarium-cum-cinema complex CinéAqua (p55), and then, in 2007, the massive new Cité de l'Architecture et du Patrimoine (p55).

The revamped and significantly enlarged aquarium opened in April 2006 – to outcry over its steep admission prices. Since then the full adult fee has dropped from €25 to €19.50, but it's still pretty pricey. That said, the underground complex is a cut above. Billing itself as a unique audio-visual watery experience, CinéAqua has its own animation studio, which produces the films that are shown on three cinema screens. Fish, though, are what this place is all about, and there are 12,000 in 43 tanks. The highlight is an 11-metre (36-foot) transparent tunnel that takes visitors under 2.2 million litres of water, among nurse sharks, guitarfish, stingrays and shoals of silver moonies. Visitors can then eat fish (not, one hopes, sourced from the tanks) at the complex's Japanese restaurant.

Sprawling across the eastern wing of the Palais de Chaillot, the Cité de l'Architecture is the result of a merger between the former Institut Français de l'Architecture and the Musée des Monuments Français. It takes a two-pronged approach, on the one hand presenting today's architecture and, on the other, showcasing the spectacular full-scale plaster mouldings of the old Galerie des Moulages, a tour de France of key churches and monuments from the 12th to 18th centuries; new galleries continue the story from the 19th on. Temporary exhibitions include a tricentenary tribute to Louis XIV's military architect Vauban from autumn 2007 and shorter exhibitions in the Galerie d'Actualités.

Galeries Nationales du Grand Palais

3 av du Général-Eisenhower, 8th (01.44.13.17.17/www.rmn.fr/galeriesnationalesdugrandpalais). M° Champs-Elysées Clemenceau. **Open** 10am-8pm Mon, Thur-Sun; 10am-10pm Wed. Booking compulsory before 1pm. **Admission** €10-€11.10; free-€8 reductions. **Map** p57 E4 ⑥

The Grand Palais was built for the 1900 Exposition Universelle, and during World War II accommodated Nazi tanks. In 1994 the magnificent glass-roofed central hall was closed when bits of metal started falling off, though exhibitions continued to be held in the other wings. The Palais reopened in 2005, and is now a venue for major shows.

Musée d'Art Moderne de la Ville de Paris

11 av du Président-Wilson, 16th (01.53.67.40.00/www.paris.fr/musees/MAMVP). M° Iéna or Alma Marceau. **Open** noon-8pm Tue-Sun. **Admission** *Permanent collection* free. *Exhibitions* €4.50; free-€2.50 reductions. **Map** p56 B4 ⑦

The monumental 1930s building that houses the city's modern art collection – the municipal collection, as opposed to the national one at the Centre Pompidou – reopened in 2006 after extensive renovation. Apart from Dufy's vast *La Fée Electricité* and the room devoted to Matisse's two versions of *La Danse*, the display is broadly chronological, from Fauvists and Cubists to the main French modern art movements. There are works by Léger, Delaunay, Klein and Fautrier, as well as a contemporary collection of Richter, Schutte and Douglas Gordon.

Musée National des Arts Asiatiques – Guimet

6 pl d'Iéna, 16th (01.56.52.53.00/www.museeguimet.fr). M° Iéna. **Open** 10am-5.45pm (last entry 5.15pm) Mon, Wed-Sun. **Admission** €6; free-€4 reductions. **Map** p56 B4 ⑧

Founded by industrialist Emile Guimet in 1889 to house his collection of Chinese and Japanese religious art, and later incorporating the oriental collections from the Louvre, the expanded Musée Guimet has 45,000 items.

Musée du Petit Palais

av Winston-Churchill, 8th (01.53.43.40.00/www.petitpalais.paris.fr). M° Champs-Elysées Clemenceau.

PARIS BY AREA

Alain Ducasse au Plaza Athénée p60

Open 10am-6pm Tue-Sun. **Admission** *Permanent collection* free. *Exhibitions* varies. **Map** p57 E4 9

Renovation has brought natural light flooding back in here to make the most of a new display of fine and decorative arts. An eclectic municipal art collection is strong on the 19th and early 20th centuries – paintings by Courbet, Sisley, Cézanne and Bonnard, sculpture by Dalou and Carpeaux, and art nouveau glass and pottery – but also includes 18th-century decorative arts, medieval and Renaissance paintings, enamels and ceramics, and a number of Greek and Russian icons and ancient Greek painted vases.

Palais de la Découverte

av Franklin-D.-Roosevelt, 8th (01.56.43.20.21/www.palais-decouverte.fr). M° Champs-Elysées Clemenceau or Franklin D Roosevelt. **Open** 9.30am-6pm Tue-Sat; 10am-7pm Sun. **Admission** €6.50; free-€4 reductions. *Planetarium* €3.50. **Map** p57 D4 10

The city's original science museum houses designs from Leonardo da Vinci's time right up to the present day. Models, real apparatus and audio-visual material bring displays to life; permanent exhibits cover astronomy, biology, chemistry, physics and earth sciences. The Planète Terre section shows the very latest developments in the field of meteorology.

Palais de Tokyo: Site de Création Contemporaine

13 av du Président-Wilson, 16th (01.47.23.54.01/www.palaisdetokyo.com). M° Iéna or Alma Marceau. **Open** noon-midnight Tue-Sun. **Admission** free-€6. **Map** p56 C4 11

When the Palais de Tokyo opened back in 2002, many thought that the stripped-back interior with visible air-conditioning at this art 'laboratory' was a statement. In fact, it was a practical decision motivated by budgetary constraints, but the 1937 building has come into its own as an open-plan space, permitting the coexistence of exhibitions and installations, fashion shows and performances.

Parc Monceau

bd de Courcelles, av Hoche, rue Monceau, 8th. M° Monceau. **Open** *Nov-Mar* 7am-8pm daily. *Apr-Oct* 7am-10pm daily. **Map** p57 D1 12

Surrounded by *grand hôtels particuliers* and elegant Haussmannian apartments, Parc Monceau is a favourite with well-dressed children and their nannies. It was laid out in the late 18th century for the Duc de Chartres in the then fashionable English style, with an oval lake, spacious lawns, an Egyptian pyramid, a Corinthian colonnade, a Venetian bridge and sarcophagi.

Eating & drinking

Alain Ducasse au Plaza Athénée

Hôtel Plaza Athénée, 25 av Montaigne, 8th (01.53.67.65.00/www.alain-ducasse.com). M° Alma Marceau. **Open** 7.45-10.15pm Mon-Fri. Closed mid July-mid Aug & 2wks Dec. **€€€€**. **Haute cuisine**. **Map** p56 C4 13

The Bowler

Its sheer glamour would be enough to recommend this restaurant, Ducasse's loftiest Paris undertaking. The dining room has a new clementine-and-white colour scheme; the ceiling drips with 10,000 crystals. An amuse-gueule of a langoustine in lemon cream with a dod of Iranian caviar starts a meal beautifully; try Breton lobster in apple, quince and spiced wine, and end with the rum baba *à Monte-Carlo*, with the finest rums for dousing.

Les Ambassadeurs

10 pl de la Concorde, 8th (01.44.71.16.17). M° Concorde. **Open** 7.30-10pm Mon; noon-2pm, 7.30-10pm Tue-Sat; 12.30-2pm Sun. **€€€€. Haute cuisine**. **Map** p57 F3 ⑭

The experience in the Hotel Crillon's prized restaurant, an 18th-century ballroom gilded and furnished with sky-high mirrors and marble, is pure classicism. The menu is predictably expensive: foie gras, lobster, duck and venison, luxury ingredients expertly prepared. Service is professional, even friendly for such a formal setting.

The Bowler

13 rue d'Artois, 8th (01.45.61.16.60/ www.thebowlerpub.com). M° Franklin D Roosevelt or St- Philippe du Roule. **Open** 11am-2am Mon-Fri; 1pm-2am Sat, Sun. **Pub**. **Map** p57 D2 ⑮

This unashamedly English pub is one of the best expat bars in Paris. Come for the draught Newcastle Brown Ale, Beamish Red and Guinness, a plate of fish'n'chips or to catch a game on one of the three flat-screen TVs.

Café de l'Homme

Musée de l'Homme, 17 pl du Trocadéro, 01.44.05.30.15/www.mnhn.fr). M° Trocadéro. **Open** 9.45am-5.15am Mon-Fri; 10am-6.30pm Sat, Sun. **Café**. **Map** p56 A5 ⑯

The fantastic terrace at the Musée de l'Homme's café has one of the best views of the Eiffel Tower in town (perfect for summer). Time your visit according to whether you want to dine or just order something to drink – food must be ordered at mealtimes.

River dance

Paris has a glitzy new waterfront nightclub.

It's only in the last decade or so that Parisians have started really paying attention to their river. The Seine is now the backdrop for merry-making of every stripe, and every year someone thinks of a new activity to associate with it. There's the summer beach jamboree Paris-Plage (p38), a new floating swimming pool (p160), tango under the stars in the Jardin Tino Rossi (quai St-Bernard) – and now Le Showcase (p64), a cavernous nightclub under the Right Bank end of the hopelessly romantic Pont Alexandre III. Other clubs can claim to be a little closer to the water than Le Showcase, by setting up on boats – as with Batofar (opposite 11 quai François-Mauriac, 01.53.60.17.30) and Bateau Concorde Atlantique – but they can't match the land-lubber's vast dimensions.

Le Showcase's impressive location is a former warehouse left empty by its former owners the Mairie de Paris; it took the man behind the club, stage musicals producer Alfred Cohen, seven years to persuade the council to sell up. Since opening in December 2006 it's been a huge success, pulling in the beautiful people with hot new rock bands and club nights like monthly Ulmann Cabarock. There are huge stone arches, a big dancefloor, snugs, stages, and plenty of sofas and armchairs – all artfully lit and impeccably sleek. Turn up early, and dress to impress.

Le Cou de la Girafe

7 rue Paul-Baudry, 8th (01.56.88. 29.55). M° St- Philippe du-Roule. **Open** noon-2.30pm, 7.30pm-11pm Mon-Sat. **€€€. Haute cuisine. Map** p57 D2 17

Frédéric Claudel took over the kitchen here in March 2006 and serves up impeccable food – *assiette du saumon*, herring with potato salad, delicious casseroles – to a local rather than touristy crowd. Come at lunchtime to take advantage of a cheaper but equally good menu.

Culture Bière

65 av des Champs-Elysées, 8th (01.42. 56.88.88/www.culturebiere.com). M° George V or Franklin D Roosevelt. **Open** 10.30am-2am Mon-Thur; 10.30am-4am Fri, Sat; 10.30am-midnight Sun. **Bar. Map** p56 C3 18

Opening a 'beer bar' on the Champs-Elysées could easily be a recipe for total disaster, but Heineken's Culture Bière venture seems to have succeeded with a gallery-lounge-restaurant concept that is innovative and decent value: you can eat here without drinking beer or food made with it, but the adventuresome will get a kick out of beer sorbet or crêpes topped with *confit de bière*.

Le Dada

12 av des Ternes, 17th (01.43.80. 60.12). M° Ternes. **Open** 6am-2am Mon-Sat; 6am-10pm Sun. **Bar. Map** p56 B1 19

Le Dada is known for its sunny terrace, though the Dada-influenced two-floor interior is ideal for an afternoon tipple. The wood-block carved tables and red walls provide a relaxed atmosphere for a well-heeled crowd.

Granterroirs

30 rue de Miromesnil, 8th (01.47. 42.18.18/www.granterroirs.com). M° Miromesnil. **Open** 9am-8pm Mon-Fri. Closed 3wks Aug. **€€. Bistro. Map** p57 E2 20

Plonk yourself at one of the massive communal tables at this *épicerie* with a difference and choose from the five succulent *plats du jour* (food served noon-3pm) on offer. There are over 600 enticing specialities (foie gras, tapenade, wine and so on) for sale here too.

Ladurée

75 av des Champs-Elysées, 8th (01.40. 75.08.75/www.laduree.fr). M° George V or Franklin D Roosevelt. **Open** 7.30am-midnight daily. **Café. Map** p56 C3 21

Everything in this 19th-century-style tearoom suggests decadence: the decor, the teas, the pastries and, above all, the hot chocolate. Creamier than heaven, it leaves you in the kind of stupor requisite for any lazy afternoon. Another branch at 16 rue Royale (01.42.60.21.79) is known for its macaroons.

La Table de Lauriston

129 rue de Lauriston, 16th (01.47. 27.00.07). M° Trocadéro. **Open** noon-2.30pm, 7-10.30pm Mon-Fri; 7-10.30pm Sat. Closed 3wks Aug. **€€€. Haute cuisine. Map** p56 A4 22

Serge Barbey's dining room has a feminine feel, with pink, orange and silver paintwork, velvety chairs and whimsical paintings. The food is excellent – try the *entrecôte* with *gratin dauphinois* or sautéed *ratte* potatoes.

Taillevent

15 rue Lamennais, 8th (01.44.95.15.01/www.taillevent.com). M° George V. **Open** 12.15-2pm, 7.15-10pm Mon-Fri. Closed Aug. **€€€. Haute cuisine. Map** p56 C2 ㉓

This ever-successful restaurant turns out flawless food. The *rémoulade de coquilles saint-jacques* is a technical feat, with delicate slices of raw, marinated scallop wrapped in a tube shape around a finely diced apple filling; an earthier dish is the trademark *épeautre* (spelt) cooked 'like a risotto' with bone marrow, black truffle, whipped cream and parmesan.

Shopping

Alléosse

13 rue Poncelet, 17th (01.46.22.50.45). M° Ternes. **Open** 9am-1pm, 4-7pm Tue-Thur; 9am-1pm, 4.30-7pm Fri, Sat. **Map** p56 B1 ㉔

People cross town for these cheeses – wonderful farmhouse camemberts, delicate st-marcellins, a choice of *chèvres* and several rarities.

Balenciaga

10 av George-V, 8th (01.47.20.21.11/www.balenciaga.com). M° Alma Marceau or George V. **Open** 10am-7pm Mon-Sat. **Map** p56 C4 ㉕

With Nicolas Ghesquière at the helm, this Spanish fashion house has jumped way ahead of Japanese and Belgian designers in the chic stakes. Floating fabrics contrast with dramatic cuts, producing a sophisticated urban style that the *haut monde* can't wait to slip into. The 'Motorcycle Le Dix' bags – popularised by an endless array of supermodels and actresses – are particularly covetable.

Christian Dior

30 av Montaigne, 8th (01.40.73.54.44/www.dior.com). M° Franklin D Roosevelt. **Open** 10am-7pm Mon-Sat. **Map** p57 D4 ㉖

To judge from the girls who flock from the suburbs, life savings in hand, to buy a Dior bag, Nick Knight's advertising campaigns have worked. Acclaimed, gifted fashion designer John Galliano is behind the label's upbeat, youthful and sexy new image.

Drugstore Publicis

133 av des Champs-Elysées, 8th (01.44.43.79.00/www.publicisdrugstore.com). M° Charles de Gaulle Etoile. **Open** 8am-2am Mon-Fri; 10am-2am Sat, Sun. **Map** p56 B2 ㉗

After a long renovation, this famous address has been clad with neon swirls and a glass-and-steel café. On the ground floor are a pharmacy, bookshop and posh deli. The basement is a macho take on Colette, with design items (some exclusive) and lifestyle magazines, some fine wines and a smart cigar cellar.

Fnac

74 av des Champs-Elysées, 8th (01.53.53.64.64/concert tickets 08.92.68.36.22/www.fnac.com). M° George V. **Open** 10am-midnight Mon-Sat; noon-midnight Sun. **Map** p56 C3 ㉘

The Fnac chain is known for its vast and varied array of books, DVDs, CDs, computers and photographic equipment. Some branches – like the one at Forum des Halles – stock all of the above; others are more specialised. All Fnac branches also operate as a concert ticket box office; this one stays open latest.

Lancel

127 av des Champs-Elysees, 8th (01.56.89.15.70). M° Charles de Gaulle Etoile. **Open** 10.30am-8pm Mon-Sat. **Map** p56 B2 ㉙

With its aerodynamic design the new Lancel flagship is about more than just handbags: it's about staking out turf as a lifestyle brand. Its open-shelved 'bag bar' display may owe a debt to the dearer Vuitton flagship down the street, but this shop shows where Lancel is heading, and if the 40-plus silver Sceau bags hung from the ceiling is any clue, it could be interesting.

Louis Vuitton

101 av des Champs-Elysées, 8th (08.10.81.00.10/www.vuitton.com). M° George V. **Open** 10am-8pm Mon-Sat. **Map** p56 C3 ㉚

After major renovation, this flagship store reopened in October 2005 to reveal a stunning spiralled interior. Artistic director Marc Jacobs has made Vuitton's luggage, accessories and fashion line what they are today.

Nike Champs-Elysées

67 av des Champs-Elysées, 8th (01.42.25.93.80/www.nike.com). M° George V. **Open** 10am-10pm Mon-Thur; 10am-11pm Fri-Sat; noon-9pm Sun. **Map** p56 C3 ㉛

The Nike concept store here is not as intimidating or as crowded as the ones in London or NYC. There are plenty of Paris-specific T-shirts and other work-out gear, as well as a Nike Lab custom design service on the lower level.

Prada

10 av Montaigne, 8th (01.53.23.99.40/www.prada.com). M° Alma Marceau. **Open** 11am-7pm Mon; 10am-7pm Tue-Sat. **Map** p56 C4 ㉜

Miuccia Prada turned Prada's handbags into the accessory of choice for discerning fashionistas – the Paris boutiques are recognisable by the trademark lime-green walls.

Sephora

70 av des Champs-Elysées, 8th (01.53.93.22.50/www.sephora.fr). M° Franklin D Roosevelt. **Open** 10am-midnight daily (until 1.30am July, Aug). **Map** p56 C3 ㉝

The flagship of the cosmetic supermarket chain houses 12,000 French and foreign beauty brands, including Shiseido, Philosophy, Paul & Joe, Nars and own brand products.

Virgin Megastore

52-60 av des Champs-Elysées, 8th (01.49.53.50.00/www.virginmega.fr). M° Franklin D Roosevelt. **Open** 10am-midnight Mon-Sat; noon-midnight Sun. **Map** p57 D3 ㉞

Browse books, CDs and DVDs until midnight; the listening posts let you sample any CD by scanning its barcode. Tickets for concerts and sports events are available here too, as are books and magazines in profusion.

Nightlife

Le Baron

6 av Marceau, 8th (01.47.20.04.11/www.clublebaron.com). M° Alma-Marceau. **Open** times vary. **Admission** free. **Map** p56 C4 ㉟

Since it opened in 2004, Le Baron has changed the face of Paris clubbing. A former hostess bar run by a group of amigos (Lionel and André are the names to drop) it fills nightly with happy, shiny people grooving to rock, funk and disco. You need to be introduced by an habitué to get in: make friends in the queue.

Le Lido

116bis av des Champs-Elysées, 8th (01.40.76.56.10/www.lido.fr). M° George V or Franklin D Roosevelt. **Open** *Dinner* 7.30pm daily. *Shows* 9.30pm, 11.30pm daily. **Admission** €80-€210; €20-€30 reductions. **Map** p56 C2 ㊱

With 1,000 seats, this classy cabaret is the largest and priciest in town. Star chef Paul Bocuse has revamped the menu; the somewhat tame show features boob-shaking, wacky costumes and odd acts.

Queen

102 av des Champs-Elysées, 8th (08.92.70.73.30/www.queen.fr). M° George V. **Open** midnight-7am Mon-Thur, Sun; midnight-8am Fri, Sat. **Admission** varies. **Map** p56 C2 ㊲

This top-notch gay club has become rather unimaginative – except when a global DJ is invited or on Wednesday nights, when a hipper bunch grinds to maximum R&B.

Le Showcase

NEW *Pont Alexandre III, Port des Champs-Elysées, 8th (01 45 61 25 43). M° Champs-Elysées Clemenceau.* **Open** times vary. **Admission** varies. **Map** p57 E4 ㊳

See box p61.

Arts & leisure

Salle Gaveau

45 rue La Boétie, 8th (01.49.53.05.07/ www.sallegaveau.com). M° Miromesnil. **Open** times vary. **Map** p57 E2 ㊴

In addition to chamber music, the Salle Gaveau can now accommodate full orchestras without losing its intimacy.

Salle Pleyel

NEW *252 rue du Fbg-St-Honoré, 8th (01.42.56.13.13/www.sallepleyel.fr).* **Open** times vary. **Map** p57 E2 ㊵

Home to the Orchestre de Paris, this gorgeously restored concert hall is the city's only venue dedicated to large-scale symphonic concerts (though top soloists also play). The art deco elegance is back, and acoustic experts have dramatically improved the sound of the place.

Théâtre des Champs-Elysées

15 av Montaigne, 8th (01.49.52. 50.50/www.theatrechampselysees.fr). M° Alma Marceau. **Open** times vary. **Map** p56 C4 ㊶

This beautiful theatre hosted the scandalous première of Stravinsky's *Le Sacre du Printemps* in 1913. Star classical performers and orchestras play here.

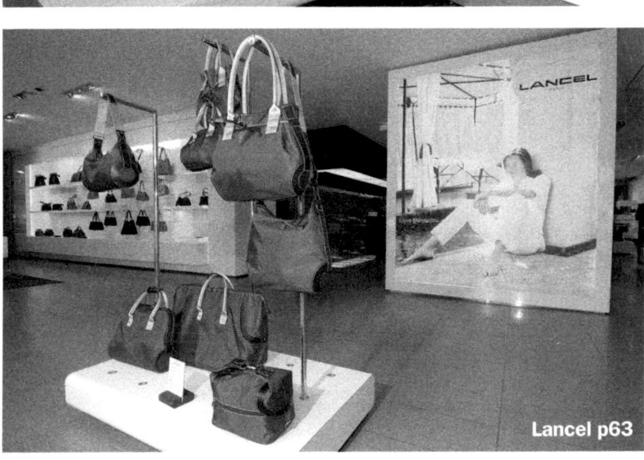

Lancel p63

PARIS BY AREA

Musée du Louvre

Opéra to Les Halles

The city's original opera house, known to Parisians as the Palais Garnier (after its architect) is a wedding-cake confection of gilt and grandeur. To the south-east, Les Halles remains the belly of Paris and its geographic centre, with a daily discharge of 800,000 people from its massive RER-métro interchange. Its reputation for soulless 1970s architecture and knots of shifty youths from the suburbs should be effaced when the vast recasting of the area and its shopping mall is finished – although that task is several years from completion. For a flavour of how Les Halles used to be, sniff out the produce stalls and cafés of the lovely rue Montorgueil.

A short distance west of Les Halles is the Louvre, no longer the centre of French power though it still exerts influence as a symbol of cultural Paris, a palace within the city. Around it grew subsidiary palaces, including the Palais Cardinal, today's Palais Royal. Between the elegant calm of the Palais Royal and shopping hub of the Grands Boulevards is squeezed the city's traditional business district, sleepy at weekends.

Sights & museums

Eglise de la Madeleine

pl de la Madeleine, 8th (01.44.51. 69.00). M° Madeleine or Concorde.
Open 9am-7pm daily. **Map** p68 A2 ❶
The building of a church here began in 1764; then Napoléon gave instructions for a 'Temple of Glory' dedicated to his army. After his fall building slowed; the edifice, by then a church again, was consecrated in 1845. The exterior is ringed

by Corinthian columns, with a frieze of the Last Judgement above the portico.

Forum des Halles

1st. M° Les Halles/RER Châtelet Les Halles. **Map** p69 E4 ❷

This vast mall covers three levels underground and includes a multiplex, clothing chains, swimming pool, giant Fnac store, the Forum des Images cinema complex, and the Forum des Créateurs, a section given over to young designers.

Jardin des Tuileries

rue de Rivoli, 1st. M° Tuileries or Concorde. **Open** 7.30am-7pm daily. **Map** p68 B4 ❸

Between the Louvre and place de la Concorde, the gravelled alleyways of the gardens have been a chic promenade since they opened in the 16th century. André Le Nôtre created the prototypical French garden with terraces and a central vista through circular and hexagonal ponds. There's a funfair in summer.

Jeu de Paume

1 pl de la Concorde, 8th (01.47.03.12.50/www.jeudepaume.org). M° Concorde. **Open** noon-9pm Tue; noon-7pm Wed-Fri; 10am-7pm Sat, Sun. **Admission** €6; €3 reductions. **Map** p68 A3 ❹

Once a tennis court, the Jeu de Paume is the new site of the Centre National de la Photographie. It offers two large galleries and a video art and cinema suite in the basement.

Musée des Arts Décoratifs

107 rue de Rivoli, 1st (01.44.55.57.50/www.lesartsdecoratifs.fr). M° Palais Royal Musée du Louvre or Pyramides. **Open** 11am-6pm Tue-Fri; 10am-6pm Sat, Sun. **Admission** (with Musée de la Mode & Musée de la Publicité) €8; free-€6.50 reductions. **Map** p68 C4 ❺

Old false floors have been removed here and the magnificent central nave opened up to provide a spacious, stylish setting for a collection of decorative arts that runs from the Middle Ages to today, with a wealth of art nouveau and art deco items. Period rooms range from a Gothic chamber from an Auvergne castle to the ornate bedroom of Baron William Hope.

Musée de l'Orangerie

Jardin des Tuileries, 1st (01.40.20.67.71/www.musee-orangerie.fr). M° Concorde. **Open** 12.30-7pm Mon-Wed, Thur, Sat, Sun; 12.30-9pm Fri. **Admission** €6.50; free-€4.50 reductions. **Map** p68 A4 ❻

With the reopening of the Orangerie in 2006, pride of place goes once more to the waterlilies and weeping willows of Monet's curved, late canvases, painted at different seasons and times of day and displayed in the natural light for which they were intended. The Jean Walter and Paul Guillaume Collection is hung in new rooms under the Tuileries gardens, a testimony to the taste of early 20th-century collector Paul Guillaume, who managed to snap up masterpieces by Renoir, Picasso and Cézanne.

Musée du Louvre

rue de Rivoli, 1st (01.40.20.50.50/www.louvre.fr). M° Palais Royal Musée du Louvre. **Open** 9am-6pm Mon, Thur, Sat, Sun; 9am-9.45pm Wed, Fri. Closed Tue. **Admission** €8.50; free-€6 reductions. **Map** p68 C6 ❼

The most famous museum in the world is several museums. Treasures from the Egyptians, Etruscans, Greeks and Romans each have their own huge galleries, as do Middle Eastern and Islamic art. There are European decorative arts from the Middle Ages up to the 19th century, and in the Sully wing you can roam through rooms distinguished by lavish interior design. Work in the galleries of *arts premiers* ('primitive' art) in the Pavillon des Sessions provides a primer for the Musée du Quai Branly.

The main draw is western painting and sculpture, mostly contained in the vast Denon wing. There are around 6,000 of the most famous paintings in the world on show, the most impressive being the vast 18th- to 19th-century canvases hanging in the Grande Galerie. In 2005, the Salle des Etats reopened after a four-year renovation programme, the

Opéra to Les Halles

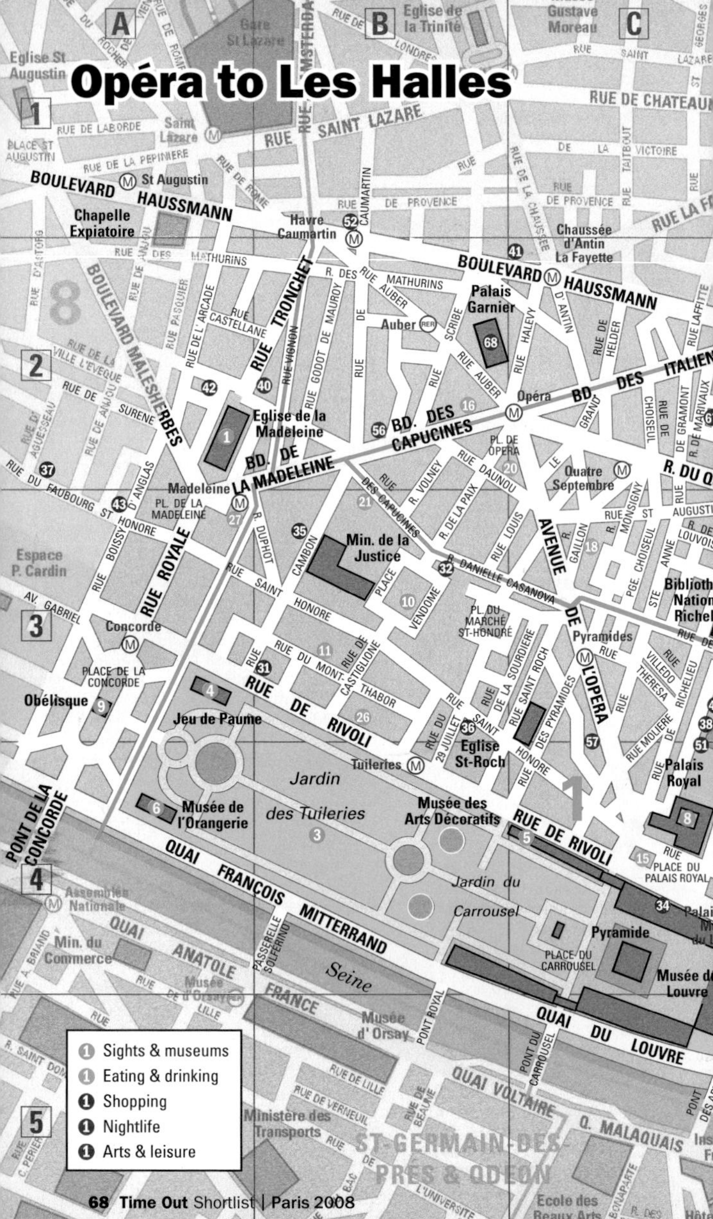

D
E
F
1
2
3
4
5
Poissonnière
Rue Bellefond
Rue des Petits Hotels
Blvd de Magenta
Rue d'Alsace
Gare de l'Est
Rue Lamartine
Rue La Fayette
Rue des Messageries
Rue de Chabrol
Rue d'Hauteville
Hôpital St Lazare
North-East Paris
Cadet
Rue Bleue
Rue Cadet
Rue Saulnier
Rue de Trevise
Cité de Trevise
Rue du Faubourg Poissonnière
Rue de Paradis
Musée du Cristal
0
300 m
300 yds
© Copyright Time Out Group 2007
Rue Richer
Rue Drouot
Rue de la Grange-Batalière
Rue du Faubourg Montmartre
R. de Montyon
R. Ste Cecile
Rue Bergère
Cité Bergère
P. Jouffroy
Rue des Petites Ecuries
Rue G. Laumain
Rue Martel
Château d'Eau
Cours des Pres. Ecuries
Rue du Château d'Eau
Boulevard de Strasbourg
Rue du Faubourg St Martin
Rue de Nancy
Rue Hittorff
10
Rue d'Enghien
Rue de l'Echiquier
Rue de Mazagran
Rue du Faubourg Saint Denis
R. de Metz
Pge Brady
Bd. Montmartre
Grands Boulevards
Bd. Poissonnière
Bonne Nouvelle
Bd. de Bonne Nouvelle
Strasbourg St Denis
Bd. St Denis
Rue René Boulanger
Blvd St Martin
Rue Bouchardon
Cité Riverin
Rue Vivienne
Rue d'Uzes
Rue St Marc
R. Feydeau
Rue Montmartre
Rue St Fiacre
Rue du Sentier
Rue Poissonnière
R. de la Lune
Rue Beauregard
Rue de Cléry
Rue des Jeuneurs
Rue du Croissant
R. St Joseph
Rue d'Aboukir
R. Ste Foy
R. Ste Apolline
Rue Saint Denis
R. de Tracy
Rue Mezlay
Rue Notre Dame de Nazareth
Rue du Vertbois
Rue Réaumur
Rue P. Lelong
Rue N. D. des Victoires
Rue de la Banque
Rue du Mail
Sentier
Rue du Caire
Boulevard de Sebastopol
Rue St Martin
Conservatoire National des Arts et Métiers
Rue L. Bellan
Rue Bachaumont
Place des Victoires
Rue St Sauveur
Réaumur-Sébastopol
Rue Turbigo
Banque de France
R. Mander
Rue Greneta
Rue Montorgueil
R. M. Stuart
Pge du G. Cerf
Rue Tiquetonne
Rue Etienne Marcel
R. Herold
Rue du Louvre
Hôtel des Postes
Rue J. J. Rousseau
Etienne Marcel
Rue de Turbigo
Rue Pierre Lescot
Rue du Temple
Rue au Maire
Arts et Métiers
Rue des Gravilliers
Rue Chapon
Rue de Montmorency
Rue Michel Le Comte
Rue Beaubourg
Rue Coquillère
R. du Jour
Les Halles
Rue Bourse du Commerce
Rue Berger
Châtelet Les Halles
Forum des Halles
Rambuteau
Rue Rambuteau
Musée d'Art et d'Histoire du Judaïsme
Rue des Archives
Rue des 4 Fils
Rue Braque
Rue Saint Honoré
Louvre Rivoli
Rue Quincampoix
Centre Pompidou
Rue du Renard
Rue des Blancs Manteaux
Archives Nationales
Rue de l'Arbre Sec
R. de la Monnaie
Rue du Pont Neuf
Rue des Bourdonnais
Rue des Halles
Rue de Rivoli
Rue des Lombards
Rue Ste Croix de la Bretonnerie
Rue des Rosiers
Pont Neuf
Châtelet
Quai de la Mégisserie
Place du Châtelet
Avenue Victoria
Rue de la Verrerie
Marais
Hôtel de Ville
Quai de Gesvres
Pl. au Change
Quai de l'Horloge
Place Dauphine
Conciergerie
Pont Neuf
Rue Coq Héron
Rue du Colonel Driant

Rue Montorgueil p66

museum's two most celebrated works, the *Mona Lisa* and Veronese's lavish *Wedding at Cana*, given pride of place in the glass-roofed room. Queues are inevitable after the release of the film version of bestselling *The Da Vinci Code* – and doubly so since the museum launched a *Code*-themed audioguide.

IM Pei's glass pyramid makes you think this is the only entrance – but you'll be standing in a queue waiting for your bag to go through a scanner. Buying a ticket in advance means you can go in via the passage Richelieu off rue de Rivoli, or the Carrousel du Louvre mall at 99 rue de Rivoli. Advance tickets, from the Louvre website, Fnac and Virgin Megastore, are valid for any day.

Palais Royal

pl du Palais-Royal, 1st. M° Palais Royal Musée du Louvre. **Open** *Gardens* 7.30am-8.30pm daily. **Map** p68 C4 ⑧

Cardinal Richelieu left this building to Louis XIII, whose widow Anne d'Autriche rechristened it when she moved in with her son, the young Louis XIV. In the 1780s the gardens were enclosed in a three-storey peristyle filled with cafés, theatres and shops; people of all classes mingled here. Daniel Buren's modern installation of black-and-white-striped columns occupies the courtyard.

Place de la Concorde

1st/8th. M° Concorde. **Map** p68 A4 ⑨

The city's largest square has grand east–west perspectives from the Louvre to the Arc de Triomphe, and north–south from the Madeleine to the Assemblée Nationale. Gabriel designed it in the 1750s, along with the two colonnaded mansions astride rue Royale. In 1792 the centre statue of Louis XV was replaced with the guillotine for Louis XVI, Marie-Antoinette and many more. The square was embellished in the 19th century with fountains and the Luxor obelisk.

Place Vendôme

1st. M° Tuileries. **Map** p68 B3 ⑩

This eight-sided square is luxury central, home to the swanky Ritz hotel and a clutch of very A-list jewellery brands. The column in the centre was modelled on Trajan's Column in Rome, with a spiral strip illustrating Napoléon's exploits. During the 1871 Commune it was pulled down; the present column is a replica.

Musée de l'Orangerie p67

Eating & drinking

L'Ardoise

28 rue du Mont-Thabor, 1st (01.42. 96.28.18). M° Concorde or Tuileries. **Open** noon-2.30pm, 6.30-11pm Tue-Sat; 6.30-11pm Sun. Closed 3wks Aug. €. **Bistro**. **Map** p68 B3 ⑪

One of the city's most outstanding modern bistros, and one of few to open on Sundays. Wise choices from the delicious €31 blackboard menu might be six oysters with warm chipolatas and a pungent shallot dressing, or hare pie with an escalope of foie gras in its centre.

Au Pied de Cochon

6 rue Coquillière, 1st (01.40.13.77.00/ www.pieddecochon.com). M° Les Halles. **Open** 24hrs daily. €. **Brasserie**. **Map** p69 D4 ⑫

This brasserie is a remnant of the time when Les Halles was a wholesale market. Now it's an ornate, pig-themed tourist favourite, but has smart and very professional standards. Try the signature trotters, or famous (and heartily delicious) cheese-capped onion soup. Finish with a plate of the excellent crêpes flambées.

Aux Lyonnais

32 rue St-Marc, 2nd (01.42.96.65.04). M° Bourse or Richelieu Drouot. **Open** noon-2pm, 7.30-11pm Tue-Fri; 7.30-11pm Sat. Closed 3wks Aug. €€. **Bistro**. **Map** p68 C2 ⑬

This classic bistro run by Alain Ducasse has gorgeous belle époque tiles and an antique zinc bar. From the menu of intelligently modernised Lyonnais, Bressane and Beaujolais classics, start with charcuterie from Sibilla (the best in Lyon); follow with steak served with sautéed shallots and a side of cheesy, garlicky mash. Wind up with the sublime st-marcellin cheese and a Cointreau soufflé.

La Bourse ou la Vie

12 rue Vivienne, 2nd (01.42.60.08.83). M° Bourse. **Open** noon-3pm, 7-10pm daily. **Bistro**. **Map** p69 D3 ⑭

The owner of La Bourse has one mission in life – to revive the dying art of the perfect steak-frites. Choose between ultra-tender coeur de filet or a huge, surprisingly unchewy bavette (unless you inexplicably decide to go for the cod) and enjoy. The frites are impressively crunchy thanks to the suet they're cooked in.

Café Marly

93 rue de Rivoli, cour Napoléon du Louvre, 1st (01.49.26.06.60). M° Palais Royal Musée du Louvre. **Open** 8am-2am daily. **Café**. **Map** p68 C4 15

A class act, this, as you might expect of a Costes café whose lofty arcaded terrace overlooks the Louvre's glass pyramid. Splash out on a Chocolate Martini or Shark of vodka, lemonade and grenadine. Brasserie fare and sandwiches are on offer, too.

Café de la Paix

12 bd des Capucines, 9th (01.40.07.36.36). M° Opéra. **Open** 7am-midnight daily. **Café**. **Map** p68 B2 16

The sumptuous terrace café-restaurant of the Grand InterContinental oozes history. Your table, beneath the ornate stucco ceiling or overlooking Garnier's opera house, may be the one patronised by Oscar Wilde, Josephine Baker or Emile Zola. Immaculate staff serve bowls of nuts and olives with your €9 kir or €7 glass of draught Grimbergen. Once-in-a-holiday stuff: lap it up.

De la Ville Café

34 bd Bonne-Nouvelle, 10th (01.48.24.48.09/www.delavillecafe.com). M° Bonne Nouvelle. **Open** 11am-2am daily. **Bar**. **Map** p69 E2 17

Run by the Café Charbon crew, De la Ville has brought good news to Bonne Nouvelle. An expansion and refurb upped the ante; the distressed walls and hippie feel remain, the curvy club section is now terribly cool. A grand staircase leads to a lounge and gallery space.

Drouant

16-18 pl Gaillon, 2nd (01.42.65.15.16). M° Opéra. **Open** noon-2.30pm, 7pm-midnight daily. **€€€**. **Brasserie**. **Map** p68 C3 18

Star Alsatian chef Antoine Westermann, who runs the successful Ile St-Louis bistro Mon Vieil Ami (see pX), has brought this landmark 1880 brasserie into the 21st century with bronze-coloured banquettes, a pale parquet floor and butter-yellow paint and fabrics. The place is dedicated to the art of the hors d'oeuvre, served in themed sets of four ranging from a surprisingly successful Thai beef salad to silky leeks in vinaigrette. The bite-sized surprises continue with the mains – four for each dish, to be shared – and the multiple mini desserts.

Le Fumoir

6 rue de l'Amiral-de-Coligny, 1st (01.42.92.00.24/www.lefumoir.fr). M° Louvre Rivoli. **Open** 11am- 2am daily. Closed 2wks Aug. **Bar**. **Map** p69 D4 19

This elegant bar is a local institution: neo-colonial fans purr, paintings adorn the walls and the bar staff mix fine cocktails. Sip Martinis at the long mahogany bar (taken from a Chicago speakeasy), eat in the restaurant and admire pretty young things in the library.

Harry's New York Bar

5 rue Daunou, 2nd (01.42.61.71.14). M° Opéra. **Open** 10.30am-4am daily. **Bar**. **Map** p68 B2 20

The city's quintessential American bar is still the atmospheric, pennant-bedecked institution beloved of expats

A Royal reception

Marc Jacobs puts the Palais Royal in the spotlight.

Palais Royal

Marc Jacobs is on a roll. Not only is he fashion king of luxury's top-selling house, Louis Vuitton, he's also the only designer to have captured the distinctive downtown New York vibe and made it real for grunge fans and Park Avenue princesses alike. In 2006 he set up his first signature boutique in Europe in the Palais Royal, formerly a sleepy pocket of central Paris best known for its pretty garden and arcades.

It was an inspired move – and one that's injected a new buzz to the area. With its marble floors, Christian Liagre furniture and muted grey and white walls, the new boutique is perfectly elegant. The stock runs to womenswear, menswear, accessories and shoes, and the designer's legions of admirers are snapping up his perfect shifts, funky T-shirts and flats like there's no tomorrow.

Still, while Jacobs's arrival was a flashpoint in the neighbourhood's fashion status, he wasn't the first style merchant to colonise the Palais. Fashion expert, vintage collector and renowned designer **Didier Ludot** has two boutiques just along the galerie de Montpensier from Jacobs. The prices are steep, but the pieces are stunning: Dior, Molyneux, Balenciaga, Pucci, Féraud and, of course, Chanel, from the 1920s onwards; Ludot also borrows other shop windows around the Palais to exhibit his best pieces. A few doors away is an elegant outpost of the fashion editor's favourite jewellery shop Casoar (No.29), which displays delicate re-editions of Napoleon III, belle èpoque and art deco jewellery. And on the other side of the garden, in the galerie de Valois, the **Salons du Palais-Royal Shiseido** is an intricately hand-painted temple of heady perfumes by Serge Lutens; while fashion darling Pierre Hardy (No.156) has a classy black-and-white foothold that sells his range of superbly conceived shoes for men and women.

PARIS BY AREA

and hard-drinking Parisians. The white-coated bartenders mix some of the best cocktails in town, from the bloody mary (invented here, so they say) to the well-named Pétrifiant, half a dozen strong spirits splashed into a beer mug.

Hemingway Bar at the Ritz

Hôtel Ritz, 15 pl Vendôme, 1st (01.43.16.33.65/www.ritzparis.com). M° Concorde or Opéra. **Open** 6.30pm-2am daily. **Bar**. **Map** p68 B3 ㉑

This is a wonderfully civilised place in which to get smashed. Bartenders Colin and Ludo whip up fabulous cocktails (and compliments and flowers for the ladies) in a gloriously sauve manner.

Un Jour à Peyrassol

13 rue Vivienne, 2nd (01.42.60.12.92/www.peyrassol.com). M° Bourse. **Open** noon-2pm, 8-10pm daily. **Brasserie**. **Map** p68 C3 ㉒

This casually chic offshoot of the Commanderie de Peyrassol, a wine-producing castle in the Var, specialises in truffles. Try them on toast, atop a baked potato, in scrambled eggs or in a rich sauce with gnocchi. Naturally, there are some great complementary wines too.

Kai

18 rue du Louvre, 1st (01.40.15.01.99). M° Louvre-Rivoli. **Open** noon-2pm, 7-10.30pm Tue-Sat; 7-10pm Sun. Closed Aug. **€€**. **Japanese**. **Map** p69 D4 ㉓

Tall sprigs of cherry blossom lend a splash of colour to this fashionably minimalist Japanese restaurant. The 'Kai-style' sushi is a modern and zesty take on a classic: try the marinated and lightly grilled yellowtail pressed on to *shiso*-scented rice.

Kong

1 rue du Pont-Neuf, 1st (01.40.39.09.00/www.kong.fr). M° Pont Neuf. **Open** noon-2am Mon-Thur, Sun; noon-3am Fri, Sat. **Bar**. **Map** p69 D5 ㉔

This Starck-designed bar on the top two floors of the Kenzo building is one of the city's hottest spots. The bright mishmash interior is manga-inspired. Perch at the long bar, and order an excellent Vodkatini. After dark you can make a music suggestion with each order. There's a dance space at weekends should you wish to show off a few moves.

Liza

14 rue de la Banque, 2nd (01.55.35.00.66). M° Bourse. **Open** noon-2.15pm, 8-10.30pm daily. **€€**. **Lebanese**. **Map** p69 D3 ㉕

A showcase of the cuisine and style of contemporary Beirut, Liza offers an impressive array of unusual meze (grilled halloumi with apricot preserve or lentil, fried onion and orange salad, for example), grills and Lebanese wines. This place is packed every night with a young crowd so make sure you book.

Le Meurice

Hôtel Meurice, 228 rue de Rivoli, 1st (01.44.58.10.10/www.meuricehotel.com). M° Tuileries. **Open** noon-2pm, 7.30-10pm Tue-Fri; 7.30-10pm Sat. Closed Aug. **€€€**. **Haute cuisine**. **Map** p68 B3 ㉖

Yannick Alléno produces glorious contemporary French luxury cuisine. Turbot is sealed in clay before cooking, then sauced with celery cream and a coulis of parsley; Bresse chicken stuffed with foie gras and served with truffled *sarladais* potatoes (cooked in the fat of the bird) is breathtaking. The cheeses on offer are from Quatrehomme, and the pastry chef amazes with his huge millefeuilles.

Senderens

9 pl de la Madeleine, 8th (01.42.65.22.90/www.lucascarton.com). M° Madeleine. **Open** noon-3pm, 7.30-11.15pm daily. Closed 3wks Aug. **€€€€**. **Haute cuisine**. **Map** p68 A3 ㉗

Veteran chef Alain Senderens has recast his art nouveau institution with a *Star Trek* interior and a fusion menu. He serves roast duck foie gras with a warm salad of black figs and liquorice powder, or monkfish steak with Spanish mussels and green curry sauce. Each dish comes with a suggested wine, whisky, sherry or punch. A meal here is always a real event.

Table d'Hôte du Palais Royal

8 rue du Beaujolais, 1st (01.42.61. 25.30/www.carollsinclair.com). M° Bourse or Pyramides. **Open** 11.30am-2.30pm, 6pm-midnight daily. €€€. **Brasserie**. **Map** p68 C3 ㉘

Caroll Sinclair's restaurant, set just outside the Palais-Royal garden, has an informal feel (the idea of *table d'hôte* is that diners should feel like guests in a private home). The excellent prix fixe pulls a younger crowd while the à la carte offers the likes of crayfish bisque, *boeuf tartare* or tuna with foie gras.

Le Tambour

41 rue Montmartre, 2nd (01.42.33. 06.90). M° Sentier. **Open** 6pm-6am daily. **Bar**. **Map** p69 D3 ㉙

A nighthawks' bar, decked out with vintage transport chic: slatted wooden banquettes and bus-stop-sign bar stools occupied by chatty regulars. At the small counter area, staff and souses banter, while a long dining room is memorable for its retro métro map.

Shopping

Agnès b

2, 3, 6, 10 & 19 rue du Jour, 1st (men 01.42.33.04.13/women 01.45.08.56.56/ www.agnesb.com). M° Les Halles. **Open** *Oct-Apr* 10am-7pm Mon-Sat. *May-Sept* 10am-7.30pm. **Map** p69 D4 ㉚

Agnès b rarely wavers from her design vision: pure lines in fine quality cotton, merino wool and silk. Best buys are shirts, pullovers and cardigans that keep their shape for years. Her mini-empire of men's, women's, children's, and sportswear shops is all nearby.

Alice Cadolle

4 rue Cambon, 1st (01.42.60.94.22/ www.cadolle.com). M° Concorde or Madeleine. **Open** 10am-1pm, 2-7pm Mon-Sat. Closed Aug. **Map** p68 B3 ㉛

This lingerie boutique was founded by Hermine Cadolle, inventor of the brassière. Her great-great-granddaughter, Poupie Cadolle, continues the family tradition in a cosy space devoted to a luxury ready-to-wear line.

Boucheron

26 pl Vendôme, 1st (01.42.61.58.16/ www.boucheron.com). M° Opéra. **Open** 10.30am-7pm Mon-Sat. **Map** p68 B3 ㉜

The grandest shop on place Vendôme, Boucheron was the first to set up here, eager for custom from the nearby Ritz hotel. The venerable jeweller still produces voluptuous pieces, using traditional motifs with new accents.

Boutique M Dia

5-7 rue des Innocents, 1st (01.40.26. 03.31/www.mdiawear.com). M° Châtelet. **Open** 1-8pm Mon; 11am-8pm Tue-Sat. **Map** p69 E4 ㉝

Mohammed Dia has his own line of urban sports clothes, plus shoe line Tariq, worn by the Dallas Mavericks.

Le Carrousel du Louvre

99 rue de Rivoli, 1st (01.43.16.47.10). M° Palais Royal Musée du Louvre. **Open** 10am-8pm daily. **Map** p68 C4 ㉞

This large, sleek underground mall is home to big-name chains such as Virgin, Esprit, Sephora, Nature et Découvertes, L'Occitane, Agatha, Bodum and Périgot.

Chanel

31 rue Cambon, 1st (01.42.86.28.00/ www.chanel.com). M° Concorde or Madeleine. **Open** 10am-7pm Mon-Sat. **Map** p68 B3 ㉟

Coco opened her first boutique in this street, at No.21, in 1910, and the tradition continues with Karl Lagerfeld rehashing classics, like the little black dress and the suit, with great success.

Colette

213 rue St-Honoré, 1st (01.55.35. 33.90/www.colette.fr). M° Tuileries or Pyramides. **Open** 11am-7pm Mon-Sat. **Map** p68 B3 ㊱

The original concept/lifestyle store is still the best. As well as exporting the one-stop concept store concept to Tokyo and Zagreb, Colette releases CDs on its own label and produces weighty style catalogues. This shrine to the limited edition displays must-have accessories inside clinical glass cases. Upstairs has a selection of 'in' clothes (think Bless and Bernard Wilhelm) and accessories such

Boulevard Haussmann

Stars attraction

Head backstage at the Grand Rex.

Paris has an awful lot going for it, but there's one thing it doesn't supply in great quantity, and that's uncomplicated, pizzazz-y family entertainment. So it's quite a thrill to be let into one of the best kept secrets in town, the brilliantly entertaining **Etoiles du Rex**: a slick and well-organised 50-minute 'backstage tour' of the grandiose Grand Rex cinema. It's loosely pitched as a tribute both to film-making and to the art deco monument that is the cinema itself, but in actual fact it's a riotous experience akin to something you might expect from a theme park. Visitors are led along corridors and through rooms by a succession of mysterious voices and a slinky Jessica Rabbit lookalike: automatic doors and lifts take you into the 'manager's office', up behind the screen and into the 'projection room'. Then, just when you think it's going to degenerate into a nostalgic hymn to the glory days of old, you find yourself caught up in a whirlwind of special effects, weird sounds – and an audition for King Kong in Paris, with a neat twist at the end. It's great for kids or budding film stars of all ages, and the tour is available in English; ask when you buy the tickets and they'll set up the correct soundtrack. Tours depart every five minutes and admission costs between €8 and €9.50.

PARIS BY AREA

as the Chrome Hearts line. Lunch, with a global selection of mineral water, can be had in the basement Water Bar.

Comme des Garçons

54 rue du Fbg-St-Honoré, 8th (01.53. 30.27.27/www.doublestreetmarket. com). M° Madeleine or Concorde. **Open** 11am-7pm Mon-Sat. **Map** p68 A2 ❸❼

Rei Kawakubo's designs and revolutionary mix of materials are superbly showcased in this red store. Exclusive perfumes get a futuristic setting at Comme des Garçons Parfums (23 pl du Marché-St-Honoré, 1st, 01.47.03.15.03).

Didier Ludot

20-24 galerie de Montpensier, 1st (01. 42.96.06.56/www.didierludot.com). M° Palais Royal Musée du Louvre. **Open** 11am-7pm Mon-Sat. **Map** p68 C3 ❸❽

See box p73.

Ekivok

39 bd de Sébastopol, 1st (01.42.21. 98.71/www.ekivok.com). M° Les Halles. **Open** 11am-7.30pm Mon-Sat. **Map** p69 E4 ❸❾

Paris fashion isn't just Dior and Chanel; *banlieue*-driven hip hop and streetwear cultures also flourish. Here you'll find the major brands like Royal Wear, Zoo York and Punky Fish. There's a branch at 6 rue de Cygne, 1st (01.40.39.97.07).

Erès

2 rue Tronchet, 8th (01.47.42.28.82/ www.eres.fr). M° Madeleine. **Open** 10am-7pm Mon-Sat. **Map** p68 B2 ❹⓿

Don't be misled by the demure interior: the label's beautifully cut bikinis and swimsuits are hot. Top and bottom can be bought in different sizes, or you can buy just one piece of a bikini.

Galeries Lafayette

40 bd Haussmann, 9th (01.42.82. 34.56/www.galerieslafayette.com). M° Chaussée d'Antin La Fayette/RER Auber. **Open** 9.30am-7.30pm Mon-Wed, Fri, Sat; 9.30am-9pm Thur. **Map** p68 C2 ❹❶

This department store has revamped its fashion, beauty and accessories sections, and opened a lingerie depart-

Printemps p81

ment on the third floor. Le Labo and Trend have introduced progressive designers, and over 90 established names occupy the rest of the first and second floors. On the third floor Lafayette Homme is a must. Lafayette Gourmet has exotic, high-end foods, and the second-biggest wine cellar in Paris. The exquisite domed ceiling in the main shop is photogenic, and there's a rooftop café.

Hédiard

21 pl de la Madeleine, 8th (01.43.12. 88.88/www.hediard.fr). M° Madeleine. **Open** 8.30am-9pm Mon-Sat. **Map** p68 A2 42

Hédiard was the first establishment in Paris to specialise in rare teas and coffees, spices, jams and candied fruits. This is the original shop, dating from 1880; upstairs is the posh tearoom La Table d'Hédiard, serving €22 buffet breakfasts during the week.

Hermès

24 rue du Fbg-St-Honoré, 8th (01.40.17.46.00/www.hermes.com). M° Concorde or Madeleine. **Open** 10.30am-6.30pm Mon-Sat. Closed most public hols. **Map** p68 A3 43

This fashion and accessories house is still a family-run business as well as a fashion star.

Jean-Paul Gaultier

6 rue Vivienne, 2nd (01.42.86.05.05/ www.jeanpaulgaultier.fr). M° Bourse. **Open** 10.30am-7pm Mon-Fri; 11am-7pm Sat. **Map** p69 D3 44

Gaultier has restyled his boutique as a boudoir with peach taffeta walls. Men's and women's ready-to-wear, accessories and the cheaper JPG Jeans lines are also sold here, with haute couture on display upstairs.

Kabuki Femme

25 rue Etienne-Marcel, 2nd (01.42.33.55. 65). M° Etienne Marcel. **Open** 10.30am-7.30pm Mon-Sat. **Map** p69 E4 45

On the ground floor are footwear and bags by Costume National, Miu Miu and Prada; Burberry belts and Miu Miu sunglasses are also stocked. Upstairs are suits by Helmut Lang, Véronique Leroy, Prada and Costume National.

Kiliwatch

64 rue Tiquetonne, 2nd (01.42.21. 17.37/www.kiliwatch.com). M° Etienne Marcel. **Open** 2-7pm Mon; 11am-7.30pm Tue-Sat. **Map** p69 E3 46

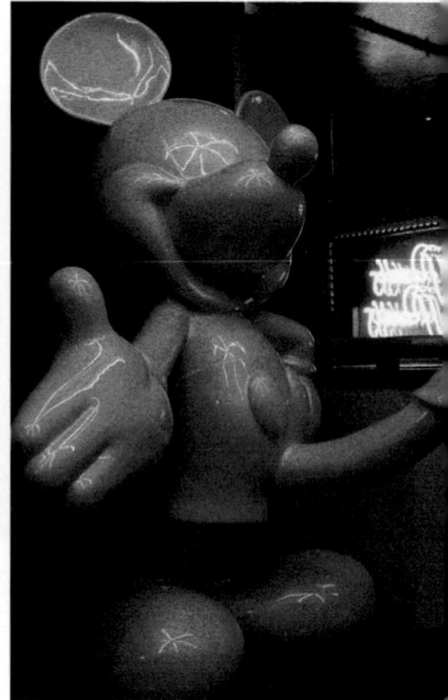

PARIS BY AREA

The trailblazer of the rue Etienne-Marcel revival is filled with hoodies, casual shirts and washed-out jeans. Featured brands such as G-Star and Kulte accompany a selection of pricey but good-condition second-hand garb.

Kokon To Zai

48 rue Tiquetonne, 2nd (01.42.36.92.41/www.kokontozai.co.uk). M° Etienne Marcel. **Open** 11.30am-7.30pm Mon-Sat. **Map** p69 E4 47

This tiny style emporium is sister to the Kokon To Zai in London. Pieces straight off the catwalk rub against creations by Alexandre et Matthieu, and a number of the new Norwegian designers.

Legrand Filles & Fils

1 rue de la Banque, 2nd (01.42.60.07.12). M° Bourse. **Open** 11am-7pm Mon-Sat. **Map** p69 D3 48

This old-fashioned shop sells fine wine and wine kit. For almost four decades, its owners have built a solid reputation for sourcing little-known *vins de terroir* and other regional specialities.

Marc Jacobs

NEW *34 galerie de Montpensier, 1st (01.55.35.02.60/www.marcjacobs.com). M° Palais Royal Musée du Louvre or Pyramides.* **Open** 11am-8pm Mon-Sat. **Map** p68 C3 49

See box p73.

Marithé et François Girbaud

38 rue Etienne-Marcel, 2nd (01.53.40.74.20/www.girbaud.com). M° Etienne Marcel. **Open** 11.30am-7.30pm Mon; 10.30am-7.30pm Tue-Sat. **Map** p69 D3 50

The pioneering *soixante-huitard* couple Girbaud came up with streetwear in high-tech fabrics using laser cutting and welding. Their flagship store has four floors; they have four others.

Martin Margiela

23 rue de Montpensier, 1st (01.40.15.07.55/www.maisonmartinmargiela.com). M° Palais Royal Musée du Louvre. **Open** 11am-7pm Mon-Sat. **Map** p68 C3 51

The first Paris boutique of the Belgian designer. His impresive collection for women (line 1) bears a blank label, recognisable by external white stitching. You can also find line 6 (women's basics) and line 10 (menswear), accessories and shoes.

Printemps

64 bd Haussmann, 9th (01.42.82.50.00/www.printemps.com). M° Havre Caumartin/RER Auber. **Open** 9.35am-7pm Mon-Wed, Fri, Sat; 9.35am-10pm Thur. **Map** p68 B1 52

The largest shoe department in Paris and the biggest beauty department in the world, with some 200 brands in stock. The lingerie department is the stuff of fantasy and on the second floor French designers APC and Zadig et Voltaire sit side by side with Dolce e Gabbana and Moschino; Miss Code targets teens with jeans and sportswear. The ninth-floor terrace restaurant sports an art nouveau cupola.

Salons du Palais Royal Shiseido

142 galerie de Valois, 1st (01.49.27.09.09/www.salons-shiseido.com). M° Palais Royal Musée du Louvre. **Open** 10am-7pm Mon-Sat. **Map** p68 C3 53

See box p73.

Le Vestibule

3 pl Ste-Opportune, 1st (01.42.33.21.89). M° Châtelet. **Open** 10.30am-8pm Mon-Sat. **Map** p69 E5 54

An eye-popping showcase for the wildest creations of vintage streetwear and club gear, with exhibits by labels like Dolce e Gabbana and Castelbajac.

Nightlife

Au Duc des Lombards

42 rue des Lombards, 1st (01.42.33.22.88/www.ducdeslombards.com). M° Châtelet. **Open** times vary. **Map** p69 E5 55

One of a number of musically inclined venues along the rue des Lombards. Au Duc des Lombards has a varied programme and attracts jazz musicians from across Europe.

Olympia

28 bd des Capucines, 9th (01.55.27.10.00/www.olympiahall.com). M° Opéra. **Open** times vary. **Map** p68 B2 56

This legendary venue is on the nostalgia circuit, though Coldplay did kick off their 2005 world tour here.

Le Paris Paris

5 av Opéra, 1st (no phone/www.leparisparis.com). M° Pyramides. **Open** 11pm-5am Tue-Sat. **Admission** free. **Map** p68 C4 57

Currently the hottest spot in Paris; getting in isn't easy, but once into the basement you'll find a spacious dancefloor and cosy alcoves, with the focus on fun. The music policy is on the button.

Pulp

25 bd Poissonnière, 2nd (01.40.26.01.93/www.pulp-paris.com). M° Grands Boulevards. **Open** midnight-5am Thur-Sat. **Admission** free Thur, €10 Fri, Sat. **Map** p69 D2 58

Essentially a lesbian club, Pulp – midway between late-hours bar and club – draws a mixed crowd midweek. You can expect top international DJs and a regular spot from local Ivan Smagghe.

Rex

5 bd Poissonnière, 2nd (01.42.36.10.96/www.club.com). M° Bonne Nouvelle. **Open** 11.30pm-dawn Wed-Sat. **Admission** free-€10. **Map** p69 E2 59

A prime venue for electronic music for a decade or more. A new management promises more live entertainment on the newly built stage.

Le Slow Club

130 rue de Rivoli, 1st (01.42.33.84.30). M° Châtelet. **Open** times vary. **Map** p69 D5 60

The medieval cellar may be tiny but compensates with boogie-woogie big bands and dance-friendly R&B.

Le Sunset/Le Sunside

60 rue des Lombards, 1st (01.40.26.21.25/01.40.26.46.60/www.sunset-sunside.com). M° Châtelet. **Open** times vary. **Map** p69 E5 61

With Sunset dabbling in all things electric, and Sunside the acoustic, this duo of venues is one of the main ports of call on any Paris jazz pilgrimage.

Théâtre du Châtelet

1 pl du Châtelet, 1st (01.40.28.28.00/ 01.40.28.28.41/www.chatelet-theatre.com). M° Châtelet. **Open** times vary. **Map** p69 E5 62

A theatre and classical music hall dabbling in jazz. Its Bleu sur Scène Festival in June sees Herbie Hancock and Ornette Coleman play.

Le Triptyque

142 rue Montmartre, 2nd (01.40.28.05.55/www.letriptyque.com). M° Bourse or Grands Boulevards. **Open** 11.30pm-3am Wed; 11pm-6am Thur-Sat. **Map** p69 D3 63

This prime club and concert venue boasts eclectic programming (Luke Vibert, the Zutons) and the sweatiest moshpit-dancehall in town; freshen up on one of the sofas in the chill-out area by the bar and watch the evening unfold before your eyes.

Arts & leisure

Châtelet – Théâtre Musical de Paris

1 pl du Châtelet, 1st (01.40.28.28.40/ www.chatelet-theatre.com). M° Châtelet. **Open** times vary. **Map** p69 D3 64

Director Jean-Luc Choplin looks set to bring in even more French music, with strongly cast revivals of *Carmen* et al. The Châtelet – Théâtre also holds high-quality chamber music and symphonic concerts.

Forum des Images

2 Grande Galerie, Forum des Halles, 1st (01.44.76.62.00/www.forumdes images.net). M° Les Halles. **Open** 1-9pm Tue-Sun. **Map** p69 D4 65

After a major facelift, the hyperactive four-screen Forum des Images finally reopened in February 2007. It's looking pretty good too. It's both a film archive dedicated to Paris on celluloid and an eclectic programmer of films, usually organised by theme. It also boasts a new (and impressive) library of books and films.

Le Grand Rex

1 bd Poissonnière, 2nd (08.92.68.05.96/www.legrandrex.com). M° Bonne Nouvelle. **Open** times vary. **Map** p69 E2 66

With its wedding-cake-esque exterior, fairy grotto interior and the largest auditorium in Europe (a whopping 2,750 seats) this is one of the few cinemas to upstage whatever it screens. It's home to the Etoiles du Rex tour, too (see box p78).

Opéra Comique

pl Boieldieu, 2nd (01.42.44.45.40/ 01.42.44.45.46/www.opera-comique.com). M° Richelieu Drouot. **Open** times vary. **Map** p68 C2 67

New director Jérôme Deschamps took over from Jérôme Savary at the end of 2007; hopefully this gem of a theatre, which saw the premieres of many great operas, will continue in the front line of Paris music-making.

Palais Garnier

pl de l'Opéra, 9th (08.92.89.90.90/ www.operadeparis.fr). M° Opéra. **Open** 10am-5pm daily. **Admission** varies. **Map** p68 B2 68

Brimming with gilt and red velvet, this opera house is a monument to the Second Empire. The auditorium seats some 2,000 people, and the exterior is just as grand, with sculptures of music and dance, Apollo on the dome and nymphs bearing torches. The Grand Foyer has been magnificently restored. For guided tours in English, call 01.40.01.22.63.

Théâtre de la Ville

2 pl du Châtelet, 4th (01.42.74.22.77/ www.theatredelaville-paris.com). M° Châtelet. **Open** times vary. **Map** p69 E5 69

Vertiginous concrete amphitheatre Théâtre de la Ville features renowned chamber music outfits like the Kronos Quartet, as well as superstar classical soloists. It's also one of the most prestigious contemporary dance venues in town and a showcase for established choreographers. A great place to experience the latest in music and dance.

Sacré-Coeur p84

Montmartre & Pigalle

For all the tourists in Montmartre – the highest point in Paris – it's not that hard to escape them and fall under the spell of what's arguably the city's most romantic district – lovelier still after dark (see Itinerary p42). With its tight-packed houses spiralling round the mound below the sugary-white dome of Sacré-Coeur, Montmartre resembles some hilltop village; climb and descend quiet stairways, peer into little alleys, ivy-covered houses and deserted squares, and explore rue des Abbesses, rue des Trois-Frères and rue des Martyrs with their cafés, boutiques and arty community.

Pigalle, south of Montmartre, has long been the sleaze centre of Paris, but that may be changing. A recent police blitz, instigated in response to increased tourist rip-offs and rough-ups, has shooed away the streetwalkers and peep shows. While locals bemoan the sanitising of their neighbourhood, the recent relandscaping of boulevards de Clichy and de Rochechouart looks set to continue the clean-up.

Sights & museums

Cimetière de Montmartre

20 av Rachel, access by stairs from rue Caulaincourt, 18th (01.53.42. 36.30). M° Blanche. **Open** *6 Nov-15 Mar* 8am-5.30pm Mon-Fri; 8.30am-5.30pm Sat; 9am-5.30pm Sun & public hols. *16 Mar-5 Nov* 8am-6pm Mon-Fri; 8.30am-6pm Sat; 9am-6pm Sun & public hols. **Map** p85 A1 ①

You stumble over the famous and infamous in this cemetery: Degas, Berlioz, Offenbach and Truffaut are just some of the artistic heavyweights buried here.

Le Brébant p86

Musée de l'Erotisme

72 bd de Clichy, 18th (01.42.58.28.73/ www.musee-erotisme.com). M° Blanche. **Open** 10am-2am daily. **Admission** €8; €6 reductions. **Map** p85 A2 ❷

Seven floors of erotic art and artefacts, running from first-century Peruvian phallic pottery through Etruscan fertility symbols to Yoni sculptures from Nepal. The top floors host exhibitions of modern erotic art.

Musée Gustave Moreau

14 rue de La Rochefoucauld, 9th (01.48. 74.38.50/www.musee-moreau.fr). M° Trinité. **Open** 10am-12.45pm, 2-5.15pm Mon, Wed-Sun. **Admission** €5; free-€3 reductions. **Map** p85 A4 ❸

A private museum, this combines the small apartment of Symbolist painter Gustave Moreau with the vast two-floor gallery he built to display his work.

Musée de Montmartre

12 rue Cortot, 18th (01.46.06.61.11/ www.museedemontmartre.fr). M° Abbesses. **Open** 11am-6pm Wed-Sun. **Admission** €7; free-€5.50 reductions. **Map** p85 B1 ❹

This 17th-century manor showcases the history of Montmartre, with rooms devoted to the composer Gustave Charpentier and a tribute to the Lapin Agile cabaret (see p88).

Musée de la Vie Romantique

16 rue Chaptal, 9th (01.55.31.95.67/ www.vie-romantique.paris.fr). M° Blanche or St-Georges. **Open** 10am-6pm Tue-Sun. **Admission** free. *Exhibitions* €7; free-€3.50 reductions. **Map** p85 A3 ❺

When Dutch artist Ary Scheffer lived in this villa, the area was home to so many writers and artists it was known as 'New Athens'. George Sand was a guest at Scheffer's famed soirées – though the watercolours, lockets and jewels she left behind reveal little – and numerous other great names crossed the threshold.

Sacré-Coeur

35 rue du Chevalier-de-la-Barre, 18th (01.53.41.89.00/www.sacre-coeur-montmartre.com). M° Abbesses or Anvers. **Open** *Basilica* 6am-10.30pm

A
B
C
Montmartre & Pigalle
Sights & museums
Eating & drinking
Shopping
Nightlife
Arts & leisure
Hôpital Bretonneau
Cimetière de Montmartre
Lamarck Caulaincourt
Musée de Montmartre
St Pierre
Sacré Coeur
18
MONTMARTRE
Moulin Rouge
Blanche
Abbesses
PLACE DES ABBESSES
Anvers
Pigalle
PLACE PIGALLE
BOULEVARD DE CLICHY
BOULEVARD DE ROCHECHOUART
RUE FONTAINE
Musée de la Vie Romantique
St Georges
R. NOTRE DAME DE LORETTE
Musée Gustave Moreau
Eglise de la Trinité
Trinité
PIGALLE
9
Notre-Dame de Lorette
© Copyright Time Out Group 2007
RUE SAINT LAZARE
RUE DE CHATEAUDIN
RUE LA FAYETTE
Cadet
Le Peletier
Havre Caumartin
Chaussée d'Antin La Fayette
BOULEVARD HAUSSMANN
Palais Garnier
Auber
Richelieu Drouot
BD. MONTMARTRE
BD. POISSONNIERE
Grands Boulevards
BD. DES ITALIENS
BD. DES CAPUCINES
Opéra
OPERA TO LES HALLES
Bonne Nouvelle

daily. *Crypt & dome* (winter) 10am-5.45pm daily; (summer) 9am-6.45pm daily. **Admission** *Basilica* free. *Crypt & dome* €5. **Map** p85 C2 ⑥

Commissioned as an act of penance after France's defeat by Prussia in 1870, this enormous mock Romano-Byzantine was started in 1877, finished in 1914, and only consecrated in 1919. The interior is lavishly adorned with gaudy neo-Byzantine mosaics. Great views.

Eating & drinking

Le Brébant

NEW *32 bd Poissonnière, 9th (01.47.70.01.02). M° Grands Boulevards.* **Open** 7.30am-6am daily. **Bar**. **Map** p85 C5 ⑦

Join the throng hanging out on the terrace (or in the split-level, arty interior) at this round-the-clock bar-bistro for pricey beers (€4 a *demi*!) and expertly made cocktails (€9). There's a big board of decent food (steak tartare and the like) too.

Casa Olympe

48 rue St-Georges, 9th (01.42.85.26.01). M° St-Georges. **Open** noon-2pm, 8-11pm Mon-Fri. Closed 3wks Aug. €. **Brasserie**. **Map** p85 B4 ⑧

Dominique Versini (aka Olympe) is one of the rare female chefs in Paris to enjoy celebrity status. Her base has Roman ochre-painted walls, a pretty Murano chandelier, oil paintings and an almost entirely male, suited crowd. In truffle season, you might wisely order a potato salad laced with this earthy treasure; don't forget to try also the squash soup with chestnut and foie gras, and for dessert, Versini's home-made sorbets.

Chez Jean

8 rue St-Lazare, 9th (01.48.78.62.73). M° Notre-Dame-de-Lorette. **Open** noon-2.30pm, 7.30-10.30pm Mon-Fri. Closed Aug. €€. **Brasserie**. **Map** p85 B4 ⑨

Despite a staff-to-diner ratio near that of a haute cuisine purveyor, and a sumptuous high-ceilinged dining room, the *prix fixe* at Chez Jean remains good value. Try delicious fine yellow Chinese-style ravioli stuffed with crab, then slow-cooked farmhouse pork with a chutney of apricots, preserved lemons and sage. Cherries soaked in eau de vie make for a fine dessert.

Chez Toinette

20 rue Germain-Pilon, 18th (01.42.54.44.36). M° Abbesses or Pigalle. **Open** noon-2.45pm, 7.30-11pm Tue-Sat. Closed Aug. €€. **Bistro**. **Map** p85 B2 ⑩

This stalwart purveyor of bistro fare has a good-value blackboard menu in an area known for rip-offs. Of the starters, try the pleasing *chèvre chaud* with a glorious creamy st-marcellin on a bed of rocket and lettuce; meaty mains include *mignon de porc*, spring lamb and sundry steaks – the lamb seared in rosemary is deliciously lean. Top it all off with Armagnac prunes.

La Divette de Montmartre

136 rue Marcadet, 18th (01.46.06.19.64). M° Lamarck Caulaincourt. **Open** 5pm-1am Mon-Sat; 5-11pm Sun. **Bar**. **Map** p85 B1 ⑪

This cavern of nostalgia has Beatles albums over the bar, Rolling Stones ones under it and an Elvis clock in between; this decorative trinity is interrupted by the green of St-Etienne football iconography and an old red phone box. Wieckse Witte, Affligem and Pelforth are available on tap.

La Fourmi

74 rue des Martyrs, 18th (01.42.64.70.35). M° Pigalle. **Open** 8.30am-2am Mon-Thur; 8.30am-4am Fri, Sat; 10am-2am Sun. **Bar**. **Map** p85 B3 ⑫

La Fourmi is retro-industrial at its best: an old bistro converted to suit contemporary tastes, with picture windows lighting the spacious, sand-coloured interior; prime seats are on the podiums at the back. The classic zinc bar counter is crowned by industrial lights, the ornately carved back bar featuring the occasional titular ant. Cool music policy and clientele, and a good place to pick up flyers to see what's on in Paris.

Georgotto

29 rue St-Georges, 9th (01.42.80. 39.13). M° St-Georges or Notre-Dame de Lorette. **Open** noon-2.45pm, 7.30-11pm Tue-Fri. Closed Aug. **€**. **Bistro**. **Map** p85 B4 13

A mix of formica tables and ancient wooden beams provides charm, but what has won Georgette a loyal following is the chef's loving use of seasonal ingredients. Hearty meat dishes satisfy the local business crowd, while lighter options might include sea bream with Provençal vegetables, or a *charlotte* of juicy lamb chunks and aubergine. The creamy fontainebleau cheese with raspberry coulis is irresistible.

Pétrelle

34 rue Pétrelle, 9th (01.42.82.11.02). M° Anvers. **Open** 8-10pm Tue-Sat. Closed 4wks July/Aug. **€€**. **Haute cuisine**. **Map** p85 C3 14

Jean-Luc André is as inspired a decorator as he is a cook, and the quirky charm of his dining room has made it popular with fashion designers and film stars. The €27 no-choice menu is excellent value (on our last visit, marinated sardines with tomato relish and rosemary scented rabbit with roasted vegetables), or you can splash out with one of the many luxurious à la carte dishes.

Le Sancerre

35 rue des Abbesses, 18th (01.42.58. 08.20). M° Abbesses. **Open** 7am-2am Mon-Thur; 7am-4am Fri, Sat; 9am-2am Sun. **Bar**. **Map** p85 B2 15

This popular choice has a busy terrace and a spacious, cosy interior.Taps of Paulaner, Grimbergen and Record partner bottled Belgian beauties Kriek and Mort Subite; standard cocktails are presented with the same care as the plats du jour. Occasional live music, too.

Spring

NEW *28 rue de la Tour d'Auvergne, 9th (01.45.96.05.72/www.springparis .blogspot.com). M° Cadet.* **Open** 7.30-10.30pm Tue-Fri. **€€**. **Bistro**. **Map** p85 C3 16

Young American chef Daniel Rose acquired a taste for restaurant cooking while living upstairs from the restaurant Le Violon d'Ingres. He shops daily at the Place des Fêtes market, coming back with ingredients like parsnip, striped beetroot, guinea hen and giant octopus. Pumpkin soup topped with foie gras has become a house classic.

Shopping

Arnaud Delmontel

39 rue des Martyrs, 9th (01.48.78.29. 33). M° St-Georges. **Open** 7am-8.30pm Mon, Wed-Sun. No credit cards. **Map** p85 B3 17

With its crisp crust and chewy crumb shot through with holes, Delmontel's Renaissance bread is one of the finest in Paris. He puts the same skill into his pastries, biscuits and almond croissants. He has another store in the 18th, at 57 rue Damrémont (01.42.64.59.63).

Base One

47bis rue d'Orsel, 18th (01.53.28. 04.52/www.baseoneshop.com). M° Anvers. **Open** 12.30-8pm Tue-Sat; 3.30-8pm Sun. Closed 2wks Aug. **Map** p85 B2 18

Princesse Léa and Jean-Louis Faverole, the couple behind Espace Lab 101 and Project 101, squeeze a mix of artefacts from unknown local and international designers, plus some of the small, established brands (Fenchurch, Consortium Motel) into their dinky boutique.

Tati

4 bd de Rochechouart, 18th (01.55. 29.52.50/www.tati.fr). M° Barbès Rochechouart. **Open** 10am-7pm Mon-Sat. **Map** p85 C2 19

Expect to find anything from T-shirts to wedding dresses, as well as bargain children's clothes and household goods at this discount chain.

Wochdom

72 rue Condorcet, 9th (01.53.21. 09.72). M° Pigalle or Anvers. **Open** noon-8pm Mon-Sat. **Map** p85 B3 20

This temple to vintage stocks a mainly female collection, with stress on the 1980s. The shop also sells *Interview*, *Elle* and *Vogue*, old vinyl and vintage shoes.

Au Lapin Agile

Nightlife

Le Bus Palladium

NEW *6 rue Fontaine, 9th (01.45.26. 80.35/www.lebuspalladium.com). M° Pigalle or St Georges.* **Open** 8.30pm-dawn Wed-Sat; 3pm-dawn Sun. No credit cards. **Map** p85 A3. 21
See box p89.

La Cigale/La Boule Noire

120 bd de Rochechouart, 18th (01.49 .25.89.99/www.lacigale.fr). M° Anvers or Barbès Rochechouart. **Open** times vary. **Map** p85 B3 22
Upstairs La Cigale stages the likes of Goldfrapp; downstairs in La Boule Noire, young bands get their turn to shine.

Le Divan du Monde

75 rue des Martyrs, 18th (01.42.52. 02.46/www.divandumonde.com). M° Anvers or Pigalle. **Open** times vary. **Map** p85 B3 23
The decadent spirit of Le Divan's Toulouse-Lautrec days remains. Indie, hip hop and electro get showcased here.

Elysée Montmartre

72 bd de Rochechouart, 18th (08.92. 69.23.92/www.elyseemontmartre.com). M° Anvers. **Open** *Bar* 11am-midnight daily. **Map** p85 C2 24
This reliable, if uninspiring, mid-sized venue once staged cancan; today it puts on gigs by the likes of Peaches.

Folies Pigalle

11 pl Pigalle, 9th (01.48.78.25.26/www. folies-pigalle.com). M° Pigalle. **Open** midnight-dawn Mon-Thur; midnight-noon Fri, Sat; 6pm-midnight Sun. **Map** p85 B3 25
Pigalle types, *banlieue* bad boys and tourists squelch to pumping and percussive house by resident DJs.

Au Lapin Agile

22 rue des Saules, 18th (01.46.06. 85.87). M° Lamarck Caulaincourt. **Open** *Shows* 9pm-2am Tue-Sun. No credit cards. **Map** p85 B1 26
This quaint bar-cabaret first opened in 1860. Tourists now outnumber the locals, but it still feels like old Montmartre.

Moulin Rouge

82 bd de Clichy, 18th (01.53.09.82.82/ www.moulin-rouge.com). M° Blanche. **Open** *Dinner* 7pm daily. *Shows* 9pm, 11pm daily. **Map** p85 A2 27
The spiritual home of the cancan. It's still the most glam Paris cabaret, with good shows, amazing costumes and humorous acts between the numbers.

Project 101

44 rue de La Rochefoucauld, 9th (01.49.95.95.85/www.project-101. com). M° Pigalle. **Open** 10pm-2am Fri. **Map** p85 A3 28
This underground venue with a shop on the ground floor hosts experimental music concerts, film screenings, DJs and VJs.

Arts & leisure

Théâtre de la Ville – Les Abbesses

31 rue des Abbesses, 18th (01.42. 74.22.77/www.theatredelaville-paris. com). M° Abbesses. **Open** times vary. **Map** p85 B2 29
The sister venue of the Théâtre de la Ville hosts dance productions by contemporary choreographers.

Ticket to jive

Iconic Paris club Le Bus Palladium is back in style.

It went through the doldrums for a while, then disappeared altogether; but one of the city's more iconic gig and club night venues is back in action – Pigalle's Le Bus Palladium (p88). Its '60s heyday was short, but this was one of the most chic and influential clubs of the time. The Beatles drank at its bar, and Serge Gainsbourg namechecked the place in a song.

'Le Bus' got started when dancer and part-time hairdresser James Arch became its boss. Despite his shortage of funds and nightclub management experience, the venue was an overnight success – thanks in no small part to a couple of inspired innovations. The first was an open-door policy that marked it out from the snobby attitude of other venues. And the second was the deal Arch struck with tour-bus drivers, who would pick up and drop off suburban revellers for a nominal charge (hence 'Bus Palladium'): no more would revellers from out of town have to leave early to catch the last bus or train home. Pretty soon everyone who was anyone was there. Roman Polanski was a regular; trend-setting singer Stone made her mark as a dancer there; Dalí made himself the club's unofficial ambassador.

Police interest, inevitable given the venue's success, meant that the giddy times couldn't last, and it was soon forced to move to other premises. Several attempts at reopening stalled; in the mid '90s Le Bus gave up on live music and became just another club; in 2004, it closed completely. But revived interest in Le Bus led to a grand relaunch in September 2006. The new interior reflects the feel of the original, but adds a good new sound system. There are concerts, stand-up comedy and the cream of homegrown DJs for club nights; and still no dress codes or face police on the door.

PARIS BY AREA

Canal St-Martin

North-east Paris

Once short of local amenities, north-east Paris is one of the city's rising neighbourhoods. Its most romantic feature is the Canal St-Martin (see Itinerary p45), which begins at the Seine at Pont Morland, goes underground at Bastille, then re-emerges east of place de la République. Its first stretch, lined with shady trees and crossed by iron footbridges and locks, has the greatest appeal – it's a popular spot with families on Sundays, when the quays are traffic-free. Many canalside warehouses have been snapped up by artists and designers, the *quais* and nearby streets colonised by trendy bars. You can take a boat up the canal as far as La Villette.

The area encompasses the lovely park of the Buttes-Chaumont, and a centre of counter-culture, Belleville. Legend has it that Edith Piaf was born in the street outside 72 rue de Belleville, marked by a plaque.

Sights & museums

Canauxrama

13 quai de la Loire, 19th (01.42. 39.15.00/www.canauxrama.fr).
Departs Port de l'Arsenal (50 bd de la Bastille, 12th, M° Bastille) 9.45am, 2.30pm daily. *Apr-Sept* Bassin de la Villette (13 quai de la Loire, 19th, M° Jaurès) 9.45am, 2.45pm daily.
Admission €14; free-€11 reductions.
Map p91 C1 ❶

If the Seine palls, take a trip up the city's second waterway, the Canal St-Martin. The tree-lined canal is a pretty sight, and the 150-minute trip even goes underground for a stretch, where tunnel walls are enlivened by a light show.

North-east Paris

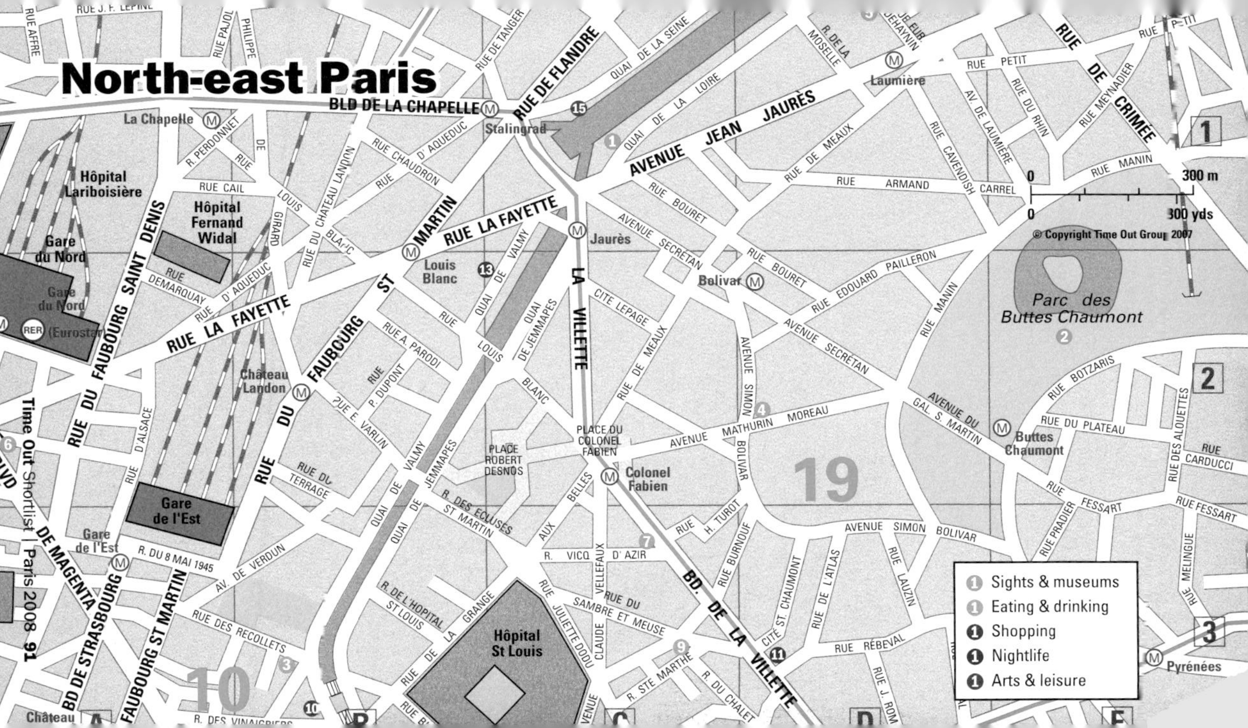

Parc des Buttes-Chaumont

rue Botzaris, rue Manin, rue de Crimée, 19th. Mº Buttes Chaumont. **Open** *Oct-Apr* 7am-8.15pm daily. *\May, mid Aug-end Sept* 7am-9.15pm daily. *June-mid Aug* 7am-10.15pm daily. **Map** p91 E2 ❷

This lovely park was laid out in the 1860s. It had formerly been a gypsum quarry, tip and public gibbet. It has winding paths, steep cliffs and waterfalls cascading from a man-made cave; the cheerfully-named Pont des Suicides crosses the lake to an island crowned by a mini-temple.

Eating & drinking

L'Atmosphère

49 rue Lucien-Sampaix, 10th (01.40.38.09.21). Mº Gare de l'Est or Jacques Bonsergent. **Open** 9.30am-1.45am Mon-Sat; 9.30am-midnight Sun. **Bar**. **Map** p91 B3 ❸

L'Atmosphère remains at the centre of the Canal St-Martin renaissance and sums up the area's spirit. Parisians of all kinds chat, read and gaze from the waterside terrace; inside is simple, tasteful decor, animated chat and cheapish drinks. It's always packed, but brave the crowds on Sunday evenings for the world and experimental music slots.

A la Bière

104 av Simon-Bolivar, 19th (01.42.39.83.25). Mº Colonel Fabien. **Open** noon-3pm, 7pm-1.30am daily. **€**. **Brasserie**. **Map** p91 D2 ❹

A la Bière looks like one of those nondescript corner brasseries with noisy pop music and lots of smoke, but what makes it stand out is an amazingly good-value €12.30 *prix fixe* full of bistro favourites. Start with thinly sliced pig's cheek with a nice French dressing on the salad, then go for charcoal-grilled *entrecôte* with top-notch hand-cut chips.

Bar Ourcq

quai de la Loire, 19th (01.42.40.12.26/ www.barourcq.com). Mº Laumière. **Open** *Winter* 5pm-midnight Wed, Thur, Sun; 3pm-2am Fri, Sat. *Summer* 5-9.30pm Wed-Fri, Sun; 3pm-2am Sat. **Bar**. **Map** p91 D1 ❺

This little turquoise-framed corner bar has an awful lot going for it. It's set back from a quay wide enough to accommodate *pétanque* (ask at the bar) for a start. Inside, it's a vivacious, boho cabin of parrot-dotted wallpaper and knackered old sofas, with a great cosy raised area at the back for lounging. Drinks start at €1 for coffee, €2 for a *demi* or glass of red, and €4 for a lively Mojito.

Chez Michel

10 rue de Belzunce, 10th (01.44.53.06.20). Mº Gare du Nord. **Open** 7pm-midnight Mon; noon-2pm, 7pm-midnight Tue-Fri. Closed 3wks Aug. **€€**. **Brasserie**. **Map** p91 A2 ❻

Thierry Breton is from Brittany, and so proud of his origins that he sports the Breton flag on his chef's whites. The food here is excellent. Marinated salmon with purple potatoes served in a preserving jar is succulently tender; as for the rabbit, braised with rosemary and Swiss chard, it might just be the best bunny in town. Blackboard specials tend to follow the seasons: game lovers are spoilt for choice in the cooler months with an array of hearty and flavoursome wood pigeon, wild boar and venison dishes.

L'Ile Enchantée

65 bd de la Villette, 10th (01.42.01.67.99). Mº Colonel Fabien. **Open** 8am-2am Mon-Fri; 5pm-2am Sat, Sun. **Bar**. **Map** p91 C3 ❼

The latest DJ bar on the fast swelling scene north-west of Belleville, this Enchanted Island has just the right mix of understated retro chic and minimal house and electro. High ceilings and windows let in acres of Belleville skyline, and there's space aplenty amid the studded banquettes and tables. The wine list is formidable, there's Kriek by the bottle and sturdy cocktails come your way at €6.50 a hit. On the busier DJ nights, a cool lounge operates upstairs.

Parc des Buttes-Chaumont

Bar Ourcq p92

Le Jemmapes

82 quai de Jemmapes, 10th (01.40.40.02.35). M° Jacques Bonsergent or République. **Open** 11am-2am daily. **Café**. **Map** p91 B3 8

A destination canalside café and a fine reason to join the lazy throng along the St-Martin embankment. Inside is small and arty, but not so much that it puts you off – not with Chimay Bleue and Duval available, anyway. Rare and unusual flavoured vodkas are another speciality, but location is the deciding factor here. Visit during the week for a more boho crowd.

Le Sainte Marthe

32 rue Ste-Marthe, 10th (01.44.84.36.96). M° Coloniel Fabien or Belleville. **Open** 11am-2am daily. **Bar**. **Map** p91 C3 9

The most accommodating bar on a narrow street lined with boho dives and ethnic eateries, this little gem is also the most culinary of the drinking options. It boasts a cool interior and a wantonly shabby clientele. Scruffy poets and fiftysomethings on the pull prop up the counter most nights, but don't let that put you off – this is a class-A bar in a class-A bar zone.

Shopping

Antoine et Lili

95 quai de Valmy, 10th (01.40.37.41.55/www.antoineetlili.com). M° Jacques Bonsergent. **Open** 11am-7pm Mon, Sun; 11am-8pm Tue-Fri; 10am-8pm Sat. **Map** p91 B3 10

Fuchsia and apple-green shopfronts, reflected in the canal, are a colour therapist's dream. Vibrant jumpers and hippie skirts hang amid Mexican shrines, Hindu postcards and all sorts of miscellaneous kitsch. The three-shop Canal St-Martin 'village' has an equally colourful home decoration shop, florist and self-service café.

Nightlife

Café Chéri(e)

44 bd de la Villette, 19th (01.42.02.02.05). M° Belleville. **Open** 11am-2am daily. **Map** p91 D3 11

A popular DJ bar, not least for its terrace. Expect anything from banging house to '80s classics. It's used as a daytime hangout, too.

New Morning

7-9 rue des Petites-Ecuries, 10th (01.45.23.51.41/www.newmorning.com). M° Château d'Eau. **Open** times vary. **Map** p91 A3 ⓬

This prestigious and reliably exciting venue hosts some of the best in electronic jazz (blues and hip hop also get a look-in): Ravi Coltrane and the James Taylor Quartet have played here.

Point Ephemère

200 quai de Valmy, 10th (01.40.34.02.48/www.pointephemere.org). M° Jaurès. **Open** 10am-2am daily. **Map** p91 C2 ⓭

Generally thought of as a bit of Berlin that relocated here, this is one of the coolest arrivals on the nightlife scene. The music policy delivers some of the best international electronic music in the city; there's a restaurant, bar, gallery, and canalside terrace in summer.

Arts & leisure

Hammam Med Centre

43-45 rue Petit, 19th (01.42.02.31.05/www.hammammed.com). M° Ourcq. **Open** *Women* 11am-10pm Mon-Fri; 9am-7pm Sun. *Mixed* 10am-9pm Sat. **Map** p91 E1 ⓮

This hammam boasts spotless mosaic-tiled surroundings, flowered sarongs and a pool. The exotic 'Forfait florale' option (€139) has you cloaked in rose petals and massaged with *huile d'Argan* from Morocco. Hammam and *gommage* €39.

MK2

14 quai de la Seine, 19th (08.92.69.84.84/www.mk2.fr). M° Stalingrad. **Open** times vary. **Admission** €9.20; €5.30-€6.70 reductions. **Map** p91 C1 ⓯

MK2's mini multiplex on the quai de la Loire was seen as a key factor in the social rise of what had previously been a scuzzy part of town. Now the chain has opened another multiplex across the water – with a boat taking punters from one to the other. Programming is innovative and international.

Le Petit Fer à Cheval p108

The Marais & Eastern Paris

Both Beaubourg – site of the Centre Pompidou – and the Marais, predominately built between the 16th and 18th centuries and now packed with boutiques and bars, are set between boulevard Sébastopol and Bastille.

The Marais is a fascinating part of town, with narrow streets dotted with aristocratic *hôtels particuliers*, boutique galleries and stylish cafés. While browsing, make sure you look up at the beautiful carved doorways and the street signs carved into the stone. The area is a great spot for a Sunday stroll, as many of the shops are open, though if you come during the week you have more chance of wandering into some of the elegant courtyards.

A little further east is the edgy Oberkampf, home to some of the city's best bars and a hub of nightlife for the last decade.

Sights & museums

Atelier Brancusi

Piazza Beaubourg, 4th (01.44.78. 12.33/www.centrepompidou.fr). M° Hôtel de Ville or Rambuteau.
Open 2-6pm Mon, Wed-Sun.
Admission free. **Map** p98 A2 ❶

When Constantin Brancusi died in 1957 he left his studio and its contents to the state. The studio has been faithfully reconstructed by the Centre Pompidou. His fragile works in wood and plaster, including endless columns and streamlined bird forms, show how Brancusi revolutionised sculpture.

Centre Pompidou (Musée National d'Art Moderne)

rue St-Martin, 4th (01.44.78.12.33/ www.centrepompidou.fr). M° Hôtel de Ville or Rambuteau. **Open** 11am-9pm (last entry 8pm) Mon, Wed, Fri-Sun; until 11pm Thur, some exhibitions. **Admission** *Museum & exhibitions* €10; free-€8 reductions. **Map** p98 A2 ②

Its primary colours and exposed pipes make this building (known to locals simply as 'Beaubourg') one of the city's best-known sights. It holds the largest collection of modern art in Europe. Take the escalators to the entirely rehung level four for post-1960s art; level five spans 1905 to 1960. Masterful ensembles let you see the span of Matisse's career on canvas and in bronze, the variety of Picasso's invention and the development of cubic orphism by Sonia and Robert Delaunay.

The Centre screens films, classic and experimental, and has a weekly documentary session. It's also the venue for the Cinéma du Réel festival in March, which has championed the cause of documentary film.

Event highlights 'Richard Rogers and architects – From the house to the city', (14 Nov 2007-12 Feb 2008). 'Alexander Calder – The Paris years, 1926-1933' (15 Apr-18 Aug 2008). 'Le Futurisme et Paris' (15 Oct 2008-26 Jan 2009).

Cimetière du Père-Lachaise

bd de Ménilmontant, 20th (01.55.25. 82.10). M° Père-Lachaise. **Open** *6 Nov-15 Mar* 8am-5.30pm Mon-Fri; 8.30am-5.30pm Sat; 9am-5.30pm Sun & public hols. *16 Mar-5 Nov* 8am-6pm Mon-Fri; 8.30am-6pm Sat; 9am-6pm Sun & public hols. **Map** p99 F2 ③

Oscar Wilde, Colette and Edith Piaf reside among the thousands of tombs in the city's enormous main cemetery.

Hôtel de Sully

62 rue St-Antoine, 4th (01.42.74. 47.75). M° St-Paul or Bastille. **Open** noon-7pm Tue-Fri; 10am-7pm Sat, Sun. **Admission** €8; €4 reductions. **Map** p98 C4 ④

This Marais mansion forms one part of the two-site home for the Jeu de Paume; the Centre National de la Photographie. Visiting exhibitions here tend to have a political slant.

Hôtel de Ville

29 rue de Rivoli, 4th (01.42.76.43.43/ www.paris.fr). M° Hôtel de Ville. **Open** 10am-7pm Mon-Sat. **Map** p98 A3 ⑤

The palatial, multi-purpose Hôtel de Ville is both the heart of the city administration and a place to entertain visiting dignitaries. Modest Paris-themed exhibitions are held in the Salon d'accueil; the rest of the building, accessible only by guided tour (weekly, book in advance), is awash with marble statues, crystal chandeliers and allegorical painted ceilings.

Maison de Victor Hugo

Hôtel de Rohan-Guéménée, 6 pl des Vosges, 4th (01.42.72.10.16/www. musee-hugo.paris.fr). M° Bastille. **Open** 10am-6pm Tue-Sun. **Admission** free. *Exhibitions* prices vary. **Map** p98 C4 ⑥

Victor Hugo lived here from 1832 to 1848, and the house today is a one-man museum. On display are his first editions, nearly 500 drawings, and, somewhat bizarrely, the famous writer's home-made furniture.

Musée d'Art et d'Histoire du Judaïsme

Hôtel de St-Aignan, 71 rue du Temple, 3rd (01.53.01.86.60/www.mahj.org). M° Rambuteau. **Open** 11am-6pm Mon-Fri; 10am-6pm Sun. Closed Jewish hols. **Admission** €6.80; free-€4.50 reductions. **Map** p98 A2 ⑦

Set in a Marais mansion, this museum sprang from the collection of a private association formed in 1948 to safeguard Jewish heritage following the Holocaust. Displays illustrate ceremonies and rites, and show how styles were adapted around the globe through fine examples of Jewish decorative arts. There are also documents and paintings relating to the emancipation of French Jewry after the Revolution, and the Dreyfus case.

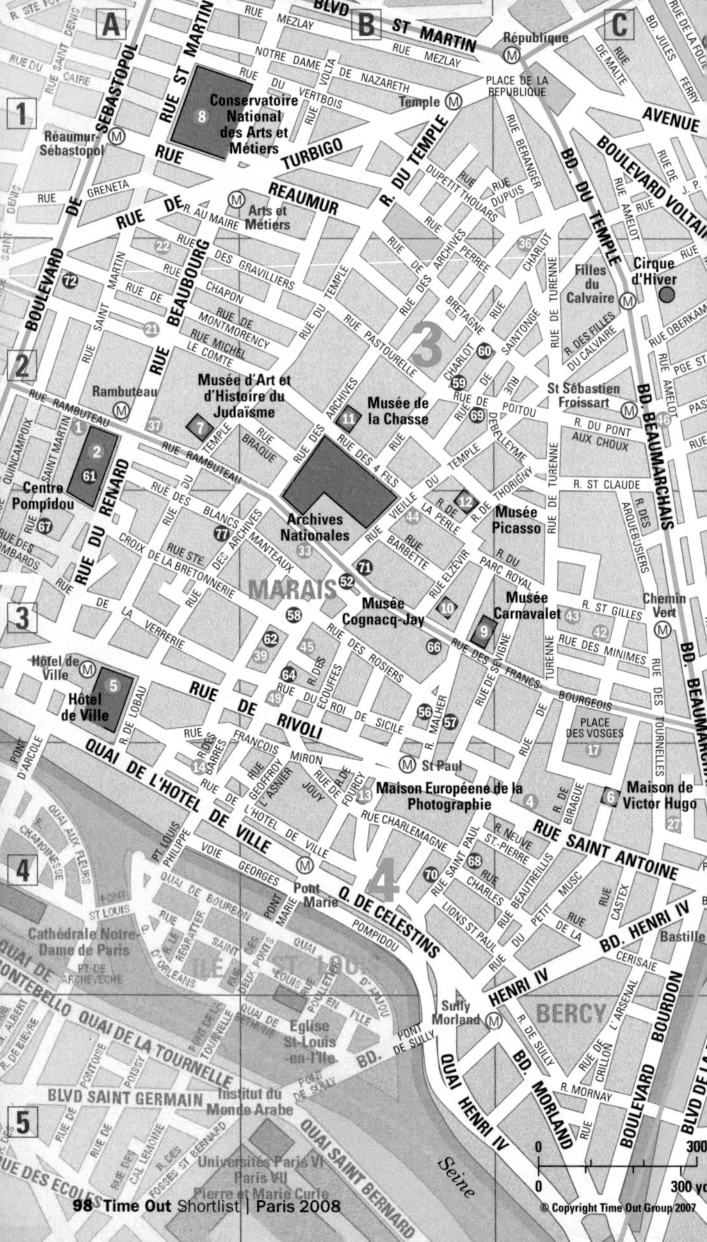
A
B
C
1
2
3
4
5
BLVD ST MARTIN
RUE MEZLAY
République
PLACE DE LA RÉPUBLIQUE
Temple
RUE ST MARTIN
BOULEVARD DE SÉBASTOPOL
Conservatoire National des Arts et Métiers
Réaumur-Sébastopol
RUE TURBIGO
RUE REAUMUR
Arts et Métiers
RUE NOTRE DAME DE NAZARETH
RUE DU VERTBOIS
RUE VOLTA
R. DU TEMPLE
RUE DUPETIT THOUARS
RUE BERANGER
BD. DU TEMPLE
AVENUE
BOULEVARD VOLTAIRE
RUE DE MALTE
BD. JULES FERRY
RUE GRENETA
RUE AU MAIRE
RUE BEAUBOURG
RUE DES GRAVILLIERS
RUE CHAPON
RUE DE MONTMORENCY
RUE MICHEL LE COMTE
RUE DES ARCHIVES
RUE PERRÉE
RUE CHARLOT
RUE DE BRETAGNE
RUE PASTOURELLE
RUE DE SAINTONGE
RUE DE TURENNE
Filles du Calvaire
Cirque d'Hiver
R. DES FILLES DU CALVAIRE
RUE OBERKAMPF
RUE AMELOT
Rambuteau
RUE RAMBUTEAU
Musée d'Art et d'Histoire du Judaïsme
Musée de la Chasse
RUE DE POITOU
St Sébastien Froissart
R. DU PONT AUX CHOUX
BD. BEAUMARCHAIS
Centre Pompidou
RUE QUINCAMPOIX
RUE DU RENARD
RUE DES 4 FILS
RUE VIEILLE DU TEMPLE
R. DE THORIGNY
R. ST CLAUDE
Archives Nationales
Musée Picasso
R. DE LA PERLE
RUE BARBETTE
RUE DES BLANCS MANTEAUX
RUE STE. CROIX DE LA BRETONNERIE
R. DU PARC ROYAL
MARAIS
Musée Cognacq-Jay
Musée Carnavalet
R. ST GILLES
Chemin Vert
RUE DE LA VERRERIE
RUE DES ROSIERS
RUE DES FRANCS-BOURGEOIS
RUE DE SÉVIGNÉ
RUE DES MINIMES
Hôtel de Ville
RUE DE RIVOLI
RUE DU ROI DE SICILE
RUE DES ECOUFFES
R. MALHER
PLACE DES VOSGES
RUE DES TOURNELLES
QUAI DE L'HOTEL DE VILLE
RUE FRANCOIS MIRON
St Paul
Maison Européene de la Photographie
Maison de Victor Hugo
RUE CHARLEMAGNE
RUE SAINT ANTOINE
RUE SAINT PAUL
RUE DE BIRAGUE
VOIE GEORGES POMPIDOU
Pont Marie
Q. DE CELESTINS
RUE CHARLES V
RUE BEAUTREILLIS
RUE DU PETIT MUSC
RUE CASTEX
BD. HENRI IV
Bastille
RUE LIONS ST PAUL
RUE CERISAIE
Cathédrale Notre-Dame de Paris
QUAI AUX FLEURS
QUAI DE BOURBON
ILE ST. LOUIS
QUAI D'ANJOU
QUAI DE BETHUNE
Eglise St-Louis-en-l'Ile
QUAI DE MONTEBELLO
QUAI DE LA TOURNELLE
BLVD SAINT GERMAIN
Institut du Monde Arabe
QUAI SAINT BERNARD
Sully Morland
PONT DE SULLY
BERCY
QUAI HENRI IV
BD. MORLAND
R. DE SULLY
R. MORNAY
BOULEVARD BOURDON
BLVD DE LA BASTILLE
Universités Paris VI Paris VII Pierre et Marie Curie
RUE DES ECOLES
Seine
0 300 m
0 300 yds

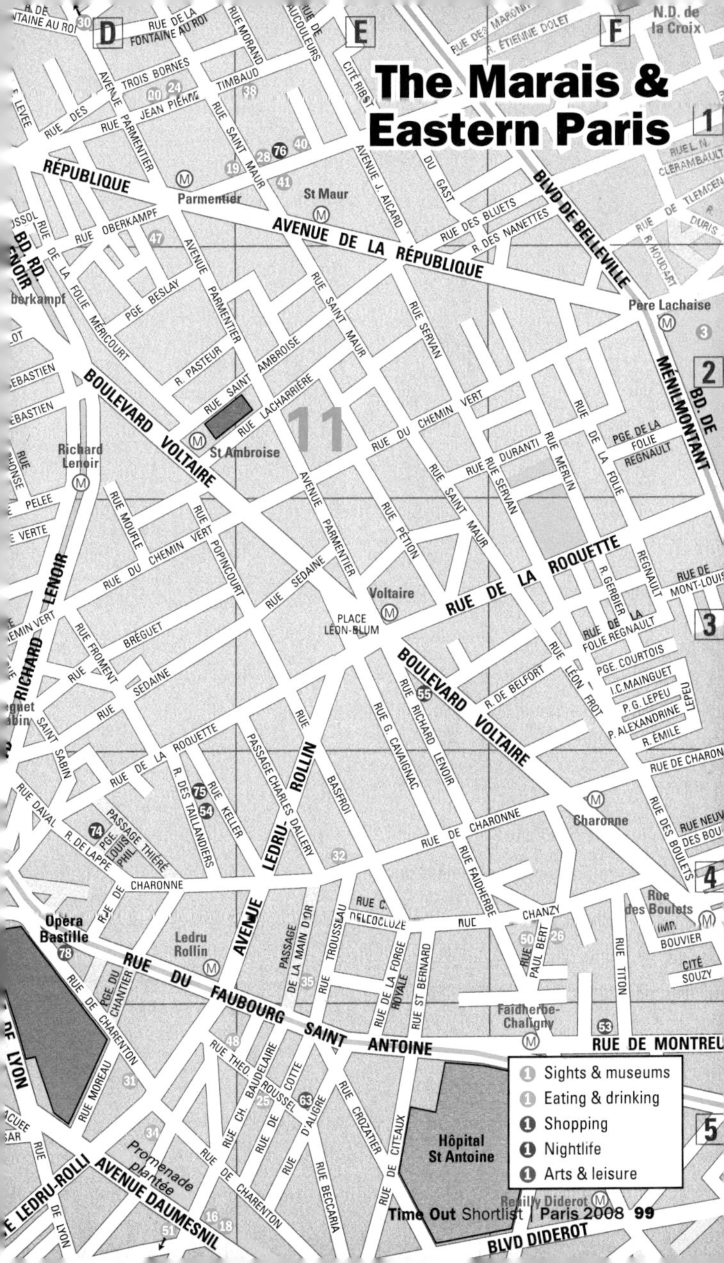

The Marais & Eastern Paris
Sights & museums
Eating & drinking
Shopping
Nightlife
Arts & leisure

Musée d'Art et d'Histoire du Judaïsme p97

Event highlights 'De Superman au Chat du Rabbin', Jews in comic strips (17 Oct 2007-27 Jan 2008)

Musée des Arts et Métiers

60 rue Réaumur, 3rd (01.53.01.82.00/ www.arts-et-metiers.net). M° Arts et Métiers. **Open** 10am-6pm Tue, Wed, Fri-Sun; 10am-9.30pm Thur. **Admission** €6.50; free-€4.50 reductions. **Map** p98 A1 ❽

After the monks of this 11th-century priory lost their heads in the 1789 Revolution, Abbé Henri Grégoire kept his by thinking up a brilliant new use for the building – as a repository of technological marvels that could act as a 3D encyclopedia for investors and industrialists in the new republic. Three floors of the neighbouring building contain glass cases of beautifully crafted scientific instruments, from astrolabes to steam engines. The best part is the magnificently restored church, the earliest example of Parisian Gothic, with exhibits on glass floors.

Event highlights 'Benjamin Franklin, Homme de Science' (5 Dec 2007-25 Apr 2008)

Musée Carnavalet

23 rue de Sévigné, 3rd (01.44.59. 58.58/www.carnavalet.paris.fr). M° St-Paul. **Open** 10am-6pm Tue-Sun. **Admission** free. *Exhibitions* €7; free-€5.50 reductions. **Map** p98 B3 ❾

This fine building contains some 140 rooms depicting the history of Paris, from pre-Roman Gaul to the 20th century. The original 16th-century rooms house Renaissance collections; the first floor shows the period up to 1789 with furniture, applied arts and paintings in period interiors; 1789 onwards is detailed in the neighbouring Hôtel Le Peletier de St-Fargeau.

Event highlights 'Benjamin Franklin, Un Américain à Paris' (5 Dec 2007-9 Mar 2008)

Musée Cognacq-Jay

Hôtel Donon, 8 rue Elzévir, 3rd (01.40. 27.07.21/www.cognacq-jay.paris.fr).

M° St-Paul. **Open** 10am-6pm Tue-Sun **Admission** free. **Map** p98 B3 ⑩
This cosy museum houses the collection diligently put together in the early 1900s by La Samaritaine founder Ernest Cognacq and his wife Marie-Louise Jay. They stuck mainly to 18th-century French, focusing on rococo artists (Watteau, Fragonard, Boucher), through the likes of Reynolds, Romney, Rembrandt and Rubens.

Musée de la Chasse

NEW *62 rue des Archives (01.53.01.92.40/www.chassenature.org). M° Rambuteau or Hôtel de Ville.* **Open** 11am-6pm Tue-Sun. **Admission** €6; free-€4.50 reductions. **Map** p98 A2 ⑪
See box p104.

Musée National Picasso

Hôtel Salé, 5 rue de Thorigny, 3rd (01.42.71.25.21/www.musee-picasso.fr). M° Chemin Vert or St-Paul. **Open** *Oct-Mar* 9.30am-5.30pm Mon, Wed-Sun. *Apr-Sept* 9.30am-6pm Mon, Wed-Sun. **Admission** €6.50; free-€4.50 reductions. *Exhibitions* prices vary. **Map** p98 B3 ⑫
This collection shows all phases of Picasso's career. Masterpieces include a gaunt, blue-period self-portrait, *Paolo as Harlequin*, his Cubist and classical phases, the surreal *Nude in an Armchair* and the ribald artist-and-model paintings of later years.

Maison Européene de la Photographie

5-7 rue de Fourcy, 4th (01.44.78.75.00/www.mep-fr.org). M° St-Paul. **Open** 11am-7.30pm Wed-Sun. **Admission** €6; free-€3 reductions. **Map** p98 B4 ⑬
The MEP is devoted to contemporary photography and stores a huge permanent collection. Also organises the biennial Mois de la Photo and the Art Outsiders festival of new media art.

Le Mémorial de la Shoah

17 rue Geoffroy-l'Asnier, 4th (01.42.77.44.72/www.memorialdelashoah.org). M° St-Paul or Pont Marie. **Open** 10am-6pm Mon-Wed, Fri-Sun; 10am-10pm Thur. *Research centre* 10am-5.30pm Mon-Wed, Fri-Sun; 10am-7.30pm Thur. **Admission** free. **Map** p98 A4 ⑭
The Mémorial du Martyr Juif Inconnu reopened with a permanent collection and temporary exhibitions devoted to the Holocaust and the 76,000 French Jews deported from 1942 to 1944.

Place de la Bastille

4th/11th/12th. M° Bastille.
Map p98 C4 ⑮
Nothing remains of the prison that was stormed on 14 July 1789 by the forces of the plebeian revolt. It remains the eternal symbol of the Revolution, fêted with a street ball on 13 July. The Colonne de Juillet in the middle is a monument to Parisians who fell in the revolutions of July 1830 and 1848.

La Promenade Plantée

av Daumesnil, 12th. M° Ledru Rollin or Gare de Lyon. **Map** p99 D5 ⑯
Where railway tracks once ran atop the Viaduc des Arts there's now a promenade planted with roses and shrubs. It continues east at ground level through the Jardin de Reuilly and the Jardin Charles Péguy to the Bois de Vincennes.

Place des Vosges

4th. M° St-Paul. **Map** p98 C3 ⑰
The Place des Vosges was the first planned square in Paris (along with its contemporary, place Dauphine) and was commissioned in 1605 by Henri IV. It's cosy, with red-brick-and-stone arcaded façades and steep slate roofs, and is quite distinct from the pomp you find in later Bourbon Paris. It has a symmetrical plan, with carriageways through the Pavillon de la Reine on the north side and Pavillon du Roi on the south.

Le Viaduc des Arts

15-121 av Daumesnil, 12th (www.viaduc-des-arts.com). M° Ledru Rollin or Gare de Lyon. **Map** p99 D5 ⑱
Glass-fronted workshops occupy the arches under the Promenade Plantée – a suite of swish showrooms for craftspeople and artists, including furniture and fashion designers, tapestry restorers, and chandelier, violin and flute makers.

PARIS BY AREA

Eating & drinking

L'Abreuvoir

103 rue Oberkampf, 11th (01.43.38. 87.01). M° Parmentier. **Open** 5pm-2am Mon-Sat. Closed 2wks Aug. **Bar**. **Map** p99 D1 ⑲

This *sympa* little bar is relatively underused. Nabbing a low stool at a candlelit table is a cinch, or you might get a spot at the bar counter done out in rock 'n' roll memorabilia. The speciality here is beer cocktails (€6), such as the Casse-Tête of beer, rum and peach liqueur.

L'Alimentation Générale

64 rue Jean-Pierre-Timbaud, 11th (01.43.55.42.50). M° Parmentier. **Open** 5pm-2am Mon-Sat. **Bar**. **Map** p99 D1 ⑳

Cupboards of kitsch china face the long counter, and the lampshades made from kitchen sponges are inspired. The beers are well chosen – Flag, Sagres, Picon and Orval by the bottle – and the €8 house speciality involves obscure combinations of fruit, spices and alcohol.

L'Ambassade d'Auvergne

22 rue du Grenier-St-Lazare, 3rd (01.42.72.31.22/www.ambassade-auvergne.com). M° Rambuteau. **Open** *Sept-July* noon-2pm, 7.30-10.30pm daily. *Aug* noon-2pm, 7.30-10.30pm Mon-Fri, Sun. **€**. **Bistro**. **Map** p98 A2 ㉑

This rustic spot is a fine embassy for the simple but hearty fare of central France. Go easy on the complimentary pâté and bread – you're going to need an appetite later for the bowl of green lentils cooked in goose fat with bacon and shallots, followed by the *rôti d'agneau* with the signature *aligot* (potatoes with garlic and cheese). Of the regional wines on offer, the quite fruity AOC Marcillac makes a worthy partner to a successful meal.

Andy Whaloo

69 rue des Gravilliers, 3rd (01.42.71. 20.38). M° Arts et Métiers. **Open** 4pm-2am Mon-Sat. **Bar**. **Map** p98 A2 ㉒

Andy Wahloo – from the team behind London's Momo and Sketch – is Arabic for 'I have nothing'. A formidably fashionable crowd fights for a coveted place

Musée Carnavalet p100

on an upturned paint can. From head to toe, it's a beautifully designed venue crammed with Moroccan artefacts.

L'Antenne Bastille

32ter bd de la Bastille, 12th (01.43.43. 34.92). M° Bastille. **Open** 8am-2am Mon-Fri; noon-2am Sat; 2-9pm Sun. Closed Aug. **Bar. Map** p98 C5 ㉓

A great little retro bar a quayside stroll from the Bastille opera, L'Antenne has a terrace on the Port de l'Arsenal marina and a simple, airy interior. There's cheap, substantial food: an €8.50 *plat du jour* and €11.50 daily *formule*.

Au P'tit Garage

63 rue Jean-Pierre-Timbaud, 11th (01.48.07.08.12). M° Parmentier. **Open** 6pm-2am daily. **Bar. Map** p99 D1 ㉔

This marvellous rock 'n' roll bar is the best you'll find on bar-lined rue Jean-Pierre-Timbaud. Stuffing bursts out of the bar stools, skip-salvage chairs accompany wobbly tables of ill-matched colours; an old radiogram is tucked away in the back. And as black-palmed mechanics clutch the first, very much welcome, cold Kro of the day, music-savvy Frenchettes giggle and gossip.

Le Baron Rouge

1 rue Théophile-Roussel, 12th (01.43. 43.14.32). M° Ledru Rollin. **Open** 10am-3pm, 5-10pm Tue-Thur; 10am-10pm Fri, Sat; 10am-3pm Sun. **Bar. Map** p99 E5 ㉕

This wine bar serves from great barrels piled on the tiled floor, chalked up at very reasonable prices by the glass. There are draught beers, too – St-Omer, Jenlain and Corsican Pietra. Popular, so don't expect much elbow room when the after-work crowd is in.

Le Bistrot Paul Bert

18 rue Paul Bert, 11th (01.43.72. 24.01). M° Charonne. **Open** noon-2pm, 7.30-11pm Tue-Thur; noon-2pm, 7.30-11.30pm Fri, Sat. Closed Aug. €€. **Bistro. Map** p99 F4 ㉖

This haunt of businessmen and artisans has a well-worn interior redolent of garlic and red wine. The food is old-fashioned, no-nonsense cuisine. Egg mayo is raised from mundanity by a particularly good potato salad; mains include a perfectly cooked piece of salmon with hollandaise sauce, served with pasta.

Bofinger

5-7 rue de la Bastille, 4th (01.42.72. 87.82/www.bofingerparis.com). M° Bastille. **Open** noon-3pm, 6.30pm-1am Mon-Fri; noon-1am Sat, Sun. €€. **Brasserie. Map** p98 C4 ㉗

Bofinger is a post-opera haunt and draws big crowds at other times for its authentic art nouveau setting and brasserie atmosphere. Downstairs is the prettiest place to eat; upstairs is air-conditioned. Go for the foolproof brasserie meal of oysters and fillet steak and you won't be disappointed.

Café Charbon

109 rue Oberkampf, 11th (01.43.57. 55.13/www.nouveaucasino.net). M° Parmentier or Ménilmontant. **Open** 9am-2am Mon-Thur, Sun; 9am-4am Fri, Sat. **Bar. Map** p99 E1 ㉘

This beautifully restored building set off the Oberkampf boom, its booths,

Thrill of the Chasse

The Musée de la Chasse reopens in the Marais.

The Musée de la Chasse, which reopened in February 2007 after a two-year refurbishment, is a delightful oddity. It occupies two Marais mansions, and its collection of hunting memorabilia goes far beyond the predictable animal trophies and firearms: a 16th-century German hunting spear, a collection of crossbows, and some ornate blunderbusses and flintlock rifles so gorgeously worked you wonder how any hunter had the heart to risk soiling them in the field.

The luscious decorative art and paintings are another highlight. There are animal studies aplenty, from the calm to the quirky – like a 17th-century painting of a drunken stag wreaking havoc in a genteel Dutch dining room – by artists including Corot and Regnault. But it's the new thematic display that really scores, organised around a special cabinet in each room that might be devoted to anything from dogs and deer to wolves – even unicorns. Other curiosities include Desportes' portraits of Louis XIV's favourite dogs, the Jeff Koons' Puppy, wild boar soup tureens, a stuffed polar bear, and a tiny panelled room containing Belgian artist/choreographer Jan Fabre's spooky owl-feather ceiling. Keep a close watch on the mounted animal heads – and don't be surprised when their eyes swivel to follow you around the room.

mirrors, chandeliers and adventurous music policy putting trendsters at their ease. Fine dining, sound DJing and retro chic are the key elements. Two decades later, the formula still works and inspires other bars in the vicinity.

C'Amelot

50 rue Amelot, 11th (01.43.55.54.04). M° Chemin Vert. **Open** 7-10.30pm Mon, Sat; noon-2pm, 7-10.30pm Tue-Fri. **€. Bistro. Map** p98 C3 29

With its panelling and bare wood tables, C'Amelot's long, narrow dining room has a pretty countrified, even dated, feel. The market-inspired meal provides two options for each course: starters of lentil soup with foie gras or unusual cured salmon with braised chicory. If available, don't miss the lamb chops in poivrade sauce with porridgy polenta.

Le Chateaubriand

129 av Parmentier, 11th (01.43.57.45.95). M° Goncourt. **Open** noon-2pm, 8-11pm Tue-Fri; 8-11pm Sat. Closed 3wks Aug. **€€€. Bistro. Map** p99 D1 30

See box p111.

China Club

50 rue de Charenton, 12th (01.43.43.82.02/chinaclub.cc). M° Bastille or Ledru Rollin. **Open** 7pm-2am daily. Closed Aug. **Bar. Map** p99 D5 31

With its huge chesterfields, low lighting and a sexy long bar, it's impossible not to feel glamorous here. They take their martinis seriously, and their well-made champagne cocktails. It's ideal seduction territory – although China Club is equally suited to a hands-off first date.

Crêperie Bretonne Fleurie

67 rue de Charonne, 11th (01.43.55.62.29). M° Ledru Rollin or Charonne. **Open** noon-2.30pm, 7pm-midnight Mon-Fri; 7-11pm Sat. Closed Aug & public hols. **€. Bistro. Map** p99 E4 32

Everything about this restaurant is apt, including the crêpe chef's striped sailor-style shirt. To fill your savoury and freshly cooked buckwheat galette,

Musée de la Chasse p101

choose a ham/cheese/egg combination or one of the more unusual choices, such as camembert with walnuts. Dessert crêpes feature enticingly sweet options such as pear 'n' chocolate and banana 'n' chocolate. Dry cider is the best accompaniment.

Le Dôme du Marais

53bis rue des Francs-Bourgeois, 4th (01.42.74.54.17). M° Rambuteau. **Open** noon-2.30pm, 7.15-11pm Tue-Sat. Closed 2wks Jan & 3wks Aug. **€€. Bistro. Map** p98 B3 33

Le Dôme is between bistro and haute cuisine. The stunning octagonal dining is good for a dressy meal, though staff won't turn a hair if you wear jeans. The building predates the Revolution, and is done up in burgundy and gilt. Owner-chef Pierre Lecoutre works with seasonal produce: *filet de courbine*, say, a white fish available three weeks a year.

L'Encrier

55 rue Traversière, 12th (01.44.68.08.16). M° Ledru Rollin or Gare de Lyon. **Open** noon-2.15pm, 7.30-11pm Mon-Fri; 7.30-11pm Sat. Closed Aug. **€. Bistro. Map** p99 D5 34

Value here is tremendous, with a €13 lunch menu and a choice of €17 or €21 menus in the evening. Start with fried rabbit kidneys on a bed of salad dressed with raspberry vinegar, an original and wholly successful combination, and follow with goose magret with honey – a nice change from the duck version.

Le Fanfaron

6 rue de la Main-d'Or, 11th (01.49.23.41.14). M° Ledru Rollin. **Open** 6pm-2am Tue-Sat. Closed 2wks Aug. No credit cards. **Bar. Map** p99 E4 35

On a small backstreet, Le Fanfaron is a haunt for musically inclined retro dudes. Buffs come for owner Xavier's rare vinyl film soundtracks, others for the cheap beer. The decor? Stones and Iggy memorabilia, old furniture, 1960s film posters, wooden panelling and Lucy the legless mannequin.

Guillaume

32 rue de Picardie, 3rd (01.44.54.20.60). M° Temple. **Open** 11am-2am Mon-Fri; 7pm-2am Sat. **Bar. Map** p98 C2 36

This trendy bar-restaurant has a large back room equipped with gallery and a huge peacock-feather chandelier, though the smart set prefers a spot on the modest terrace facing the Carreau du Temple market. During 'bubble hours', 5.30-7.30pm, custom is encouraged with cheapish Jaeger-Ligneut champers and crostini with red tuna or guacamole. At other times, cocktails are €8 a pop.

Le Hangar

12 impasse Berthaud, 3rd (01.42.74.55.44). M° Rambuteau. **Open** noon-2.30pm, 7-11.30pm Tue-Sat. Closed Aug. **€. Bistro. Map** p98 A2 37

This bistro has a terrace, stone walls, smartly set tables and excellent food. A bowl of tapenade and toast is supplied while you choose from the carte. It yields, for starters, tasty *rillettes de lapereau* (rabbit) and perfectly balanced

18 rue Bourg-Tibourg, 75004 Paris
Metro : Hotel de Ville t 01 42 72 81 34

lunch, brunch,
snacks & booze

Happy Hours 17h – 20h 5€ on selected cocktails
UNDERGROUND Happy Hours 20h – 22h

COME WATCH WORLD CUP RUGBY

STOLLY'S
stone-bar

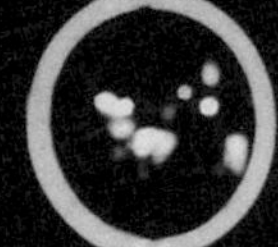

Enjoy lethal cocktails on our marais terrasse

16, rue Cloche-Perce - 75004 Paris Open 7 Days A Week 16h30 – 02h
Metro : Saint-Paul t 01 42 76 06 76 Happy hours 17h – 20h

pumpkin and chestnut soup; mains include a well-seasoned steak tartare, served with a fresh, crisp salad and pommes dauphines, and a superb *ris de veau* on a bed of melting chicory.

Juan et Juanita

82 rue Jean-Pierre-Timbaud, 11th (01.43.57.60.15). M° Couronnes. **Open** 8pm-2am Tue-Sat. **€**. **Brasserie**. **Map** p99 E1 38

With candelabras on every table, the look here is polished and flirty – as are the staff. Starters include mesclun salads with toasted hazelnuts, one with a crispy st-marcellin *brik*. They're followed by the special of the night, perhaps buttery rabbit with thyme, or tender leg of lamb. Desserts here really are too good to miss; try the lime sorbet with vodka or the vanilla ice-cream with a red fruit coulis. The ambitious wine list is very strong on Graves and Gaillacs.

Lizard Lounge

18 rue du Bourg-Tibourg, 4th (01.42.72.81.34/www.hip-bars.com). M° Hôtel de Ville. **Open** noon-2am daily. **Bar**. **Map** p98 B3 39

Anglophile favourite deep in the Marais, this loud and lively (mainly hetero) pick-up joint provides lager in pint glasses, strong, well-mixed cocktails by the bucketload and a viewing platform to ogle your prey. There's trip hop and house music of consistent quality and a decent happy hour.

La Maizon

123 rue Oberkampf, 11th (01.58.30.62.12). M° Ménilmontant. **Open** 4pm-2am Mon-Thur, Sun; 4pm-6am Fri, Sat. **Bar**. **Map** p99 E1 40

The best DJ bar on the Oberkampf strip – although inexplicably less frequented than the cod salsa and pseudo Brazilian bars you have to pass to get here. This means you're guaranteed a cosy spot, if not by the bar, then certainly at a table in the back. Its location opposite madly popular music venue Cithéa helps, but stick around here for Maes on draught, Gin Fizz and other long drinks at €7.

La Mercerie

98 rue Oberkampf, 11th (01.43.38.81.30). M° Parmentier. **Open** 7pm-2am daily. **Bar**. **Map** p99 E1 41

Opposite the landmark Charbon, the Mercerie has bare walls – bare everything, in fact – that contain the usual Oberkampf shenanigans of death-wish drinking against a loud, eclectic soundtrack. A DJ programme is lipsticked on to the bar mirror. Happy hour stretches to 9pm, so you can cane the house vodkas and still have enough euros to finish the job after dusk. The back area, with its tea lights, provides intimacy.

Le Petit Marché

9 rue de Béarn, 3rd (01.42.72.06.67). M° Chemin Vert. **Open** noon-3pm, 8pm-midnight Mon-Fri; noon-4pm, 8-10pm Sat, Sun. **€**. **Bistro**. **Map** p98 C3 42

This bistro attracts a fashion-conscious crowd. The wood-decorated interior is welcoming, the menu short and modern with Asian touches. Start with refreshing raw tuna flash-fried in sesame seeds and served with a Thai sauce; then why not try pan-fried scallops with lime or a vegetarian risotto rich in basil, coriander, cream and green beans.

Le Petit Pamphlet

NEW *15 rue St-Gilles, 3rd (01.42.71.22.21). M° Filles du Calvaire.* **Open** 7.30-11pm Mon, Sat; noon-2.30pm, 7.30-11pm Tue-Fri. Closed 2wks Jan & 2wks Aug. **€€**. **Bistro**. **Map** p98 C2 43

His solid success at the chic bistro Le Pamphlet inspired chef Alain Carrère to open this casual annexe. Flavours are as bold as ever in starters like tomato stuffed with confit lamb, or black cod in a tomato and caper dressing. Typical of the seasonal desserts are roasted figs with caramel ice-cream and mirabelle plums with a crumble topping. The very professional staff are anxious to please.

La Perle

78 rue Vieille-du-Temple, 3rd (01.42.72.69.93). M° Chemin Vert or St-Paul.

PARIS BY AREA

Open 6am-2am Mon-Fri; 8am-2am Sat, Sun. **Bar**. **Map** p98 B3 44

This Marais hit is commendably simple in its execution. Arty dabblings on the walls and the old locomotive over the bar meet rows of grey chairs outside, and patterned banquettes within. The Pearl is an all-day and late-night hetero/homo mix: it feels very much like a neighbourhood bar. The menu runs from hearty omelettes to a delicate *salade marine*. Expect DJs later on in the evening.

Le Petit Fer à Cheval

30 rue Vieille-du-Temple, 4th (01.42. 72.47.47). M° St-Paul. **Open** 9am-2am daily. **Bar**. **Map** p98 B3 45

This charming spot has old film and promo posters, a vintage clock and an ornate mirror backdrop; behind the glassy façade hides a friendly dining room lined with old métro benches, offering space, but not scenery. In business since 1903, the Little Horseshoe had a retro makeover in the 1990s.

Pop In

105 rue Amelot, 11th (01.48.05.56.11). M° St-Sébastien Froissart. **Open** 6.30pm-1.30am Tue-Sun. Closed Aug. **Bar**. **Map** p98 C2 46

Since it hosted a Christian Dior aftershow party and was colonised by fashion types, the Pop In has been known as a place that doesn't care but is cool anyway. It's scruffy, cheap and the staff are genuinely nice. Add a cellar bar that does open-mic DJs and you have a recipe for a top (and trendy) night out.

Rosso

4bis rue Neuve Popincourt, 11th (01.49. 29.06.36). M° Parmentier. **Open** 6pm-2am daily. **Bar**. **Map** p99 D1 47

Zéro Zéro boss Ben's newest venture, Rosso, is just as funky and snug as its sibling, though less blokey and more arty in style. Among the dozen or so cocktails on offer (€6.50) are the Rosso (vodka, Triple Sec and framboise) and daiquiris in several fruit flavours. Beers available here include Kilkenny and Hoegaarden.

Le Square Trousseau

1 rue Antoine-Vollon, 12th (01.43.43. 06.00). M° Ledru Rollin. **Open** noon-2.30pm, 8-11.30pm Tue-Sat. **€**. **Brasserie**. **Map** p99 D5 48

This friendly restaurant, with its superb 1900s interior, is a definite favourite with the Parisian fashion and media crowd. Start with a silky *timbale* of smoked salmon and candied lemon, or poached eggs in a delicious, nutmeg-scented cheese sauce. A main dish of plump farm chicken comes with a creamy risotto or set in Moroccan-style pastry; tender strips of duck arrive with a complementary cherry sauce.

Stolly's

16 rue Cloche-Perce, 4th (01.42.76. 06.76/www.hip-bars.com). M° Hôtel de Ville or St-Paul. **Open** 4.30pm-2am daily. **Bar**. **Map** p98 B3 49

This drinking den has been serving an Anglo crowd with expert vodka tonics and old Velvets tunes for nights immemorial. The friendly staff help smooth a passage from sobriety to sinking drinks until you're rotten with consummate ease. An outdoor terrace eases libation, as do long happy hours.

Le Temps au Temps

NEW *13 rue Paul-Bert, 11th (01.43. 79.63.40). M° Faidherbe-Chaligny.* **Open** noon-2pm, 8-10.30pm Tue-Sat. **€€**. **Bistro**. **Map** p99 F4 50

This bistro's friendly new owners have retained the name, but replaced the inaccurate timepieces with just two or three clocks. Chef Sylvain Sendra is a bright talent. The €27 menu might begin with a home-made *fromage de tête*, or a cleverly balanced dish of warm *ratte* potatoes and sundried tomatoes topped with anchovies. Ice-creams are home-made, and include an exquisite violet sorbet.

Le Train Bleu

Gare de Lyon, cour Louis-Armand, 12th (01.43.43.09.06/www.le-train-bleu.com). M° Gare de Lyon. **Open** 11.30am-3pm, 7-11pm daily. **€€**. **Brasserie**. **Map** p99 D5 51

PARIS BY AREA

China Club p104

Le Dôme du Marais p105

This listed dining room – with vintage frescoes of destinations served by the Paris-Lyon-Marseille railway and big oak benches with shiny brass coat racks – exudes pleasant expectation. Expect fine renderings of traditional French classics using first-rate produce. Lobster served on a bed of delicate, walnut-oil-dressed salad leaves is a lovely starter; you can follow it with *sandre* (pike-perch) accompanied by a 'risotto' of *crozettes*.

Shopping

A-poc

47 rue des Francs-Bourgeois, 4th (01.44.54.07.05). M° St-Paul or Rambuteau. **Open** 11am-7pm Mon-Sat. Closed 3wks Aug. **Map** p98 B3 52
Issey Miyake's cool lab-style boutique (the name's an acronym for 'A Piece of Cloth') takes a conceptual approach to clothes. Alongside ready-to-wear cotton Lycra clothes are rolls of seamless tubular wool jersey that is cut *sur mesure*; Miyake's trustworthy assistants will be more than happy to give any advice you require.

L'Autre Boulange

43 rue de Montreuil, 11th (01.43.72.86.04). M° Nation or Faidherbe Chaligny. **Open** 7.30am-1.30pm, 3.30-7.30pm Tue-Sat. Closed Aug. **Map** p99 F5 53
Michel Cousin bakes organic loaves in his wood-fired oven – varieties like the *flutiot* (rye bread dotted with raisins, walnuts and hazelnuts), the *sarment de Bourgogne* (sourdough and a little rye) and a spiced cornmeal bread ideal for foie gras.

Come On Eileen

16-18 rue des Taillandiers, 11th (01.43.38.12.11). M° Ledru Rollin. **Open** *Sept-July* 11.30am-8.30pm Mon-Thur; 11.30am-7.30pm Fri; 4-8pm Sun. *Aug* 2-8pm Mon-Fri. **Map** p99 D4 54
The owners of this vintage wonderland have an keen eye for what's funky, from cowboy gear to stunning debutantes' frocks. With customers including the likes of Kylie Minogue, they

can get away with setting their prices high. Having said this, the stock is very well sourced and generally in excellent condition.

Les Domaines qui Montent

136 bd Voltaire, 11th (01.43.56.89.15). M° Voltaire. **Open** 10am-8pm Tue-Fri; 10.30am-10pm Sat. **Map** p99 E3 55
A shop and café, where wines cost the same as they would at the producers. Ideal for restocking your cellar or gifts.

L'Eclaireur

3ter rue des Rosiers, 4th (01.48.87. 10.22/www.leclaireur.com). M° St-Paul. **Open** 11am-7pm Mon-Sat. **Map** p98 B3 56
L'Eclaireur stocks the most uncompromising of top labels' designs, including such luminaries as Comme des Garçons, Martin Margiela, Dries van Noten and Carpe Diem.

L'Eclaireur Homme

12 rue Malher, 4th (01.44.54.22.11/ www.leclaireur.com). M° St-Paul. **Open** 11am-7pm Mon-Sat. **Map** p98 B3 57
Amid this old printworks you'll find items by Prada, Comme des Garçons, Dries van Noten and Martin Margiela.

Free 'P' Star

8 rue Ste-Croix-de-la-Bretonnerie, 4th (01.42.76.03.72). M° St-Paul. **Open** noon-11pm Mon-Sat; 2-10pm Sun. **Map** p98 B3 58
This Aladdin's cave of retro glitz, ex-army jackets and glad rags is the best-priced of the bargain basements.

L'Habilleur

44 rue de Poitou, 3rd (01.48.87.77.12). M° St-Sébastien Froissart. **Open** noon-8pm Mon-Sat. **Map** p98 B2 59
Urbanites prowl this slick store for its severely cut men's and women's togs by Dries van Noten, Helmut Lang and John Richmond, and dagger-toed shoes by Patrick Cox. All items are end of line or straight from the catwalk.

Julien, Caviste

50 rue Charlot, 3rd (01.42.72.00.94). M° Filles du Calvaire. **Open** 9.30am-

Cook's tour de force

Le Chateaubriand's hotshot chef.

Parisian nouvelle cuisine has a new celebrity exponent, the 34-year-old Iñaki Aizpitarte. You may struggle to pronounce his Basque name, but you'll certainly remember his cooking, as showcased at the very stylish Le Chateaubriand (p104). Since it opened in 2006, the buzzing bistro has been packed with singers, artists, designers – and even some chefs.

Aizpitarte has his own style. His cuisine is sharp, simple, yet extremely creative, founded on unusual combinations, new takes on classical dishes and the best seasonal produce. He defines his culinary mission as 'pleasure through invention and adventure'. 'I try to make dishes with well-defined flavours that first clash with each other, then end up in alliance,' he says. It works a treat. Asparagus with a sublime tahini foam and little splinters of sesame seed brittle, or the seemingly risky dark chocolate brick with red pepper mousse, will be firmly logged in your gastronomic memory.

Presentation is important, too. In the minimalist set menu, which changes every fortnight, the attention to detail is clear. He finds inspiration for his dishes at Paris farmers' markets, or when eating foreign food. His is some of the best French nouvelle cuisine going, and the art deco setting is wonderful. Book well ahead.

1.30pm, 3.30-7.30pm Tue-Sat; 10.30am-1.30pm Sun. **Map** p98 A2 60
Tireless wine merchant Julien overflows with enthusiasm for the producers he's discovered, and holds wine tastings.

Librairie Flammarion

Centre Pompidou, 4th (01.44.78.43.22/www.flammarioncentre.com). M° Rambuteau. **Open** 11am-10pm Mon, Wed-Sun. Closed 2wks Sept. **Map** p98 A3 61
On the ground floor of the Pompidou, this is one of the nicest places in Paris to peruse first-rate art, design, architecture, photography and cinema books. It also stocks a huge selection of postcards and arty magazines.

Mariage Frères

30 rue du Bourg-Tibourg, 4th (01.42.72.28.11/www.mariagefreres.com). M° Hôtel de Ville. **Open** *Shop* 10.30am-7.30pm daily. *Salon* noon-7pm daily. **Map** p98 B3 62
Aromatic, old-fashioned wood-panelled tea emporium. Come here to buy (or, in the salon, sample) teas of every provenance, colour and strength.

Moisan

5 pl d'Aligre, 12th (01.43.45.46.60). M° Ledru Rollin. **Open** 7am-8pm Tue-Sat; 7am-2pm Sun. **Map** p98 E5 63
Moisan's organic bread, *viennoiseries* and rustic tarts are outstanding. At this branch, by place d'Aligre market, there's always a queue out the door.

Nodus

22 rue Vieille-du-Temple, 4th (01.42.77.07.96/www.nodus.fr). M° St-Paul or Hôtel de Ville. **Open** 10.45am-2pm, 3-7.30pm Mon-Sat; 1-7.30pm Sun. **Map** p98 B3 64
Under the beams of this cosy men's shirt specialist (there are several other branches to be found across town) are rows of plain, striped and checked dress shirts, stylish silk ties and a range of silver-plated cufflinks.

Ô Château – The Wine Loft

100 rue de la Folie-Méricourt, 11th (01.44.73.97.80/www.o-chateau.com). M° République. **Open** 9am-7.30pm Mon-Sat. **Map** p98 C1 65
Olivier Magny's wine boutique is a user-friendly operation for wine buffs and beginners alike.

Paris-Musées

29bis rue des Francs-Bourgeois, 4th (01.42.74.13.02). M° St-Paul. **Open** 2-7pm Mon; 11am-1pm, 2-7pm Tue-Fri; 11am-7pm Sat; noon-7.30pm Sun. **Map** p98 B3 66
Run by the city's museums federation, this operation sells funky lamps and ceramics by young local designers, alongside reproductions from various Paris museums.

Rag

83-85 rue St-Martin, 4th (01.48.87.34.64). M° Rambuteau or Châtelet/RER Châtelet Les Halles. **Open** 10am-8pm Mon-Sat; noon-8pm Sun. **Map** p98 A3 67
A shop in two halves. One does casual *fripes* – pilots' jumpers and 1970s shirts, colourful puffer jackets, '70s heels and more; the other might yield a vintage Hermès scarf, a '60s Paco Rabanne dresses or any number of Dior accessories.

Red Wheelbarrow

22 rue St-Paul, 4th (01.48.04.75.08/www.theredwheelbarrow.com). M° St Paul. **Open** 10am-6pm Mon; 10am-7pm Tue-Sat; 2-6pm Sun. Map p98 B4 68
This friendly little Anglo bookshop has a good range of new books from the UK and US, and also serves as a venue for an interesting roster of readings and other events.

Shine

15 rue de Poitou, 3rd (01.48.05.80.10). M° Filles du Calvaire. **Open** 11am-7.30pm Mon-Sat. **Map** p98 B2 69
If you're looking for funky, youthful and cutting-edge togs, Vinci d'Helia should have exactly what you need: sexy T-shirts with unusual detailing, Luella's chunky knits and Earl Jeans fabulously cut trousers and jackets. And you could even find yourself sharing shop space with Laetitia Casta and Emma de Caunes.

Le Village St-Paul

rue St-Paul, rue Charlemagne & quai des Célestins, 4th. M° St-Paul. **Open** 10am-7pm Mon-Sat. **Map** p98 B4 70

Antiques sellers are spread across a series of small courtyards linking rue St-Paul, rue Charlemagne and quai des Célestins. As well as a source of decent old furniture and kitchenware, Le Village St-Paul is a great place for a morning's browse.

Zadig & Voltaire

42 rue des Francs-Bourgeois, 3rd (01.44.54.00.60/www.zadig-et-voltaire.com). M° St-Paul or Hôtel de Ville. **Open** 1.30-7.30pm Mon, Sun; 10.30am-7.30pm Tue-Sat. **Map** p98 B3 71

Z&V branches are popping up all over Paris. Popular separates include the cotton tops, shirts and faded jeans; its winter range of gorgeously soft cashmere jumpers is superb.

Nightlife

Les Bains Douches

NEW *7 rue du Bourg-l'Abbé, 3rd (01.48.87.01.80/www.lesbainsdouches.net). M° Etienne Marcel.* **Open** 11pm-6am Wed-Sun. **Map** p98 A2 72

Once a world leader, Les Bains lost its way in the 1990s, relying on its reputation to pull in tourists. This all changed when it reopened in 2006, and now star local DJs like Busy P and international names like Erol Alkan grace its decks. The crowd is increasingly, though not exclusively, gay.

Le Bataclan

50 bd Voltaire, 11th (01.43.14.00.30). M° Oberkampf. **Open** times vary. **Map** p99 D2 73

Rock legends and stars of chanson and world music play at this atmospheric former theatre.

Café de la Danse

5 passage Louis-Phillipe, 11th (01.47.00.57.59/www.cafedeladanse.com). M° Bastille. **Open** times vary. Closed July & Aug. **Map** p99 D4 74

This utterly lovely venue, with its high ceilings and cheery acoustics, is the place in which to check out international indie acts such as Mercury Rev and Granddaddy.

Follow Me

24 rue Keller, 11th (no phone/www.followme-paris.com). M° Bastille. **Open** 6am-noon Mon, Fri; 6am-11am Thur; 6am-4pm Sat; 6am-6pm Sun. **Admission** €18-€25. **Map** p99 D4 75

This is an after-only club, and a sure bet if you find yourself wide-eyed when other venues are closing. Admission includes two drinks. There's a pit-like dancefloor, podiums and full-on tribal house and trance.

Nouveau Casino

109 rue Oberkampf, 11th (01.43.57.57.40/www.nouveaucasino.net). M° Parmentier, Ménilmontant or St-Maur. **Open** midnight-5am Wed-Sat. **Map** p99 E1 76

Run by the adjacent Café Charbon: fab acoustics, a leftfield line-up (post-rock, dub, garage) and fair drinks prices.

Arts & leisure

Les Bains du Marais

31-33 rue des Blancs-Manteaux, 4th (01.44.61.02.02/www.lesbainsdumarais.com). M° St-Paul. **Open** *Men* 11am-11pm Thur; 10am-8pm Fri. *Women* 11am-8pm Mon; 11am-11pm Tue; 10am-7pm Wed. *Mixed* 10am-8pm Sat; 11am-7pm Sun. Closed Aug. **Map** p98 A3 77

This chic hammam and spa mixes modern and traditional to great effect. Hairdressing services, facials, waxing and essential oil massages are also available. The hammam is €30, a massage also comes in at €30.

Opéra Bastille

pl de la Bastille, 12th (08.36.69.78.68/www.opera-de-paris.fr). M° Bastille. **Open** times vary. **Map** p99 D5 78

This modern building is one that everyone (other than the city's skateboarder contingent) loves to hate. Still, Gérard Mortier's work as the Opéra National director (he's heading to New York in 2009) has proved adventurous with high levels of dramatic intensity.

PARIS BY AREA

Pont Neuf p117

The Seine & the Islands

The Seine

The city's river serves several purposes: boundary, transport route and tourist attraction. On the first count, the division is as much psychological as physical, between a Left Bank still popularly seen as chic and intellectual and a Right Bank seen as mercantile. On the second, the Seine is still used to transport building materials; and on the third, as the boat tours prove, it's a must-see feature.

In 1990 UNESCO put 12 kilometres of Paris riverbank on its World Heritage register, and the Parc Tino-Rossi was set up on the Left Bank, now a regular venue for open-air tango. Then the floating venues – Batofar being the best known – became super-trendy; and in the last ten years, it's been one Seineside cultural attraction after another. Stretches of riverside roads are closed on Sundays to give space to cyclists and rollerskaters, the Port de Javel becomes an open-air dancehall in the summer and there's the summer riverside jamboree of Paris-Plage, which brings the seaside to the embankments (on both sides of the river since 2006) – sand, palm trees, loungers, beach huts and all.

Sights & museums

Vedettes du Pont-Neuf

square du Vert Galant, 1st (01.46.33. 98.38/www.vedettesdupontneuf.com).

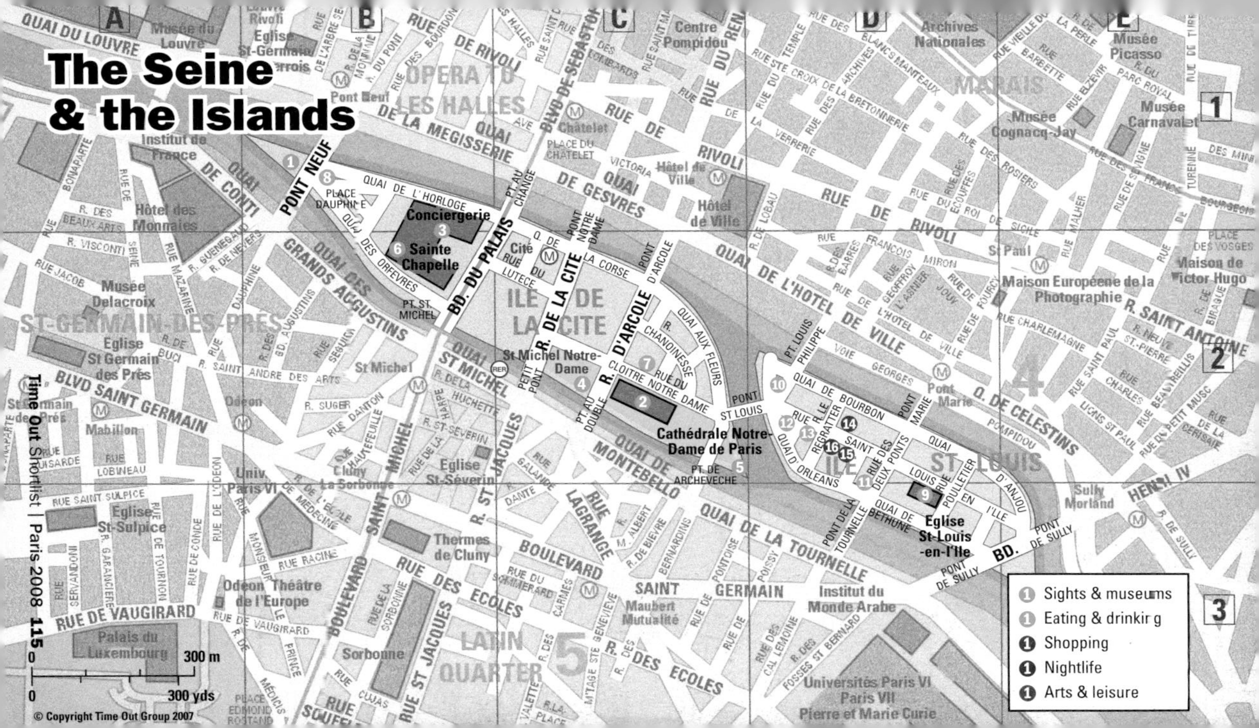
The Seine
& the Islands
A
B
C
D
E
1
2
3
4
5
Quai du Louvre
Musée du Louvre
Louvre Rivoli
Eglise St-Germain l'Auxerrois
Pont Neuf
Institut de France
Quai de Conti
Hôtel des Monnaies
Place Dauphine
Quai de l'Horloge
Conciergerie
Sainte Chapelle
Quai des Orfèvres
Bd. du Palais
Quai des Grands Augustins
Opera to Les Halles
Rue de Rivoli
Quai de la Mégisserie
Blvd de Sébastopol
Châtelet
Place du Châtelet
Pt. au Change
Quai de Gesvres
Hôtel de Ville
Centre Pompidou
Cité
Ile de la Cité
R. de la Cité
Pont Notre Dame
R. d'Arcole
Pont d'Arcole
Quai aux Fleurs
St Michel Notre-Dame
Cathédrale Notre-Dame de Paris
Pont St Louis
Pt. de Archevêché
Quai de l'Hôtel de Ville
Pt. Louis Philippe
Quai de Bourbon
Ile St Louis
Quai d'Orléans
Quai de Béthune
Eglise St-Louis-en-l'Ile
Pont Marie
Q. des Célestins
Pont de Sully
Bd. Henri IV
Sully Morland
Archives Nationales
Marais
Musée Cognacq-Jay
Musée Carnavalet
Musée Picasso
Maison de Victor Hugo
Maison Européene de la Photographie
R. Saint Antoine
St Paul
St-Germain-des-Prés
Eglise St Germain des Prés
Musée Delacroix
Blvd Saint Germain
Odéon
Mabillon
Eglise St-Sulpice
Rue de Vaugirard
Palais du Luxembourg
Odéon Théâtre de l'Europe
Univ. Paris VI
Cluny La Sorbonne
Boulevard Saint Michel
St Michel
Quai St Michel
Eglise St-Séverin
R. St Jacques
Thermes de Cluny
Rue des Écoles
Sorbonne
Latin Quarter
Quai de Montebello
Rue Lagrange
Boulevard Saint Germain
Maubert Mutualité
Quai de la Tournelle
Institut du Monde Arabe
Universités Paris VI Paris VII Pierre et Marie Curie
300 m
300 yds
Sights & museums
Eating & drinking
Shopping
Nightlife
Arts & leisure
© Copyright Time Out Group 2007

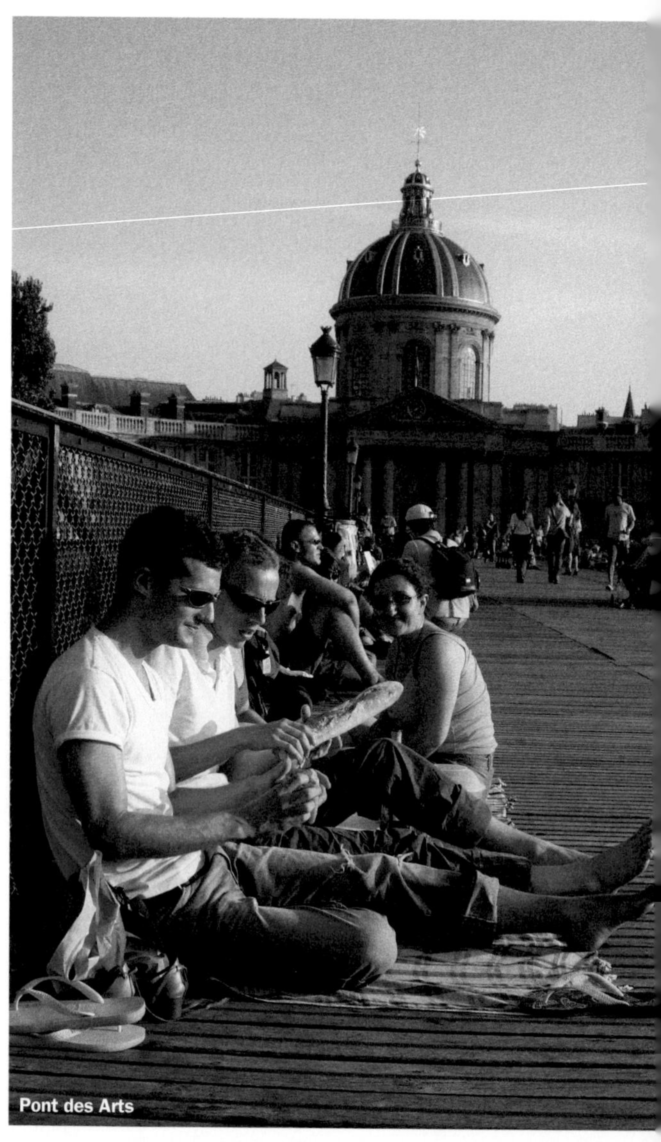

Pont des Arts

M° Pont Neuf. **Departs** *Mar-Oct* every 30-45mins 10am-10.30pm daily. *Nov-Feb* every 45 mins 10.30am-10pm Mon-Thur; 10.30am-10.30pm Fri-Sun. **Admission** €10; free-€5 reductions. **Map** p115 B1 ❶

Big boats that give you the option of sitting inside just a foot or two above water level or outside on the top deck.

The bridges

From the recently cleaned, honey-coloured arches of ancient Pont Neuf to Pont Charles-de-Gaulle, with its smooth aerodynamic lines, the 37 Paris bridges afford some of the most seductive reasons to visit the city – and some of the best views.

The most romantic is the Pont des Arts, the first solely pedestrian crossing (built in 1803, rebuilt in the 1980s); the most glitteringly exuberant is the Pont Alexandre III, with its finely wrought lamps, and gilded embellishments; the cleanest is the recently renovated, 400-year-old Pont Neuf; and the most pleasingly practical is the Pont de l'Alma, with its Zouave statue. The Zouave has long been a popular flood-level measure: when his toes get wet the city raises the flood alert and starts to close the quayside roads; when he's up to his ankles in Seine, it's no longer possible to navigate the river by boat.

The Passerelle Simone de Beauvoir, the city's 37th bridge, was winched into place in 2006. It's a sleek, low-lying, cabled construction without ground support between the south-east riverbanks, and a walkway that stretches 180 metres between the Bibliothèque Nationale and the Parc de Bercy.

Ile de la Cité

The Ile de la Cité is where Paris began, when the Parisii, a tribe of Celtic Gauls, settled around 250 BC at this convenient bridging point of the Seine. Romans, Merovingians and Capetians followed, in what became a centre of political and religious power right into the Middle Ages: royal authority concentrated at one end, around the Capetian palace; and the church at the other end, around Notre-Dame.

Perhaps the most charming spot on the island is the western tip, where the Pont Neuf spans the Seine. The bridge's arches are lined with grimacing faces, supposedly modelled on some of the courtiers of Henri III. Down the steps is a leafy triangular garden, square du Vert-Galant, ideal for picnics.

Sights & museums

Cathédrale Notre-Dame de Paris

pl du Parvis-Notre-Dame, 4th (01.42. 34.56.10/www.notredamedeparis.com). M° Cité/RER St-Michel Notre-Dame. **Open** 7.45am-6.45pm daily. *Towers Apr-Sept* 9am-6.45pm daily. *Oct-Mar* 10am-4.45pm daily. **Admission** free. *Towers* €7.10; free-€5.10 reductions. **Map** p115 C2 ❷

One of the absolute masterpieces of Gothic architecture, Notre-Dame was commissioned in 1160 by Bishop de Sully, who wanted to match the new abbey that had just gone up in St-Denis. It was built between 1163 and 1334, and the time and money spent on it reflected the city's growing prestige. However, the cathedral was plundered during the French Revolution, and by the 19th century was looking pretty shabby.

The Gothic revivalist Viollet-le-Duc restored Notre-Dame to her former glory in the mid 19th century, although work has been going on ever since, with the replacement and cleaning of damaged and eroded finials and sculptures. In 1430, Henry VI of England was crowned here; Napoléon made himself Emperor here in 1804; and in 1909 it hosted the beatification of Joan of Arc (you'll find a statue of her inside).

Cathédrale Notre-Dame de Paris p117

To appreciate the masonry, climb the towers (a limited number can ascend at one time). The route goes up the north tower and down the south. Between the two you get a close-up of the gallery of chimeras – the fantastic birds and leering hybrid beasts designed by Viollet-le-Duc along the balustrade, including the pensive Stryga, who looks down on the capital from the first corner. After a detour to see the Bourdon, the big bell, a spiral staircase leads to the top of the south tower from where you can see pretty much every monument in Paris.

On the parvis Notre-Dame in front of the cathedral, the bronze 'Kilomètre Zéro' marker is the point from which distances to Paris from the rest of France are measured.

La Conciergerie

2 bd du Palais, 1st (01.53.40.60.97). M° Cité/RER St-Michel Notre-Dame.
Open *Mar-Oct* 9.30am-6pm daily. *Nov-Feb* 9am-4.30pm daily. **Admission** €6.50; free-€4.50 reductions. *With Sainte-Chapelle* €9.50; €7.50 reductions.
Map p115 B1 ❸

Marie-Antoinette was imprisoned here during the Revolution, as were Danton and Robespierre before their executions. The wealthy had private cells with their own furniture, which they paid for; others made do with straw. In the Chapelle des Girondins, Marie-Antoinette's cell, are her crucifix, some portraits and a guillotine blade. The Conciergerie looks every inch the forbidding medieval fortress, yet much of the façade was added in the 1850s. The visit takes you through the Salle des Gardes, the medieval kitchens and the Salle des Gens d'Armes, a vaulted Gothic hall constructed between 1301 and 1315.

La Crypte Archéologique

pl Jean-Paul II, 4th (01.55.42.50.10). M° Cité/RER St-Michel Notre-Dame.
Open 10am-6pm Tue-Sun. **Admission** €3.30; free-€2.20 reductions.
Map p115 C2 ❹

Under the parvis in front of the cathedral is a large void that contains bits of Roman quaysides and hypocausts, medieval cellars, shops and pavements, foundations of the Eglise Ste-Geneviève-

Passerelle Simone de Beauvoir p117

des-Ardens, an 18th-century foundling hospital and a 19th-century sewer – all excavated since the 1960s.
Event highlights 'Construire à Lutèce', Roman-era Paris (present-25 May 2008)

Mémorial des Martyrs de la Déportation

square de l'Ile de France, 4th (01.46. 33.87.56). M° Cité/RER St-Michel Notre-Dame. **Open** *Winter* 10am-noon, 2-5pm daily. *Summer* 10am-noon, 2-7pm daily. **Admission** free. **Map** p115 C2 ⑤

This sobering tribute to the 200,000 Jews, Communists, homosexuals and Résistants deported to concentration camps from France during World War II is located at the island's eastern tip. A blind staircase descends to river-level chambers lined with tiny lights, and a barred window looks on to the Seine.

Sainte-Chapelle

4 bd du Palais, 1st (01.53.40.60.80). M° Cité/RER St-Michel Notre-Dame. **Open** *Mar-Oct* 9.30am-5.30pm daily. *Nov-Feb* 9am-4.30pm daily. **Admission** €6.10; free-€4.10 reductions. *With Conciergerie* €9.50; €7.50 reductions. **Map** p115 B2 ⑥

In the 1240s devout King Louis IX bought what was advertised as the Crown of Thorns, and ordered up a suitable shrine: the result was the exquisite Flamboyant Gothic Sainte-Chapelle. With its 15m-high windows, the upper level appears to consist almost entirely of stained glass. The windows depict scenes from the Bible, culminating with the Apocalypse in the rose window.

Eating & drinking

Le Vieux Bistro

14 rue du Cloître-Notre-Dame, 4th (01.43.54.18.95). M° Cité or St Michel. **Open** noon-10.15pm daily. **€€€. Bistro**. **Map** p115 C2 ⑦

The food here is generally excellent and the dining room comfortable and well run. Start with sliced, pistachio-studded sausage and potatoes dressed in vinegar and oil. Then sample the renowned bourguignon, a first-rate rib of beef for two, or scallops sautéed in whisky. The

Mon Vieil Ami

superb house Bordeaux goes down a treat with cheese or one of the fabulous homely desserts.

Taverne Henri IV

13 pl du Pont-Neuf, 1st (01.43.54. 27.90). M° Pont Neuf. **Open** 11.30am-9.30pm Mon-Fri, noon-5pm Sat. Closed Aug & some public hols. **€. Bistro. Map** p115 B1 ❽

Blink and you'll miss this bistro: under new ownership, it's a lovely spot at the tip of the Ile de la Cité. The emphasis here is on good, simple French fare washed down with fine wine – all at very reasonable prices. The eggs baked with blue cheese and ham are delectable and a glass of white Beaujolais (€4) even better. If you're having trouble deciding which wine to pick, the chatty barman will be happy to make a few suggestions. The decor? Dark wooden bar, certificates on the wall, wine bottles, and a few dusty books for good measure.

Ile St-Louis

The Ile St-Louis is one of the most exclusive residential addresses in the city. Delightfully unspoiled, it has fine architecture, narrow streets and pretty views from the tree-lined quays, and retains the air of a tranquil backwater. Rue St-Louis-en-l'Ile – lined with fine historic buildings that now contain quirky gift shops and gourmet food stores (many of them open on Sunday), quaint tearooms, stone-walled bars, restaurants and hotels – runs the length of the island. There are great views of the flying buttresses of Notre-Dame at the western end from the terraces of the Brasserie de l'Ile St-Louis and the Flore en l'Ile café. A footbridge runs to the Ile de la Cité.

Sights & museums

Eglise St-Louis-en-l'Ile

19bis rue St-Louis-en-l'Ile, 4th (01.46.34.11.60). M° Pont Marie. **Open** 9am-noon, 3-7pm Tue-Sun. **Map** p115 D3 ❾

The island's discreet church was built between 1664 and 1765, following plans by Louis Le Vau, and later completed by

Gabriel Le Duc. The interior follows the classic baroque model, with Corinthian columns and a sunburst over the altar, and is also used as a venue for classical music concerts.

Eating & drinking

Brasserie de l'Ile St-Louis

55 quai de Bourbon, 4th (01.43.54. 02.59). Mº Pont Marie. **Open** noon-midnight Mon, Tue, Fri-Sun; 6pm-midnight Thur. Closed Aug. €. **Brasserie**. **Map** p115 D2 ⑩

This old-fashioned brasserie has a terrace with one of the best summer views in all Paris (and thus invariably packed). Inside, nicotined walls make for an agreeably authentic Paris mood, as does the slightly gruff waiter, though nothing here is gastronomically gripping: a well dressed *frisée aux lardons*, say, a slab of rather ordinary terrine, or a somewhat greasy slice of *foie de veau* prepared *à l'anglaise* with a rasher of bacon.

L'Escale 14

1 rue des Deux-Ponts, 4th (01.43.54. 94.23). Mº Pont Marie. **Open** 7.30am-10pm Tue-Sun. €€. **Brasserie**. **Map** p115 D3 ⑪

This old-fashioned brasserie/wine bar does comfort food in the form of *chou farci*, a divine leek quiche and, that Paris café rarity, golden, crispy home-made chips with fluffy interior. Quality wines are reasonably priced, and desserts, including a deliciously eggy clafoutis, are all own-made.

Le Flore en l'Isle

42 quai d'Orléans, 4th (01.43.29. 88.27). Mº Hôtel de Ville or Pont Marie. **Open** 8am-2am daily. €. **Café**. **Map** p115 D2 ⑫

Although the terrace here pulls in the summer hordes with Berthillon ice-cream, sitting at a window table over-looking the Seine and Notre-Dame with a coffee and its accompanying plate of chocolate truffles is a top Ile St-Louis activity. Egg- and seafood-based brunch dishes are also popular, as are the house desserts. Don't be fobbed off into the sometimes empty tearoom next door.

Mon Vieil Ami

69 rue St-Louis-en-l'Ile, 4th (01.40.46.01.35). Mº Pont Marie. **Open** noon-2.30pm, 7.30-10.30pm Wed-Sun. Closed 3wks Aug. €. **Bistro**. **Map** p115 D2 ⑬

Alsatian chef Antoine Westermann has created a true foodie destination here, with modern bistro cooking that draws from all the regions of France – and he pays as much attention to vegetables as to meat and fish. Typical of the mains is a casserole of roast duck with turnips and couscous, or fresh, chunky flakes of hake on a generous barigoule of stewed artichoke hearts.

Shopping

Arche de Noé

70 rue St-Louis-en-l'Ile, 4th (01.46.34. 61.60). Mº Pont Marie or Sully Morland. **Open** 10.30am-7pm daily. **Map** p115 D2 ⑭

Far from the chaos of the grands magasins, 'Noah's Ark' is the perfect place for old-fashioned Christmas shopping, with traditional wooden toys from Eastern Europe, games and jigsaw puzzles.

L'Epicerie

51 rue St-Louis-en-l'Ile, 4th (01.43. 25.20.14). Mº Pont Marie or Sully Morland. **Open** *Oct-Apr* 10.30am-7pm daily. *May-Sept* 11am-8pm daily. **Map** p115 D2 ⑮

This glorious gift shop is crammed with delightful bottles of blackcurrant vinegar, five-spice mustard, tiny pots of jam, orange sauce, honey with figs and boxes of chocolate snails.

L'Occitane

55 rue St-Louis-en-l'Ile, 4th (01.40.46. 81.71/www.loccitane.com). Mº Pont Marie or Sully Morland. **Open** 11am-7pm Mon; 10am-7pm Tue; 10am-7.30pm Wed-Fri; 10am-8pm Sat, Sun. **Map** p115 D2 ⑯

This shop, like the many other branches of the popular Provençal chain spread across five continents, proffers an array of natural beauty products (soap, essential oils, perfume and the like) candles and home fragrances.

Musée National Rodin p125

The 7th & Western Paris

The 7th arrondissement, to the west of St-Germain-des-Prés, has a rather stuffy reputation – fostered by a goodish number of government offices and lofty residential blocks. It's pleasantly tranquil, though, and not without quirks – the sewer museum is here, as are French icons Napoleon (what's left of him) and the Eiffel Tower. The 7th divides into the rather cosy Faubourg St-Germain, with historic mansions and fine shops, and the grander area around Les Invalides.

Sights & museums

Les Egouts de Paris

Entrance opposite 93 quai d'Orsay, by Pont de l'Alma, 7th (01.53.68.27.81). M° Alma Marceau/RER Pont de l'Alma. **Open** 11am-4pm Wed-Sat (until 5pm May-Sept). Closed 3wks Jan. **Admission** €3.80; free-€3.05 reductions. No credit cards. **Map** p123 B1 ❶

The Paris sewerage system is open to visitors (except after periods of heavy rain). Each sewer in the 2,100km system is marked with a replica of the street sign above.

Eiffel Tower

Champ de Mars, 7th (01.44.11.23.45/ recorded information 01.44.11.23.23/ www.tour-eiffel.fr). M° Bir-Hakeim/ RER Champ de Mars Tour Eiffel. **Open** *14 June-Aug* 9am-12.45am daily. *Sept-13 June* 9.30am-11.45pm daily. **Admission** *By stairs* (1st & 2nd levels, 9.30am-6.30pm) €3.80; €3 reductions. *By lift* (1st level) €4.20;

The 7th & Western Paris

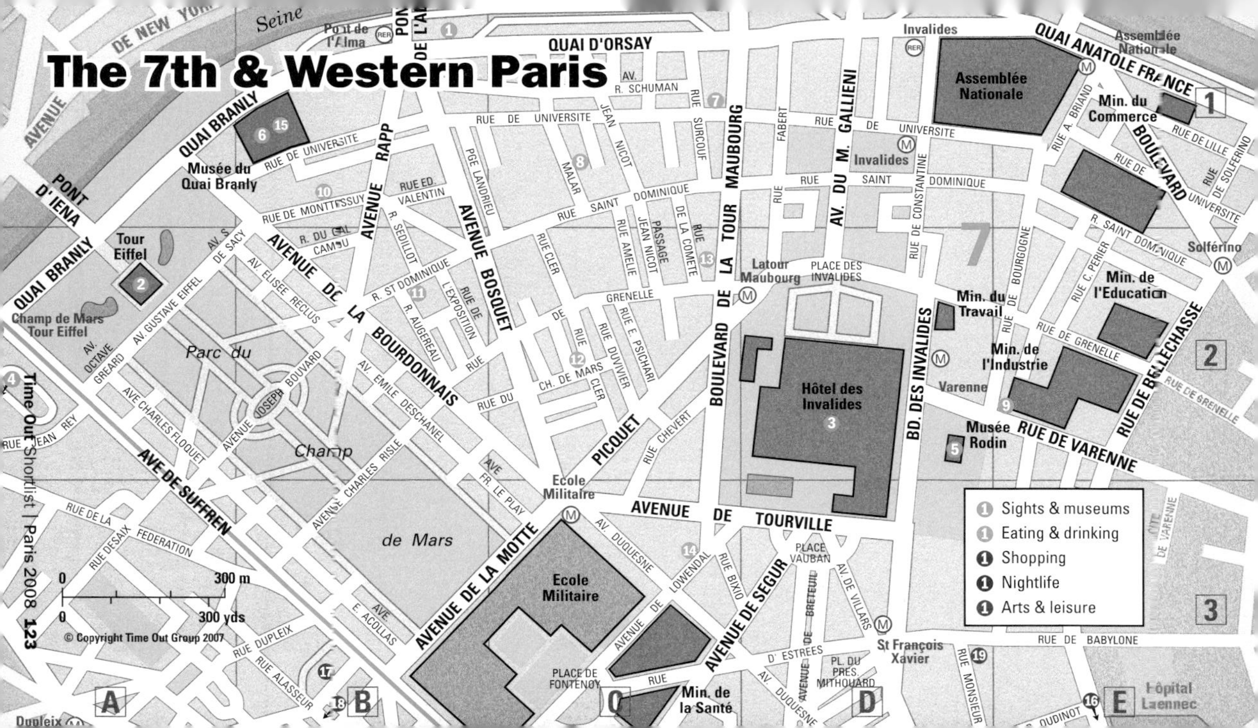

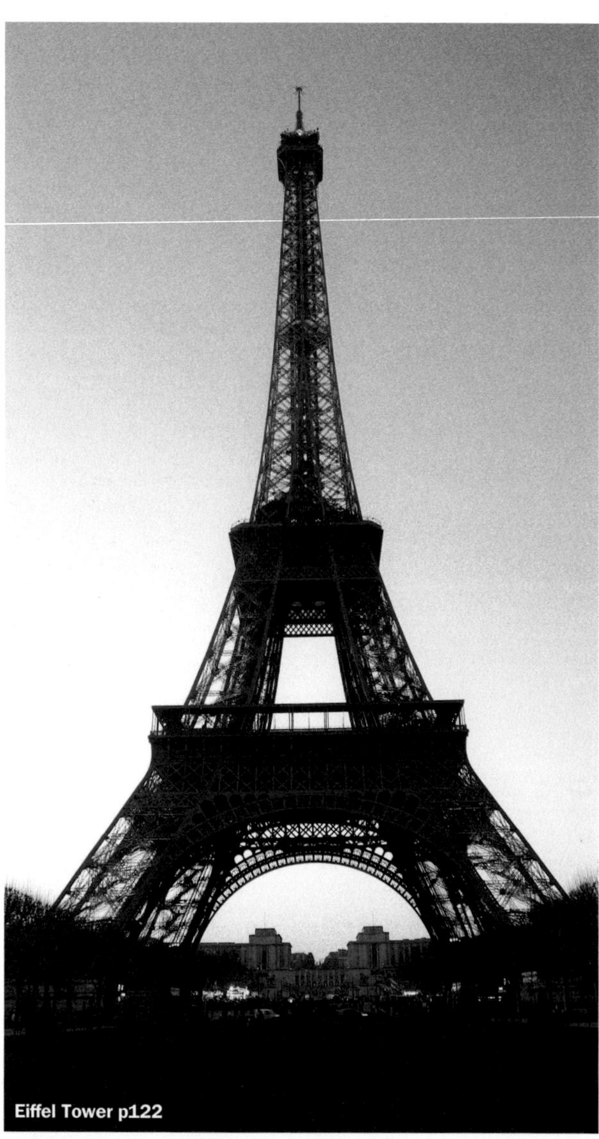

Eiffel Tower p122

€2.30 reductions; (2nd level) €7.70; €4.20 reductions; (3rd level) €11; free-€6 reductions. **Map** p123 A2 ❷
No building better symbolises Paris than the 300-metre Tour Eiffel, and it's the capital's most visited attraction. The radical cast-iron tower was built – for the 1889 World Fair and the centenary of the 1789 Revolution – by engineer Gustave Eiffel. Construction took more than two years and used some 18,000 pieces of metal and 2,500,000 rivets. It stands on four massive concrete piles, and was the tallest structure in the world until New York's Empire State Building went up in the 1930s. Vintage lifts ply their way up and down, or you can walk as far as the second level. On the third level, there's Eiffel's cosy salon and a viewing platform. Views can reach over 65km on a good day. At night, on the hour, 20,000 flashbulbs attached to the tower create a stunning sequined robe effect.

Les Invalides & Musée de l'Armée

esplanade des Invalides, 7th (01.44.42.40.69/www.invalides.org). M° Invalides or La Tour Maubourg. **Open** *Apr-Sept* 10am-6pm daily. *Oct-Mar* 10am-5pm daily. Closed 1st Mon of mth. **Admission** *Musée de l'Armée & Eglise du Dôme* €7.50; free-€5.50 reductions. **Map** p123 D2 ❸
Its imposing gilded dome is misleading: the Hôtel des Invalides was (and in part still is) a hospital, commissioned by Louis XIV for wounded soldiers (the main façade has a relief of Louis XIV and the Sun King's sunburst). The complex contains two connecting churches: the Eglise St-Louis was for the soldiers, the Eglise du Dôme for the king. Since 1840 the latter has been dedicated to the worship of Napoléon, whose body supposedly lies here. Included in the entry price is the excellent Musée de l'Armée, the Paris equivalent of London's Imperial War Museum. For the military historian, the Musée is a must; and even if uniforms and cannons aren't your thing, the building itself is splendid.

Maison de la Culture du Japon

101bis quai Branly, 15th (01.44.37.95.00/www.mcjp.asso.fr). M° Bir-Hakeim/RER Champ de Mars Tour Eiffel. **Open** noon-7pm Tue, Wed, Fri, Sat; noon-8pm Thur. Closed Aug. **Admission** free. **Map** p123 A2 ❹
Built in 1996, this opulent glass cultural centre dishes up a feast of Japan: film, theatre, exhibitions and tea ceremonies.

Musée National Rodin

Hôtel Biron, 77 rue de Varenne, 7th (01.44.18.61.10/www.musee-rodin.fr). M° Varenne. **Open** *Apr-Sept* 9.30am-5.15pm Tue-Sun (gardens until 6.45pm). *Oct-Mar* 9.30am-4.15pm Tue-Sun (gardens until 5pm). **Admission** €6; free-€4 reductions. *Exhibitions* €7; €5 reductions. *Gardens* €1. **Map** p123 D2 ❺
The Rodin museum occupies the *hôtel particulier* where the sculptor lived in his later years. *The Kiss*, the *Cathedral*, the *Walking Man* and portrait busts are exhibited indoors; walls are hung with paintings by Van Gogh, Monet, Renoir, and Rodin himself. The gardens are spotted with treasures: the *Burghers of Calais*, the *Gates of Hell* and the *Thinker*.

Musée du Quai Branly

29-55 quai Branly, 7th (01.56.61.70.00/www.quaibranly.fr). RER Pont de l'Alma. **Open** 10am-6.30pm Tue, Wed, Fri-Sun; 10am-9.30pm Thur. **Admission** €10; free reductions. **Map** p123 B1 ❻
The great opening of 2006 was this collection of art and artefacts from non-Western cultures. It's housed in an extraordinary building by Jean Nouvel, and treasures include a 10th-century Dogon statue from Mali, costumes from Vietnam, Gabonese masks, Aztec statues and more. Music is a key feature of the interdisciplinary approach, and an auditorium hosts regular concerts.

Eating & drinking

Le 144 Petrossian

18 bd de La Tour-Maubourg, 7th (01.44.11.32.32/www.petrossian.fr).

Chez les Anges

M° La Tour Maubourg. **Open** noon-2.30pm, 7.30pm-10.30pm Tue-Sat. **€€**. **Russian**. **Map** p123 C1 7
Senegalese-French chef Rougui Dia directs the kitchen here with some intriguing results. You'll find Russian specialities, such as blinis, salmon and caviar, along with some unusual Med-meets-Russia options like lamb 'cooked for eleven hours' on a raisin-filled blini or roast sea bream with lemon-vodka sauce.

L'Ami Jean

27 rue Malar, 7th (01.47.05.86.89). M° Invalides. **Open** noon-2pm, 7pm-midnight Tue-Sat. Closed Aug. **€**. **Brasserie**.. **Map** p123 C1 8
This long-running Basque address has been a hit since chef Stéphane Jégo came here. Terrific bread from Poujauran is slathered with tangy, herby *fromage blanc*, as are starters like little rolls of aubergine stuffed with perfectly seasoned braised lamb; tender veal shank comes de-boned with a lovely side of baby onions and broad beans with tiny cubes of ham. There's a great wine list to work your way through too.

L'Arpège

84 rue de Varenne, 7th (01.45.51. 47.33/www.alain-passard.com). M° Varenne. **Open** noon-2.30pm, 8-10.30pm Mon-Fri. **Haute cuisine**. **€€€€**. **Map** p123 E2 9
If you can swallow a sky-high bill – €42 for a starter! – and forsake the full-dress drill of a haute cuisine meal, you'll have a fine time at chef Alain Passard's Left Bank table. The minimalist dining room looks somewhat old East Germany; but then the food arrives – things like tiny smoked potatoes with a horseradish *mousseline*, vegetable-stuffed ravioli in lobster bouillon, or mains like sautéed free-range chicken garnished with potato *mousseline* and pan juices.

Au Bon Accueil

14 rue de Monttessuy, 7th (01.47.05. 46.11). M° Alma Marceau. **Open** noon-2.30pm, 7.30-10.30pm Mon-Fri. **€€**. **Bistro**. **Map** p123 B1 10
Ever since Jacques Lacipière opened this relaxed bistro in 1990, it's been one of the best deals in the 7th, an excellent updater of French classics. Start with a tasty *chaud-froid* combination of raw

Maison de la Culture du Japon p125

marinated sardines between tiny spring leeks; then go for richly braised beef cheek in dark wine sauce, nicely offset by the tart flavours of stewed rhubarb.

Le Café Constant

139 rue St-Dominique, 7th (01.47.53.73.34). M° Ecole Militaire or RER Pont de l'Alma. **Open** noon-2.30pm, 7-10.30pm Tue-Sat. **€**. **Café**. **Map** p123 B2 ⑪

This simple, brightly lit café purrs with good times, good food and good value. The blackboard menu changes regularly; if you're hungry, start with a peppery *pâté de campagne* or maybe salmon-wrapped poached eggs with salad, and follow with the steak or grilled steak tartare. Everything is fresh and flavourful, portions are more than fair and the wine list is a blessing. No booking.

Le Café du Marché

38 rue Cler, 7th (01.47.05.51.27). M° Ecole Militaire. **Open** 7am-midnight Mon-Sat; 7am-5pm Sun. **€€**. **Café**. **Map** p123 C2 ⑫

The well-loved Café du Marché is frequented by trendy locals and shoppers hunting special cheeses on this busy market street. It really is a hub of neighbourhood activity; its *pichets* of decent house plonk go down a treat, and the food's good – try the house salad with lashings of foie gras and Parma ham.

Chez les Anges

54 bd La Tour-Maubourg, 7th (01.47.05.89.86/www.chezlesanges.com. M° La Tour Maubourg. **Open** noon-3pm, 7.30pm-11pm Mon-Sat. **€€**. **Brasserie**. **Map** p123 C2 ⑬

This restaurant was known for its superb Burgundian cooking in the 1960s and '70s (hence the decor) and is having something of a revival. You can order à la carte or opt for the good value 'Menu Surprise'. This is served tapas-style and includes creations such as cauliflower bavarois and frogs' leg fritters.

D'Chez Eux

2 av de Lowendal, 7th (01.47.05.52.55/www.chezeux.com). M° Ecole Militaire. **Open** noon-2.30pm, 7.30-10.30pm Mon-Sat. Closed 3wks Aug. **€€**. **Brasserie**. **Map** p123 C3 ⑭

D'Chez Eux is friendly and comfortingly provincial, its menu an archetype

Fromagerie Quatrehomme p130

Dragons and silk screens

Paris's loveliest cinema.

La Pagode

It's the lasting fruit of a doomed romance, a husband's lavish gift built for high-society frolics and the whirl of silk. La Pagode (p130) is by a long way the city's most beautiful cinema, an elaborate replica of a Far Eastern pagoda that has the hipped roof, carved wooden beams and tiled veranda familiar to travellers in China and Japan; and yet, for all the attention to exotic detail, the edifice is not – as myth would have it – a building transported block by block from Japan.

The building was commissioned from French architect Alexandre Marcel by a Monsieur Morin, then director of department store Le Bon Marché (p138), as a gift to his wife; it was completed in 1895. What's now the main auditorium was a ballroom where the Morins gave lavish costumed receptions dressed as 'the Emperor and Empress of the Land of the Rising Sun'. One year later, madame ran off with a son of a different kind: the offspring of one of her husband's colleagues. The pagoda languished for a while, then started a new life as a cinema in 1931. Cocteau held the premiere of Le Testament d'Orphée here in 1959, and in the 1960s it screened the New Wave, Eisenstein, Bergman – and matinee Laurel & Hardy. These days its all arthouse, with a strong penchant for films from the Far East; it's also home to the annual eco-themed Festival International du Film d'Environnement (www. festivalenvironnement.com).

Listed since 1986, it was renovated just before the turn of the millennium. The long ground-floor auditorium, with its unusual curving floor, is sumptuously decorated with gilt reliefs and dragons; the painted ceiling is especially gorgeous. There's also a small salon de thé, and a 'Japanese' garden (with Chinese lion statues) outside. Seeing a film might not be the first thing you think of on a visit to Paris, but this cinema really is worth the ticket.

of a certain traditional French cuisine. Start with the salad trolley, which has plump fresh anchovies and delicious, tender pearl onions, or equally tempting charcuterie. Mains include a guinea fowl *grand-mère*, served in a copper pan and carved at the table on its bed of potatoes, bacon and mushrooms.

Les Ombres

NEW *Musée du Quai Branly, 27 quai Branly, 7th (01.47.53.68.00). RER Pont de l'Alma or M° Alma Marceau.* **Open** noon-2pm, 7.30pm-10pm daily. **€€**. **Bistro**. **Map** p123 B1 ⑮

Even the most blasé Parisians can't fail to be impressed by this restaurant's full-on view of the Eiffel Tower from the top floor of the Musée du Quai Branly. The interior by architect Jean Nouvel mirrors the tower with iron beams and a sober burgundy-and-brown décor. Perhaps the room lacks intimacy, but the Mediterranean-inspired food makes up for it – expect dishes such as perfectly cooked red mullet fillet on a bed of minutely diced courgette. Aim for the terrace in summer.

Shopping

Fromagerie Quatrehomme

62 rue de Sèvres, 7th (01.47.34.33.45). M° Vaneau or Duroc. **Open** 8.45am-1pm, 4-7.45pm Tue-Thur; 8.45am-7.45pm Fri, Sat. **Map** p123 E3 ⑯

This inviting *fromagerie* is justly famous for classics like beaufort and st-marcellin.

Marie-Anne Cantin

12 rue Champ-de-Mars, 7th (01.45.50.43.94/www.cantin.fr). M° Ecole Militaire. **Open** 8.30am-7.30pm Mon-Sat. **Map** p123 B3 ⑰

Cantin is proud of her aged *chèvres*, roquefort réserve and amazing morbier, mont d'or and comté.

Village Suisse

38-78 av de Suffren or 54 av de La Motte-Picquet, 15th (www.levillage suisse.com). M° La Motte Picquet Grenelle. **Open** 10.30am-7pm Mon, Thur-Sun. **Map** p123 B3 ⑱

The Swiss village built for the 1900 Exposition Universelle is long gone; but the street level has been colonised by some 150 boutiques, offering antiques and collectables.

Arts & leisure

La Pagode

57bis rue de Babylone, 7th (01.45.55.48.48). M° St François Xavier. **Open** times vary. No credit cards. **Map** p123 D3 ⑲

See box p129.

Musée du Quai Branly p125

PARIS BY AREA

Jardin du Luxembourg p132

St-Germain-des-Prés & Odéon

The lore of Paris café society has been amply fed by St-Germain-des-Prés. Verlaine and Rimbaud drank here; later, Sartre, Camus and de Beauvoir scribbled and squabbled in the area, and musicians congregated around Boris Vian in the post-war jazz boom. Now, though, St-Germain is best known for having some of the most expensively priced property in Paris; it's also serious fashion territory (in fact, it could almost rival avenue Montaigne for designer boutiques). A few publishers do remain, and earnest types still pose with books while the literati and glitterati assemble on local café terraces to give intellectual interviews.

The patch south of boulevard St-Germain is crammed with historic buildings and interesting shops, epitomising civilised Paris. This and the area further west are shopping hubs: clothes on rue Bonaparte and rue du Four; accessory and fashion shops on rue du Dragon, rue de Grenelle and rue du Cherche-Midi.

Sights & museums

Ecole Nationale Supérieure des Beaux-Arts (Ensb-a)

14 rue Bonaparte, 6th (01.47.03.52.15/www.ensba.fr). M° St-Germain-des-Prés. **Open** *Courtyard* 9am-5pm Mon-Fri. *Exhibitions* 1-7pm Tue-Sun. **Admission** *Exhibitions* prices vary. **Map** p133 C1 ①

The city's most prestigious fine-arts school resides in what's left of the 17th-century Couvent des Petits-Augustins, the 18th-century Hôtel de Chimay and some 19th-century additions. The entrance is on quai Malaquais.

Event highlights 'Le Triangle des Bermudes', Caribbean artists (23 Oct-23 Dec 2007). 'Mai '68', contemporary art (19 Feb-27 Apr 2008). 'Figures du Corps', anatomical studies (20 Oct-23 Dec 2008).

Eglise St-Germain-des-Prés

3 pl St-Germain-des-Prés, 6th (01.55.42.81.33/www.eglise-sgp.org). M° St-Germain-des-Prés. **Open** 8am-7.45pm Mon-Sat; 9am-8pm Sun. **Map** p133 C2 ❷

The Eglise St-Germain-des-Prés is the oldest church in Paris. Most of the present structure dates from the 12th-century, but some ornate carved capitals and the tower remain from the 11th. Illustrious tombs include that of Jean-Casimir, the deposed King of Poland, Abbot of St-Germain in 1669. The funeral stone of Descartes is in the second chapel; his ashes have been here since 1819.

Eglise St-Sulpice

pl St-Sulpice, 6th (01.46.33.21.78). M° St-Sulpice. **Open** 7.30am-7.30pm daily. **Map** p133 C3 ❸

It took some 120 years (starting in 1646) and six architects to finish the church of St-Sulpice. It has a grandiose Italianate façade, a two-tier colonnade and mismatched towers. Three murals by Delacroix in the first chapel foster a suitably sombre atmosphere.

Jardin & Palais du Luxembourg

pl Auguste-Comte, pl Edmond-Rostand or rue de Vaugirard, 6th (01.42.34.23.89/www.senat.fr/visite). M° Odéon/RER Luxembourg. **Open** *Summer* 8am-dusk daily. *Winter* 9am-dusk daily. **Map** p133 C4 ❹

The Jardin du Luxembourg is one of the nicest places to relax in the city: part formal, part 'English garden', it's the quintessential Paris park, with its green chairs and interesting sculptures. The palace at its northern edge was built in the 1620s for Marie de Médicis, widow of Henri IV; its Italianate style was intended to remind her of the Pitti Palace in her native Florence. Reworked in the 18th century, it's now the French parliament's upper house, the Sénat (guided visits only); next to it is Le Petit Luxembourg, residence of the Sénat's president.

Musée Maillol

59-61 rue de Grenelle, 7th (01.42.22.59.58/www.museemaillol.com). M° Rue du Bac. **Open** 11am-6pm (last admission 5.15pm) Mon, Wed-Sun. **Admission** €8; free-€6 reductions. **Map** p133 A2 ❺

Dina Vierny was 15 when she met Aristide Maillol and became his main model. Years later, in 1995, she opened this lovely museum, exhibiting his pastels, drawings, ceramics, engravings, tapestry panels and sculpture. There are also works by Gauguin, Degas, Rodin, Cézanne, Picasso and Matisse on display.

Musée National Delacroix

6 pl Furstenberg, 6th (01.44.41.86.50/www.musee-delacroix.fr). M° St-Germain-des-Prés. **Open** 9.30am-4.30pm Mon, Wed-Sun. **Admission** €5; free reductions. **Map** p133 C2 ❻

Painter Eugène Delacroix moved to this apartment/studio in 1857 to be near the Eglise St-Sulpice, where he was painting murals. The Louvre and Musée d'Orsay house his major canvas works, but this museum has a selection of small oil paintings, pastel studies, sketches and lithographs, as well as his palette.

Musée National du Luxembourg

19 rue de Vaugirard, 6th (01.42.34.25.95/www.museeduluxembourg.fr). M° Cluny La Sorbonne/RER Luxembourg. **Open** 11am-10.30pm Mon, Fri; 11am-7pm Tue-Thur, Sat; 9am-7pm Sun. **Admission** €10; free-€8 reductions. **Map** p133 C3 ❼

PARIS BY AREA

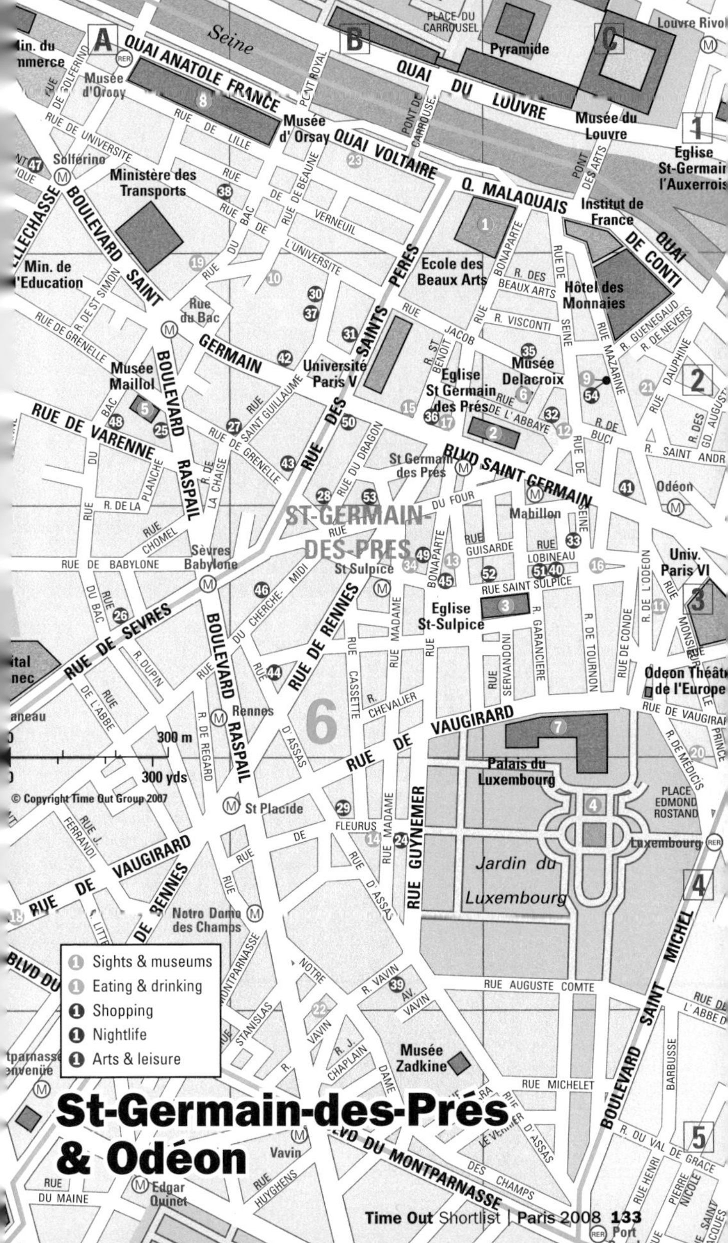
St-Germain-des-Prés
& Odéon
Sights & museums
Eating & drinking
Shopping
Nightlife
Arts & leisure
© Copyright Time Out Group 2007
300 m
300 yds
Seine
Quai Anatole France
Quai du Louvre
Quai Voltaire
Q. Malaquais
Quai de Conti
Place du Carrousel
Pyramide
Musée du Louvre
Louvre Rivoli
Eglise St-Germain l'Auxerrois
Institut de France
Hôtel des Monnaies
Musée d'Orsay
Ministère des Transports
Min. de l'Education
Ecole des Beaux Arts
Université Paris V
Musée Delacroix
Eglise St Germain des Prés
Musée Maillol
St-Germain-des-Prés
St Sulpice
Eglise St-Sulpice
Univ. Paris VI
Odéon Théâtre de l'Europe
Palais du Luxembourg
Place Edmond Rostand
Jardin du Luxembourg
Musée Zadkine
Solférino
Rue du Bac
Sèvres Babylone
Rennes
St Placide
Notre Dame des Champs
Vavin
Edgar Quinet
Mabillon
Odéon
Luxembourg
Port Royal
Boulevard Saint Germain
Blvd Saint Germain
Boulevard Raspail
Boulevard Saint Michel
Blvd du Montparnasse
Rue des Saints Pères
Rue de Rennes
Rue de Sèvres
Rue de Vaugirard
Rue Guynemer
Rue de Varenne
Rue de Grenelle
Rue de Babylone
Rue de l'Université
Rue de Lille
Rue du Bac
Rue Jacob
Rue Bonaparte
Rue de Seine
Rue Mazarine
Rue Dauphine
Rue du Four
Rue Madame
Rue Cassette
Rue d'Assas
Rue de Fleurus
Rue Auguste Comte
Rue Michelet
Rue de Tournon
Rue de Condé
Rue Garancière
Rue Servandoni
Rue Saint Sulpice
Rue du Dragon
Rue du Cherche-Midi
Rue Notre Dame des Champs
Rue Vavin
Rue Stanislas
Rue de Médicis
Rue Monsieur le Prince
Rue de l'Odéon
Rue du Val de Grâce
Rue du Maine
Rue Huyghens
Rue Barbusse
A
B
C
1
2
3
4
5
6

Le Comptoir p136

When it was inaugurated in 1750, this modest but imposing museum inside the Jardin du Luxembourg was the first public gallery to open in France. Its current stewardship by the national museums and the French Senate has managed to bring imaginative touches and a reliable number of prestigious exhibitions here.

Event highlights 'Arcimboldo', 16th-century Italian painter (11 Sep 2007-13 Jan 2008).

Musée d'Orsay

1 rue de la Légion-d'Honneur, 7th (01.40.49.48.14/recorded information 01.45.49.11.11/www.musee-orsay.fr). M° Solférino/RER Musée d'Orsay. **Open** 9.30am-6pm (until 9.45pm June) Tue-Sun. **Admission** €8; free-€6 reductions. **Map** p133 A1 ❽

The building was originally a train station, designed to coincide with the 1900 Exposition Universelle. Now it's a huge treasure trove of an art museum, spanning the fertile period between 1848 and 1914. It follows a chronological passage, showing the links between Impressionist painters and their forerunners: here you'll find a profusion of famous paintings by Delacroix, Degas, Corot, Manet, Renoir, Pissarro, Gauguin, Monet, Cézanne, Van Gogh, Toulouse-Lautrec and many others. Running down the centre of the building, a sculpture aisle takes in monuments and maidens, plus outstanding pieces by Carpeaux. The museum runs a full and enterprising series of concerts at lunchtime and in the evening.

Event highlights 'Alexandre Charpentier (1856-1909) – Naturalisme and Art Nouveau' (22 Jan-13 Apr 2008). 'British pioneer photography, 1840-1865' (27 May-7 Sept 2008). 'Japonisme and French tableware, 1865-1875' (16 Sept-20 Oct 2008). 'Masks from Carpeaux to Picasso' (21 Oct 2008-10 Feb 2009).

Eating & drinking

Alcazar

62 rue Mazarine, 6th (01.53.10.19.99/ www.alcazar. fr). M° Odéon. **Open** noon-3pm, 7pm-2am daily. €€. **Brasserie**. **Map** p133 C2 9

The success of Terence Conran's Paris gastrodome has more to do with its cachet than the food. Seafood is a safe bet and staff can rustle up a good brunch: perfect scrambled eggs, fluffy muffins and a rich chocolate cake. The mezzanine 'AZ bar' has sleek velvet banquettes and a vantage point over the restaurant – and the drinks are great. The impressive DJ line-up at the Wagg draws local yuppies; the music gets pumping after midnight.

L'Atelier de Joël Robuchon

5 rue de Montalembert, 7th (01.42.22.56.56/www.robuchon.com). M° Rue du Bac. **Open** 11.30am-3.30pm, 6.30pm-midnight daily. €€. **International**. **Map** p133 B2 10

This is star chef Joël Robuchon's Paris take on a New York coffee-shop-cum-sushi-and-tapas-bar: lacquer interior and two U-shaped bars with stools. The food is fine, the menu split into three different *formules*: start with Spanish ham, a large seasonal salad, or maybe an assortment of tasting plates. Then you can either go classic (a steak), fanciful (*vitello tonnato*, veal in tuna and anchovy sauce) or lush (cannelloni of Bresse chicken and foie gras).

Le Bar Dix

10 rue de l'Odéon, 6th (01.43.26.66.83). M° Odéon. **Open** 6pm-2am daily. No credit cards. **Bar**. **Map** p133 C3 11

It's been here forever, this homely cavern of a bar, and generations of students have glugged back jugs of home-made sangría in the cramped, twilit upper bar, tattily authentic with its Jacques Brel record sleeves, Yves Montand handbills and pre-war light fittings. Spelunkers and romantics brave the perilous stone staircase for the candlelit cellar bar.

Le Bar du Marché

75 rue de Seine, 6th (01.43.26.55.15). M° Mabillon or Odéon. **Open** 8am-2am daily. **Bar**. **Map** p133 C2 12

The market in question is the Cours des Halles, the bar a convivial corner café opening out on to St-Germain-des-Prés bustle. It's all wonderfully simple, with easy dishes like a ham omelette or plate of herring in the €7 range, a half-decent Brouilly or Muscadet at €4-€5 a glass, a few retro posters and the regular passing of a beret-topped waiter.

Boucherie Roulière

24 rue des Canettes, 6th (01.43.26.25.70). M° St-Sulpice, Mabillon or St-Germain-des-Prés. **Open** noon-2.30pm, 7-11.30pm Tue-Thur, Sun; noon-2.30pm, 7pm-midnight Fri, Sat. €€. **Bistro**. **Map** p133 B3 13

The blackboard menu offers a simple collection of grilled meat and fish, accompanied by traditional bistro favourites to begin and end your meal. Main courses include a perfectly grilled *rognon de veau* (veal kidney). Desserts and the single house cheese keep up the standard. Service is friendly.

Bread and Roses

7 rue de Fleurus, 6th (01.42.22.06.06). M° St-Placide. **Open** 8am-8pm Mon-Sat. **Café**. **Map** p133 B4 14

You'll find giant wedges of cheesecake, delicious savoury puff-pastry tarts and towering birthday cakes at this Anglo-influenced *boulangerie/épicerie*/café. The pavement tables are spot on for sunny days.

Café de Flore

172 bd St-Germain, 6th (01.45.48.55.26/www.cafe-de-flore.com). M° St-Germain-des-Prés. **Open** 7.30am-1.30am daily. **Café**. **Map** p133 B2 15

This historic café, formerly the HQ of the Lost Generation intelligentsia, attracts a steady stream of tourists. Prices are steep (*café crème* €4.60). Ideally pass over the standard omelette and croque-monsieur offerings in favour of the far better main dishes (priced between €15-€25). Upstairs, play readings are held on Mondays and philosophy discussions on the first Wednesday of the month, both at 8pm, in English.

PARIS BY AREA

Le Comptoir

Hôtel Relais Saint-Germain, 9 carrefour de l'Odéon, 6th (01.44.27.07.97/ www.hotel-paris-relais-saint-germain.com). M° Odéon. **Open** noon-midnight daily. Closed 3wks Aug. €. **Brasserie**. **Map** p133 C3 16

The art deco dining room at chef Yves Camdeborde's bijou 17th-century hotel serves brasserie fare from noon to 6pm and on weekend nights – salads and a hot *plat du jour*, like duck confit with smooth mashed potatoes – and a five-course, no-choice meal for €42 on weekday evenings; an outstanding bargain. On the daily menu, you might find dishes like iced cream of chicken soup spiked with *vin jaune du Jura*, or rolled saddle of lamb with vegetable-stuffed 'Basque ravioli'. Book well ahead.

Les Deux Magots

6 pl St-Germain-des-Prés, 6th (01.45.48.55.25/www.lesdeuxmagots.com). M° St-Germain-des-Prés. **Open** 7.30am-1am daily. **Café**. **Map** p133 B2 17

The former haunt of Sartre, de Beauvoir et al now draws a less pensive, more touristy crowd, particularly at weekends. The hot chocolate is still good (and the only item served in generous portions) – but, like everything else, it's costly. If you must, visit on a weekday afternoon when the editors repair, manuscripts in hand, to the inside tables.

La Ferrandaise

8 rue de Vaugirard, 6th (01.43.26.36.36). M° Odéon or RER Luxembourg. **Open** noon-2.30pm, 7-10.30pm Tue-Thu; noon-2.30pm, 7-midnight Fri; 7pm-midnight Sat. €€. **Bistro**. **Map** p133 A4 18

This modern bistro serves up solid, classic food with a twist. A platter of excellent ham, sausage and terrine arrives as you study the blackboard menu and almost every dish is an excellent variation on a standard. Try the potato stuffed with escargots in pungent camembert sauce or the wonderfully flavoured veal.

Gaya Rive Gauche

44 rue du Bac, 7th (01.45.44.73.73/ www.pierregagnaire.com). M° Rue du Bac. **Open** 12.15-2.30pm, 7.15-10.45pm Mon-Fri; 7.15-10.45pm Sat. €€€. **Seafood**. **Map** p133 A2 19

This witty makeover of a fish institution, with seaweed-motif tables and a fish-scale carpet, lets diners sample the skills of chef Pierre Gagnaire for a fraction of the cost of his HQ in the 20th. The menu is split into 'noble' (sea bass, lobster) and 'modest' (squid, skate) and dishes run from funky – 'black' croque monsieur with aubergine and pesto or a land-sea mix of oysters and foie gras – to variations on classics, like petals of sea bass in a spice-and-sherry sauce.

Le Rostand

6 pl Edmond-Rostand, 6th (01.43.54.61.58). RER Luxembourg. **Open** 8am-2am daily. **Bar**. **Map** p133 C4 20

Le Rostand has a truly wonderful view of the Jardin du Luxembourg from its classy interior, decked out with oriental paintings, a long mahogany bar and wall-length mirrors. It's a terribly well-behaved place, and the drinks list is stuffed with whiskies and cocktails – pricey but not as steep as the brasserie menu also available.

La Taverne de Nesle

32 rue Dauphine, 6th (01.43.26.38.36). M° Odéon. **Open** 6pm-4am Mon-Thur, Sun; 6pm-6am Fri, Sat. **Bar**. **Map** p133 C2 21

La Taverne, a spot for people who just can't go home before daylight, has four drinking areas: a zinc bar, a sort of Napoleonic campaign tent, a trendily lit ambient area, and a dreadful 1980s disco. The 100 or so brews include the best of Belgium, but it's the French beers that really set it apart. Don't miss the house special – L'Epi, brewed in three different versions: Blond (barley), Blanc (oats) and Noir (buckwheat).

Le Timbre

3 rue Ste-Beuve, 6th (01.45.49.10.40). M° Vavin. **Open** 7.30-11pm Mon; noon-2pm, 7.30-11pm Tue-Sat. Closed 3wks Aug. €. **Bistro**. **Map** p133 B4 22

The throwaway pastime

Egalitarian pétanque seeks new players.

Walk past the *boulodrome* in the Jardin du Luxembourg on any sunny day and you'll see them in action: the *pétanque* players. It's one of those sights that seems so perfectly French – and yet the game is in trouble. The younger generation simply isn't playing, especially in the game's spiritual heartland, the south. It's a rather baffling state of affairs when you consider *pétanque*'s great simplicity and accessibility: men, women and children – able-bodied or wheelchair-bound – can play each other on more or less equal terms, and the equipment is cheap. It's fun. It's sociable. And it's a fine, not overly strenuous thing to do on a warm afternoon.

The game is played all over Paris, at the 40 designated pitches in public gardens and squares or at ad hoc locations like the banks of the Canal St-Martin up towards La Villette. Whether singles (*tête-à-tête*), pairs (*doublettes*) or – most popularly – triples (*triplettes*), the game's the same. In a circle of rough ground or gravel, players must try to throw their solid steel ball nearest the jack (*cochonnet*); knocking an opponent's ball from a prime position is an admired tactic. Turns are not taken alternately; those furthest from the jack must throw. In the team version, six balls are divided between two or three players. Whoever is closest to the jack when all the balls are used up gains a point, and 13 points win a match. At the Jardin du Luxembourg, only members of the garden's official *pétanque* association are allowed to play (the same goes for the other official pitches across town) – but for non-members there are always the canal banks, the Arènes de Lutèce (p144) and a hundred other suitable patches of ground. Local sports shops and the larger chain supermarkets sell cheap sets of boules, so why not have a go? You'll be protecting an endangered species.

La Ferrandaise p136

Chris Wright's Le Timbre restaurant is small, but this Mancunian always thinks big. His menu of three to four starters, main courses and desserts changes every week. Main courses are pure in presentation and bold in flavour – a thick slab of pork, pan-fried but not the least bit dry, comes with petals of red onion that have a light crunch, and juicy guinea fowl is served on a bed of tomato and pineapple 'chutney'.

Le Voltaire

27 quai Voltaire, 7th (01.42.61.17.49). M° Rue du Bac. **Open** 12.30-2.30pm, 7.30-10.30pm Tue-Sat. Closed 3 wks Aug. **€€**. **Bistro**. **Map** p133 B1 23

With its riverside setting, the Voltaire might seem to be just another tourist-chasing Paris bistro, but is in fact a chic spot whose regulars treat it like a private club. Try the exemplary bowl of lamb's lettuce and beetroot salad, or a golden *feuilleté* encasing fresh, tangy goat's cheese; then a luxury like lobster omelette (€41), creamy and thick with firm morsels of shellfish.

Shopping

APC

3 & 4 rue de Fleurus, 6th (01.42.22.12.77/www.apc.fr). M° St-Placide. **Open** 11am-7.30pm Mon-Sat. **Map** p133 B4 24

APC is very, very cool. Think of Muji crossed with a rough-cut Agnès b and see why Jean Touitou's gear is loved by the Japanese in-crowd. Men's clothes are at No.4, with quirky accessories; cross the road to No.3 for the women's collection. All items can be bought online.

L'Artisan Parfumeur

24 bd Raspail, 7th (01.42.22.23.32). M° Rue du Bac. **Open** 10.30am-7.30pm Mon-Sat. **Map** p133 A2 25

Among scented candles, pot pourri and charms, you'll find the best vanilla perfume Paris can offer – Mûres et Musc, a bestseller for over 20 years.

Le Bon Marché

24 rue de Sèvres, 7th (01.44.39.80.00/www.bonmarche.fr). M° Sèvres

Babylone. **Open** 9.30am-7pm Mon-Wed, Fri; 10am-9pm Thur; 9.30am-8pm Sat. **Map** p133 A3 ㉖
The capital's oldest department store (it opened in 1848) is also its most swish. The prestigious Balthazar men's section offers a cluster of designer boutiques, while the Théâtre de la Beauté provides a comfort zone for women. Seven luxury boutiques, occupied by Dior, Chanel and others, take pride of place on the ground floor; escalators take you up to the fashion floor, which has a fabulous selection of global designer labels. The adjacent Grande Epicerie luxury food hall (01.44.39.81.00, www.lagrandeepicerie.fr, 8.30am-9pm Mon-Sat) also accommodates its own café and restaurant.

Bruno Frisoni

34 rue de Grenelle, 7th (01.42.84.12.30/www.brunofrisoni.fr). M° Rue du Bac or Sèvres Babylone. **Open** 10.30am-7pm Tue-Sat. **Map** p133 B2 ㉗
Innovative shoe designer Frisoni creates shoes with a cinematic, pop edge.

Catherine Malandrino

10 rue de Grenelle, 6th (01.42.22.26.95/www.catherinemalandrino.com). M° St-Germain-des-Prés or Sèvres Babylone.
Open 11am-7pm Mon-Sat.
Map p133 B2 ㉘
After hitting it big in New York, where fans of her floaty stars-and-stripes dresses included Madonna and Mary J Blige, French designer Catherine Malandrino recently opened her first boutique on home soil. With its yellow mirror wall and plexiglass display shelves, the shop is a shiny showcase for strappy sandals and clothes that show her love of patchwork, quilting and embroidery details.

Christian Constant

37 rue d'Assas, 6th (01.53.63.15.15/www.christianconstant.com). M° St-Placide or Rennes. **Open** 8.30am-9pm Mon-Fri; 8.30am-8.30pm Sat, Sun.
Map p133 B4 ㉙
Master chocolate-maker and *traiteur* Constant makes *ganaches* subtly scented with verbena, jasmine or cardamom.

Corinne Sarrut

4 rue du Pré-aux-Clercs, 7th (01.42.61.71.60). M° Rue du Bac or St-Germain-des-Prés. **Open** 10.30am-7pm Mon-Sat. **Map** p133 B2 ㉚
Fans of *Amélie* will be charmed by the clothes of Corinne Sarrut, who dressed Audrey Tautou for the role: 1940s-look trapeze creations in silky viscose.

Debauve & Gallais

30 rue des Sts-Pères, 7th (01.45.48.54.67/www.debauve-et-gallais.com). M° St-Germain-des-Prés or Rue du Bac. **Open** 9am-7pm Mon-Sat.
Map p133 B2. ㉛
This former pharmacy, a historic monument whose façade dates from 1800, sold chocolate for medicinal purposes. Now it's all chocs – in intense tea, honey and praline flavours that heal the soul.

La Dernière Goutte

6 rue Bourbon le Château, 6th (01.43.29.11.62). M° Mabillon.
Open 4-8.30pm Mon; 10am-1.30pm,

3-8.30pm Tue-Fri; 10am-8.30pm Sat; 11am-7pm Sun. **Map** p133 C2 32
This friendly wine shop belongs to the American owners of restaurant Fish around the corner on rue de Seine, and is an ideal place to sip finds from Burgundy, Languedoc, the Rhône valley and Provence. There are free tastings on Saturdays; private tastings are also available upon request.

Gérard Mulot

76 rue de Seine, 6th (01.43.26.85.77). M° Odéon. **Open** 6.45am-8pm Mon, Tue, Thur-Sun. Closed Aug. **Map** p133 C2 33
Mulot makes stunning pastries: typical is the *mabillon*, caramel mousse with apricot marmalade.

Hervé Chapelier

1bis rue du Vieux-Colombier, 6th (01.44.07.06.50/www.hervechapelier.fr). M° St-Sulpice or St-Germain des-Prés. **Open** 10.15am-7pm Mon-Sat. **Map** p133 B3 34
Great for chic, hard-wearing, bicoloured totes. Often copied, never equalled, they're available in almost every colour.

Huilerie Artisanale Leblanc

6 rue Jacob, 6th (01.46.34.61.55/www.huile-leblanc.com). M° St-Germain-des-Prés. **Open** noon-7pm Tue-Fri; 10am-7pm Sat. Closed 2wks Aug. **Map** p133 C2 35
The Leblanc family started out making walnut oil from its family tree in Burgundy before branching out to press oils from hazelnuts, almonds, pine nuts, grilled peanuts, pistachios and olives.

La Hune

170 bd St-Germain, 6th (01.45.48.35.85). M° St-Germain-des-Prés. **Open** 10am-11.45pm Mon-Sat; 11am-7.45pm Sun. **Map** p133 B2 36
This Left Bank institution stocks a global selection of art and design books, and a stock of French lit and theory.

Irié Wash

8 rue du Pré-aux-Clercs, 7th (01.42.61.18.28). M° Rue du Bac or St-Germain-des-Prés. **Open** 10.15am-7pm Mon-Sat. Closed 3wks Aug. **Map** p133 B2 37
Parisians have fallen for this Japanese designer, whose liking for new methods and materials includes laser cutting or hologram prints. The label also sells three perfumes for three different moods and times in any one day, for men and women: 9.25, 15.10 and 20.50.

Iunx

48-50 rue de l'Université, 7th (01.45.44.50.14/www.iunx.com). M° Rue du Bac. **Open** 10.30am-7pm Mon-Sat. **Map** p133 A1 38
Iunx is Greek for 'seduction by scent', and this mysterious, futuristic temple to fragrance sells its own delicious lines of perfumes, gels and candles. Sniff out the Eau Interdite, an absinthe-scented eau de cologne.

Jean-Paul Hévin

3 rue Vavin, 6th (01.43.54.09.85/www.jphevin.com). M° Vavin. **Open** 10am-7pm Mon-Sat. Closed Aug. **Map** p133 B4 39
Jean-Paul Hévin dares to fill chocolates with potent cheeses; some people like to serve them with wine as an apéritif. The aphrodisiac chocs are very popular.

Marie Mercié

23 rue St-Sulpice, 6th (01.43.26.45.83). M° Odéon. **Open** 11am-7pm Mon-Sat. **Map** p133 C3 40
Marie Mercié's creations make you wish you lived in an era when hats were de rigueur. You can step out in one shaped like curved fingers (complete with shocking-pink nail varnish and pink diamond ring) or a beret like a face with red lips and turquoise eyes.

Le Mouton à Cinq Pattes

138 bd St-Germain, 6th (01.43.26.49.25/www.mouton-a-cinq-pattes.com). M° Odéon or Mabillon. **Open** 10am-7pm Mon-Sat. **Map** p133 C2 41
Designer vintage and last season's collection are all here, in mint condition: Vittadini, Buscat, Donn Adriana, Chanel and Lagerfeld. Turnover is fast, and labels are cut out: make sure you know what you're buying.

Le Voltaire p138

Patrick Roger

108 bd St-Germain, 6th (01.43.29.38. 42/www.patrickroger.com). M° Odéon or Cluny La Sorbonne. **Open** 10.30am-7.30pm Tue-Sat. **Map** p133 B2 ㊷

With a sculptor's sensibility, Sceaux-based Patrick Roger is shaking up the art of chocolate-making. While other *chocolatiers* aim for a glossy finish, Roger creates a brushed effect by sprinkling cocoa powder on amazingly realistic choccie hens.

Paul & Joe

64 rue des Sts-Pères, 7th (01.42.22. 47.01/www.paulandjoe.com). M° Rue du Bac or St-Germain-des-Prés. **Open** 10am-7pm Mon-Sat. **Map** p133 B2 ㊸

Trendy types have taken a great shine to Sophie Albou's weathered 1940s-style creations (named after her sons) – so much so that she's opened a menswear branch in addition to this sleek flagship, with its bubblegum-pink gramophone.

Peggy Huyn Kinh

9-11 rue Coëtlogon, 6th (01.42.84. 83.83/www.phk.fr). M° St-Sulpice. **Open** 10am-7pm Mon-Sat. **Map** p133 B3 ㊹

PHK, formerly creative director for Cartier, creates luxurious bags with boarskin and python, and minimalist silver jewellery.

Pierre Hermé

72 rue Bonaparte, 6th (01.43.54. 47.77). M° St-Sulpice. **Open** 10am-7pm Tue-Fri, Sun; 10am-7.30pm Sat. Closed 3wks Aug. **Map** p133 B3 ㊺

Pastry superstar Pierre Hermé attracts connoisseurs from St-Germain-des-Prés and afar with his special seasonal confections. His other branch is in the 15th at 185 rue de Vaugirard (01.47.83.89.96).

Poilâne

8 rue du Cherche-Midi, 6th (01.45.48. 42.59/www.poilane.com). M° Sèvres

Hervé Chapelier p140

Babylone or St-Sulpice. **Open** 7.15am-8.15pm Mon-Sat. Closed public hols. **Map** p133 B3 46

At the tiny original Poilâne shop, locals queue for freshly baked country *miches*, flaky-crusted apple tarts and buttery shortbread biscuits – and, of course, for the signature Poilâne bread, dark, firm and flavourful.

Richart

258 bd St-Germain, 7th (01.45.55. 66.00/www.richart.com). M° Solférino. **Open** 10am-7pm Mon-Sat. **Map** p133 A1 47

At this chic chocs boutique, chocolate *ganaches* have intricate designs, packages look like jewel boxes, and each purchase comes with tasting tips.

Ryst Dupeyron

79 rue du Bac, 7th (01.45.48.80.93/ www.dupeyron.com). M° Rue du Bac. **Open** 12.30-7.30pm Mon; 10.30am-7.30pm Tue-Sat. Closed 2wks Aug. **Map** p133 A2 48

The Dupeyron family has sold armagnac for four generations, and stocks bottles dating from 1868. Treasures include some 200 fine Bordeaux wines, vintage port and rare whiskies.

Sadaharu Aoki

35 rue de Vaugirard, 6th (01.45.44. 48.90/www.sadaharuaoki.com). M° St-Placide. **Open** 11am-7pm daily. **Map** p133 B3 49

Japanese pastry chef Aoki uses French techniques and ingredients such as green tea to produce original (and completely pristine) pastries.

Sonia Rykiel

175 bd St-Germain, 6th (01.49.54. 60.60/www.soniarykiel.fr). M° St-Germain-des-Prés or Sèvres Babylone. **Open** 10.30am-7pm Mon-Sat. **Map** p133 B2 50

The reigning queen of all things stripy still produces fantastic skinny rib knitwear evoking the Left Bank babes of Sartre's time. The menswear store is situated just across the street; elsewhere you'll find the younger, and much more affordable 'Sonia by Sonia Rykiel' range (59 rue des Sts-Pères, 6th, 01.49.54.61.00) and stylish kids' togs (4 rue de Grenelle, 6th, 01.49. 54.61.10). Next door to the latter, the Rykiel Woman store (No.6, 01.49.54. 66.21) stocks a range of unusual designer sex toys – like a vibrating black rubber duck (€45).

Vanessa Bruno

25 rue St-Sulpice, 6th (01.43.54.41.04/ www.vanessabruno.com). M° Odéon or St-Sulpice. **Open** 10.30am-7.30pm Mon-Sat. **Map** p133 C3 51

Bruno's feminine and highly characterful clothes have a cool, Zen-like quality that no doubt derives from her stay in Japan. She also makes great bags.

Yves Saint Laurent

6 pl St-Sulpice, 6th (01.43.29.43.00/ www.ysl.com). M° St-Sulpice. **Open** 11am-7pm Mon; 10.30am-7pm Tue-Sat. **Map** p133 C3 52

Yves Saint Laurent retired in 2002 after a 40-year career that began at Dior and continued with the revolution he fomented in the 1960s under his own name, getting women into dinner and jump suits. This is the women's store; menswear is at No.12 (01.43.26.84.40).

Nightlife

Le Sabot

6 rue du Sabot, 6th (01.42.22.21.56). M° St-Germain-des-Prés or St-Sulpice. **Open** noon-3pm, 6pm-2am Mon-Sat. **Map** p133 B2 53

Jazz, blues and *chanson* with your *gigot d'agneau*? Not a problem. The multi-talented owner of Le Sabot joins jazz, blues and *chanson* guests with his own piano and sax, concerts start at 9pm most nights.

Wagg

62 rue Mazarine, 6th (01.55.42. 22.00/ www.wagg.fr). M° Odéon. **Open** 11.30pm-6am Fri, Sat; 3pm-midnight Sun. **Map** p133 C2 54

This old Jim Morrison hangout attracts crowds with house and disco at weekends, and a salsa session on Sunday afternoons. Admission prices of €10-€15 include one drink.

Le Panthéon p148

The Latin Quarter

The Latin Quarter is thought to have come by its name through the use of Latin among students who came here for education from all over Europe in the Middle Ages – but it could refer to the vestiges of Roman Lutetia, of which it was the larger part. The first two Roman streets ran where rue St-Jacques (later on the pilgrims' route to Santiago de Compostela) and rue Cujas run today; scholars think the forum was under rue Soufflot.

The district has been the city's university district since medieval times. It's awash with lovely churches, wonky ancient buildings, studenty bars, learning or learned institutions and bustling street life (the best taste of this can be had on rue Mouffetard); and despite the rocketing prices of flats, it still has a distinctly intellectual edge.

Sights & museums

Arènes de Lutèce

rue Monge, rue de Navarre or rue des Arènes, 5th. M° Cardinal Lemoine or Place Monge. **Open** *Summer* 8am-10pm daily. *Winter* 8am-5.30pm daily. **Map** p145 B4 ❶

This Roman arena, where wild beasts and gladiators once did battle, could accommodate 10,000 seated spectators. It was still visible as late as the reign of Philippe-Auguste in the 12th century, but then it disappeared under rubble. The site was rediscovered in 1869 and now incorporates a garden. It attracts skateboarders and boules players.

Eglise St-Etienne-du-Mont

pl Ste-Geneviève, 5th (01.43.54.11.79). M° Cardinal Lemoine/RER Luxembourg. **Open** 10am-7pm Tue-Sun. **Map** p145 B4 ❷

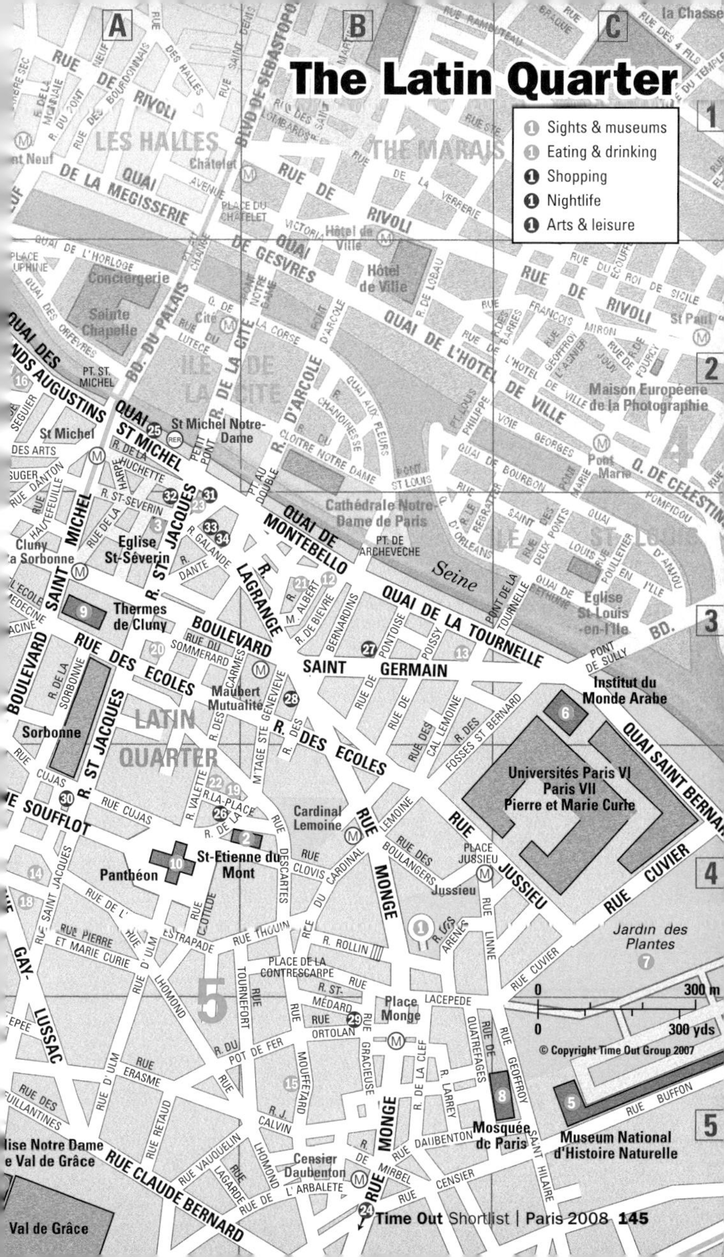

The Latin Quarter
Sights & museums
Eating & drinking
Shopping
Nightlife
Arts & leisure
A
B
C
1
2
3
4
5
LES HALLES
THE MARAIS
ILE DE LA CITE
ILE ST LOUIS
LATIN QUARTER
Châtelet
PLACE DU CHATELET
Hôtel de Ville
Conciergerie
Sainte Chapelle
PT. ST. MICHEL
St Michel Notre-Dame
St Michel
Cluny La Sorbonne
Eglise St-Séverin
Cathédrale Notre-Dame de Paris
PT. DE ARCHEVECHE
Seine
Maison Européene de la Photographie
Pont Marie
St Paul
Eglise St-Louis-en-l'Ile
Thermes de Cluny
Maubert Mutualité
Institut du Monde Arabe
Universités Paris VI Paris VII Pierre et Marie Curie
Sorbonne
Cardinal Lemoine
Panthéon
St-Etienne du Mont
PLACE JUSSIEU
Jussieu
Jardin des Plantes
PLACE DE LA CONTRESCARPE
Place Monge
Mosquée de Paris
Museum National d'Histoire Naturelle
Censier Daubenton
Val de Grâce
RUE DE RIVOLI
BLVD DE SEBASTOPOL
QUAI DE LA MEGISSERIE
QUAI DE GESVRES
QUAI DE L'HOTEL DE VILLE
QUAI DES GRANDS AUGUSTINS
QUAI ST MICHEL
BD. DU PALAIS
R. DE LA CITE
R. D'ARCOLE
QUAI DE MONTEBELLO
QUAI DE LA TOURNELLE
QUAI D'ORLEANS
QUAI DE BETHUNE
QUAI DE BOURBON
Q. DE CELESTINS
QUAI SAINT BERNARD
BOULEVARD SAINT GERMAIN
BOULEVARD SAINT MICHEL
RUE DES ECOLES
R. DES ECOLES
R. ST JACQUES
RUE SAINT JACQUES
RUE SOUFFLOT
RUE CUJAS
RUE MONGE
RUE JUSSIEU
RUE CUVIER
RUE LINNE
RUE LACEPEDE
RUE GEOFFROY SAINT HILAIRE
RUE BUFFON
RUE CLAUDE BERNARD
GAY-LUSSAC
RUE DE L'ESTRAPADE
RUE THOUIN
R. ROLLIN
RUE CARDINAL LEMOINE
RUE MOUFFETARD
RUE DAUBENTON
RUE CENSIER
RUE DE L'ARBALETE
RUE DESCARTES
RUE CLOVIS
PONT DE SULLY
PONT DE LA TOURNELLE
0
300 m
300 yds
© Copyright Time Out Group 2007

Geneviève, patron saint of Paris, is credited with having miraculously saved the city from Attila the Hun in 451, and her shrine has been a site of pilgrimage ever since. The church was built in an amalgam of Gothic and Renaissance styles between 1492 and 1626; the interior is tall and light, with soaring columns and a classical balustrade.

Eglise St-Séverin

3 rue des Prêtres-St-Séverin, 5th (01.42. 34.93.50). M° Cluny La Sorbonne or St-Michel. **Open** 11am-7.30pm daily. **Map** p145 A3 ❸

This lovely Flamboyant Gothic edifice dates from the 15th century (though the doorway, carved with foliage, is an 1837 extra). The double ambulatory is famed for its 'palm tree' vaulting, and the bell-tower, a survivor from an earlier church, has the oldest bell in Paris (1412).

Eglise du Val-de-Grâce

pl Alphonse-Laveran, 5th (01.40.51. 47.28). RER Luxembourg or Port-Royal. **Open** noon-6pm Tue, Wed, Sat, Sun. Closed some public hols. **Admission** €5; free-€2.50 reductions. No credit cards. **Map** p145 A5 ❹

Anne of Austria, wife of Louis XIII, vowed to erect 'a magnificent temple' if God blessed her with a son; she got two. The resulting church and Benedictine monastery – now a military hospital and a museum – were built by François Mansart and Jacques Lemercier. This is the most luxuriously baroque of the city's 17th-century domed churches.

Grande Galerie de l'Evolution

36 rue Geoffroy-St-Hilaire, 2 rue Bouffon or pl Valhubert, 5th (01.40. 79.54.79/56.01/www.mnhn.fr). M° Gare d'Austerlitz or Jussieu. **Open** *Grande Galerie* 10am-6pm Mon, Wed-Fri, Sun; 10am-8pm Sat. *Other galleries* 10am-5pm Mon, Wed-Fri; 10am-6pm Sat, Sun. **Admission** *Grande Galerie* €8; free-€7 reductions. *Other galleries (each)* €6; free-€4 reductions. No credit cards. **Map** p145 C5 ❺

The brilliant renovations to the Grande Galerie de l'Evolution, located within the Jardin des Plantes, have taken the city's natural history museum out of the stone age. Architect Paul Chemyetov set the glass-sided lifts and the latest audio-visual techniques into the 19th-century iron-framed structure. Sections are dedicated to sea creatures (including a 14m-long skeleton of a whale), mammals, ecological and demographic problems, and endangered and extinct species. The separate Galerie d'Anatomie Comparée et de Paléontologie contains more than a million skeletons and a fossil collection of world importance.

Institut du Monde Arabe

1 rue des Fossés-St-Bernard, 5th (01.40.51.38.38/www.imarabe.org). M° Jussieu. **Open** *Museum* 10am-6pm Tue-Sun. *Library* 1-8pm Tue-Sat. *Café* noon-6pm Tue-Sun. **Admission** *Roof terrace, library* free. *Museum* €5; free-€4 reductions. **Map** p145 C3 ❻

A clever blend of high-tech, steel-and-glass architecture and Arab influences, this *grand projet* was built between 1980 and 1987. Window screens, based on those of Moorish palaces, use camera apertures to control the amount of available light. Inside is a collection of Middle Eastern art, archaeological finds and a café. Of particular interest are the urns and masks from Carthage, early scientific tools and 19th-century Tunisian costume and jewellery.

Event highlights 'Les Phéniciens de Tir à Carthage', North Africa in antiquity (15 Oct 2007-30 Mar 2008).

Jardin des Plantes

36 rue Geoffroy-St-Hilaire, 2 rue Bouffon, pl Valhubert or 57 rue Cuvier, 5th. M° Gare d'Austerlitz, Place Monge or Jussieu. **Open** *Main garden (winter)* 8am-dusk; *(summer)* 7.30am-dusk daily. *Alpine garden (Apr-Sept)* 8-11am, 1.30-5pm daily. Closed Oct-Mar. *Greenhouses (Apr-Sept)* 1-5pm Mon, Wed-Fri; 10am-5pm Sat, Sun. *Menagerie (Apr-Sept)* 9am-5pm daily. Closed Oct-Mar. **Admission** *Jardin des Plantes* free. *Greenhouses* €3. *Menagerie* €7; free-€5 reductions. **Map** p145 C4 ❼

Rue Mouffetard p144

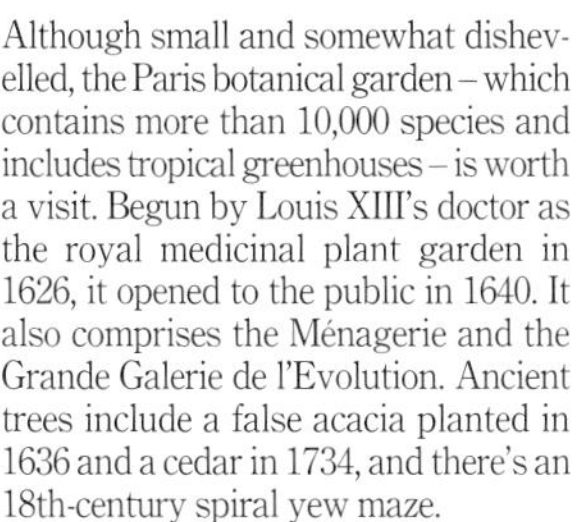

Although small and somewhat dishevelled, the Paris botanical garden – which contains more than 10,000 species and includes tropical greenhouses – is worth a visit. Begun by Louis XIII's doctor as the royal medicinal plant garden in 1626, it opened to the public in 1640. It also comprises the Ménagerie and the Grande Galerie de l'Evolution. Ancient trees include a false acacia planted in 1636 and a cedar in 1734, and there's an 18th-century spiral yew maze.

La Mosquée de Paris

2 pl du Puits-de-l'Ermite, 5th (01.45.35.97.33/tearoom 01.43.31.38.20/baths 01.43.31.18.14/www.mosquee-de-paris.net). M° Monge. **Open** *Tours* 9am-noon, 2-6pm Mon-Thur, Sat, Sun (closed Muslim hols). *Tearoom* 10am-11.30pm daily. *Restaurant* noon-2.30pm, 7.30-10.30pm daily. *Baths (women)* 10am-9pm Mon, Wed, Sat; 2-9pm Fri; *(men)* 2-9pm Tue, Sun. **Admission** €3; free-€2 reductions. *Tearoom* free. *Baths* €15-€35. **Map** p145 C5 ❽

The mosque's stunning green and white square minaret is the spiritual heart of France's Algerian-dominated Muslim population. Built from 1922 to 1926 in Hispano-Moorish style, with elements inspired by the Alhambra and Fez's Mosque Bou-Inania, the mosque is a series of buildings and courtyards in three sections: religious (for serious worshippers and not inquisitive tourists); scholarly (Islamic school and library); and, via rue Geoffroy-St-Hilaire, commercial (the domed hammam, Turkish baths and relaxing Moorish tearoom).

Musée National du Moyen Age – Thermes de Cluny

6 pl Paul-Painlevé, 5th (01.53.73.78.00/www.musee-moyenage.fr). M° Cluny La Sorbonne. **Open** 9.15am-5.45pm Mon, Wed-Sun. **Admission** €6.50; free-€4.50 reductions. No credit cards. **Map** p145 A3 ❾

The national museum of medieval art is best known for the lovely allegorical *Lady and the Unicorn* tapestry cycle, but it also has important collections of

Grand Galerie de l'Evolution p146

medieval sculpture and enamels. The building itself – built atop a Gallo-Roman baths complex – is a rare example of 15th-century secular Gothic architecture; the baths, in characteristic Roman bands of stone and brick masonry, are the finest Roman remains to be found in Paris. Recent acquisitions include the illuminated manuscript *L'Ascension du Christ* from the Abbey of Cluny, dating from the 12th century. The museum also presents a programme of medieval concerts.
Event highlights 'Frères d'Amboise: La Chapelle de l'Hôtel de Cluny', Renaissance religious art (3 Oct 2007-14 Jan 2008). 'Les Routes du Lustre', Moorish ceramics (9 Apr-1 Sept 2008).

Le Panthéon

pl du Panthéon, 5th (01.44.32.18.00). M° Cardinal Lemoine/RER Luxembourg. **Open** 10am-5.30pm daily. **Admission** €7.50; free-€4.50 reductions. **Map** p145 A4 ⑩

This neoclassical megastructure was the architectural *grand projet* of its day, commissioned by Louis XV to thank Saint Geneviève for his recovery from illness. By the time it was ready in 1790, much had changed; the Revolution saw the Panthéon rededicated as a 'temple of reason' and resting place of the nation's great men: the list includes Voltaire, Rousseau, Hugo, Zola and Malraux; Alexandre Dumas joined them in 2002.

Eating & drinking

Allard

41 rue St-André-des-Arts, 6th (01.43. 26.48.23). M° Odéon. **Open** noon-2.30pm, 7-11.30pm Mon-Sat. Closed 3wks Aug. **€€**. **Bistro**. **Map** p145 A2 ⑪

This fine, traditional bistro has a pre-war feel, an impression confirmed by the kitchen, which sends out the sort of glorious Gallic grub you come to Paris for. Start with sliced, pistachio-studded Lyonnaise sausage served with potato salad in delicious vinaigrette, or maybe a sauté of wild mushrooms; then try roast Bresse chicken with sautéed ceps or roast duck with olives. Finish up with the *tarte fine de pommes*.

Atelier Maître Albert

1 rue Maître-Albert, 5th (01.56.81.30. 01/www.ateliermaitrealbert.com). M° St Michel or Maubert Mutualité. **Open**

noon-2.30pm, 6.30-11.30pm Mon-Wed; noon-2.30pm, 6.30pm-1am Thur, Fri; 6.30pm-1am Sat; 6.30-11.30pm Sun. €€. **Brasserie**. **Map** p145 B3 ⑫

This Guy Savoy outpost has a slick decor and an attractive marble-floored dining room with open kitchen. It's noisy too: book a table in the quieter bar area if possible. The short menu lists a Savoy classic or two as starters – oysters in sea-water gelée, or inventive dishes like ballotine of chicken, foie gras and celery root in chicken liver sauce. Next up, perhaps, roast *faux-filet*, or a hunk of tuna with tiny casseroles of dauphinois potatoes.

Chez René

14 bd St-Germain, 5th (01.43.54.30.23). M° Maubert Mutualité. **Open** 12.15-2.15pm, 7.45-10.30pm Tue-Sat. Closed Aug. **€€**. **Brasserie**. **Map** p145 B3 ⑬

René Cinquin opened this place in 1957. Nowadays it's René's son Jean-Paul who chats with diners, but the silver cutlery, starched linen and hard work in the kitchen are still here. The *coq au vin* is the main attraction, the secret of whose succulent sauce is no stock, just 20 minutes stirring flour and butter over a feeble flame before adding wine. Similar skill goes into the *boeuf bourguignon*.

Le Crocodile

6 rue Royer-Collard, 5th (01.43.54.32.37). RER Luxembourg. **Open** 10pm-late Mon-Sat. Closed Aug. **Bar**. **Map** p145 A4 ⑭

Ignore the seemingly boarded-up windows – if you're here late, it's open. Friendly regulars line the sides of this small, narrow bar and try to decide on a drink: not easy, given the complexity of the cocktail list. It trots out 311 choices (the number increases every year), each one more potent than the last.

5th Bar

62 rue Mouffetard, 5th (01.43.37.09.09). M° Place Monge. **Open** 5pm-2am Mon-Thur, Sun; 4pm-3am Fri, Sat. **Bar**. **Map** p145 B5 ⑮

The 5th is perhaps the cosiest of the city's many expat pubs. Small, dark and squeezed into two floors, it has Sky Sports, a pool table at the back and pub-type bonhomie and banquettes downstairs. Staff and punters here are residents from over the Channel or the Atlantic, happy to pay a little extra for the convenience of discussing familiar topics with their own kind.

El Fogón

45 quai des Grands-Augustins, 6th (01.43.54.31.33). M° St Michel. **Open** 7.30pm-midnight Tue-Fri; noon-2pm, 7.30pm-midnight Sat, Sun. **€€**. **Spanish**. **Map** p145 A2 ⑯

One of the hottest tables of the moment is not French, but Spanish. Chef Alberto Herraíz specialises in rice dishes, including what many consider the best paella in Paris. The decor may be bourgeois, but the atmosphere and the food are big-hearted – here it is more about ordering for a table than individually: the tapas menu (€35) and rice menus (€40) are prepared for a minimum of two people.

Lapérouse

51 quai des Grands-Augustins, 6th (01.43.26.68.04/www.restaurant

laperouse.com). M° St Michel. **Open** noon-2.30pm, 7.30-10.30pm Mon-Fri; 7.30-10.30pm Sat. Closed Aug. **€€**. **Brasserie**. **Map** p145 A2 ⑰

One of the most romantic spots in Paris, Lapérouse was once a rendezvous for French politicians and their mistresses; the tiny private dining rooms upstairs used to lock on the inside. Chef Alain Hacquard does a modern take on classic French cooking: his beef fillet is smoked for a complex flavour; tender saddle of rabbit is scented with both lavender and rosemary. The seductive riverside dining room is best savoured at night.

Le Pantalon

7 rue Royer-Collard, 5th (no phone). RER Luxembourg. **Open** 5.30pm-2am Mon-Sat. No credit cards. **Café**. **Map** p145 A4 ⑱

Le Pantalon is a local café that seems familiar yet utterly surreal. It has the standard fixtures and fittings, plus a strange vacuum-cleaner sculpture, disco-light toilets and the world's most prosaic proposal of marriage. Happy hours are generous, but drinks are cheap enough to make you tipsy without the worry of a cash hangover.

Le Piano Vache

8 rue Laplace, 5th (01.46.33.75.03/ www.lepianovache.com). M° Maubert Mutualité or Cardinal Lemoine. **Open** noon-2am Mon-Fri; 9pm-2am Sat, Sun. **Bar**. **Map** p145 A4 ⑲

A Left Bank drinking haunt for many a decade, this has all the hallmarks of what any beer-stained, smoky hovel should be: dark, cramped, filled with a hardcore drinker/student clientele, walls covered four times over with posters and indeterminate pub grime, and the hits of alternative 1980s synth-pop on repeat on the stereo.

Le Pré Verre

8 rue Thénard, 5th (01.43.54.59.47). M° Maubert Mutualité or Cluny La Sorbonne. **Open** noon-2pm, 7.30-10.30pm Tue-Sat. Closed 3wks Aug. **€€**. **Bistro**. **Map** p145 A3 ⑳

Chef Philippe Delacourcelle uses spices like few other of his French counterparts. Take his salt cod with cassia bark and smoked potato purée: what the fish lacks in size it makes up for in crunchy texture and rich, cinnamon-like flavour, and the smooth potato cooked in a smoker makes a great accompaniment. Finish it all off with roast figs with olives.

La Mosquée de Paris p147

Old books, new blood

Paris's most famous bookshop takes a fresh direction.

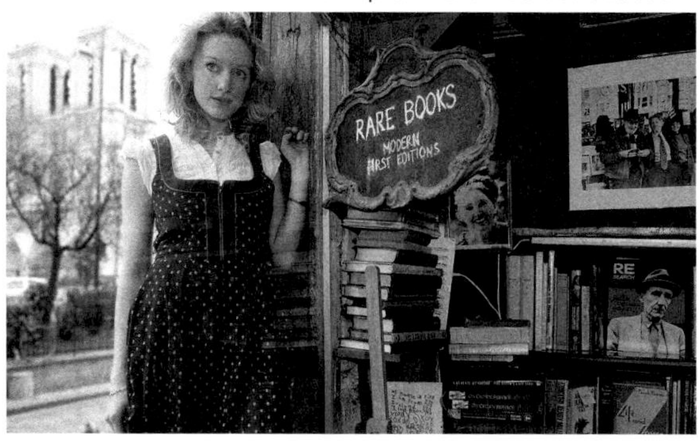

Founded in 1951, Shakespeare & Co (p153) is one of the world's most famous bookshops. Its story includes some of the leading literary names of the 20th century, three premises and two owners.

Sylvia Beach, founder of the original store at nearby Odéon, died in Paris in 1962; the current owner, George Whitman, is now in his 94th year, grey-haired and lucid; and the present manager, responsible for introducing a telephone, a credit card machine and, most notably, a biennial summer literary festival, is Sylvia Whitman, George's daughter.

'When I took over in 2003, everyone was always talking about the shop's history,' she says. 'It was always Sylvia Beach and the Lost Generation, George Whitman and the Beat Generation. It was nfuriating!' And yet, rather than tamper with the homely feel of the shop's interior, or her father's philosophy of giving penniless writers a dark recess of the shop in which to sleep, Sylvia has set about giving Shakespeare & Co a modern direction. As well as the festival, housed in a marquee beside the store – 'Real Lives, Memoirs and Biographies' is the theme for 2008 – Sylvia has plans for a café and cultural centre.

Whitman bought the current shop with a modest inheritance; at first it was called Le Mistral, but she renamed it in Beach's honour when she died in 1962. The Beats, Burroughs and Ginsberg were regulars, giving readings and drinking their way through literary evenings. Walk in today and you hear the clacking of old typewriters upstairs, your eyes falling upon a few bronze coins in a symbolic dry wishing well. Outside, amid the stalls and small ads, the 'Paris Wall Newspaper' is a chalked history written by Whitman on New Year's Day 2004. No bar codes, no security gates, no shrink wrap. In other words, the sort of bookshop that every city really ought to have.

Le Reminet

3 rue des Grands-Degrés, 5th (01.44.07.04.24). M° Maubert Mutualité or St Michel/RER St Michel. **Open** noon-2.30pm, 7.30-11pm Mon, Thur-Sun. Closed 3wks Aug. €. **Bistro**. **Map** p145 B3 21

This has long been a popular Left Bank bistro, serving a splash-out €50 tasting menu. and an absolute bargain €15 lunch menu three days a week. Start with crisp fried filo parcels of black pudding, or ravioli of whole *gambas* in a light dough, bathed in coconut milk. Main courses include perfectly timed fillet of beef with a shallot purée, and tender scallops on well-sauced tagliatelle.

Rhubarb

18 rue Laplace, 5th (01.43.25.35.03). M° Maubert Mutualité. **Open** 5pm-2am daily. **Bar**. **Map** p145 A4 22

Wonderful little Rhubarb is the latest offering from the same organisation that put the Fu Bar (5 rue St-Sulpice, 6th, 01.40.51.82.00) on the map. The cocktails here are excellent: try Sean's great Apple Martini. A relaxed vibe abounds; the cellar is all crumbling pale stone and high ceilings, and while a quiet corner is ideal seduction territory, the space works equally well for gaggles of mates.

Ribouldingue

10 rue St-Julien-le-Pauvre, 5th (01.46. 33.98.80). M° St-Michel. **Open** noon-2pm, 7-11pm Mon-Fri; 7-11pm Sat. **Bistro**. € **Map** p145 A3 23

Ribouldingue (meaning 'binge'), the joyous creation of Nadège Varigny, is situated across the bridge from Notre Dame. Critics and chefs love its gutsy bistro fare which focuses on unusual cuts of meat and offal.

Shopping

Le Boulanger de Monge

123 rue Monge, 5th (01.43.37.54.20/ www.leboulangerdemonge.com). M° Censier Daubenton. **Open** 7am-8.30pm Tue-Sun. **Map** p145 B5 24

Dominique Saibron uses spices to give inimitable flavour to his organic sourdough *boule.* Great baguettes too.

Bouquinistes

Along the quais, especially quai de Montebello & quai St-Michel, 5th. M° St Michel. **Open** times vary from stall to stall, generally Tue-Sun. No credit cards. **Map** p145 A2 25

The green, open-air boxes along the *quais* are one of the city's great institutions. Most, as the name suggests, sell books (second-hand); others sell postcards, replica tin signs and the blue-and-white enamelled numbers above Paris doorways. You're allowed to haggle if you wish.

Crocojazz

64 rue de la Montagne-Ste-Geneviève, 5th (01.46.34.78.38). M° Maubert-Mutualité. **Open** 11am-7pm Tue-Sat. **Map** p145 A4 26

There's a great range of jazz and blues records on sale at this friendly and utterly savvy shop.

Diptyque

34 bd St-Germain, 5th (01.43.26.45.27/ www.diptyqueparis.com). M° Maubert Mutualité. **Open** 10am-7pm Mon-Sat. **Map** p145 B3 27

Diptyque's divinely scented candles are sold in 48 different varieties.

Kayser

8, 14 rue Monge, 5th (01.44.07.01.42/ 01.44.07.17.81/www.maison-kayser. com). M° Maubert Mutualité. **Open** 6.45am-8.30pm Mon, Wed-Sun. **Map** p145 B3 28

In a few years, Eric Kayser has established himself as one of the city's star bakers – even if his baguette is a touch on the salty side. The bakery at number 14 is devoted to organic loaves.

La Maison des Trois Thés

1 rue St-Médard, 5th (01.43.36.93.84). M° Place Monge. **Open** 11am-7.30pm Tue-Sun. Closed Mon, Aug. **Map** p145 B5 29

Yu Hui Tseng, one of the world's top tea experts, has moved to these larger premises. Hush reigns as connoisseurs sample its 1,000 varieties of tea (most costing a small fortune – the cheapest goes for €10). Very busy at weekends.

Left Bank bouquiniste p152

Princesse Tam Tam

52 bd St-Michel, 6th (01.42.34.99.31/ www.princessetam-tam.com). M° Cluny La Sorbonne or St Michel. **Open** 1.30-7pm Mon; 10am-7pm Tue-Sat. **Map** p145 A4 30

The commendable but inexpensive underwear and swimwear brand now much favoured by Parisian trendies has launched with provocative, traffic-stopping promotions. Bright colours and sexily transparent and sporty gear are very much order of the day here – though not, it seems, for the more well-endowed girl.

Shakespeare & Co

37 rue de la Bûcherie, 5th (01.43. 26.96.50/www.shakespeareco.org). M° St Michel. **Open** noon-midnight daily. **Map** p145 B3 31

See box p151.

Nightlife

Caveau de la Huchette

5 rue de la Huchette, 5th (01.43.26. 65.05/www.caveaudelahuchette.fr). M° St Michel. **Open** 9.30pm-2.30am Mon-Wed, Sun; 9.30pm-dawn Thur-Sat. **Map** p145 A2 32

This medieval cellar is a Left Bank classic. Music, usually good, varies from funky jazz to rock 'n' roll classics.

Caveau des Oubliettes

52 rue Galande, 5th (01.46.34.23.09). M° St Michel. **Open** *Bar* 5pm-2am Mon-Thur, Sun; 5pm-5am Fri, Sat. *Concerts* 10pm daily. **Map** p145 A3 33

A foot-tapping frenzy thrives in this medieval dungeon, complete with instruments of torture. Jam sessions in the week. Upstairs bar, too.

Arts & leisure

Studio Galande

42 rue Galande, 5th (01.43.26.94.08). M° St Michel or Cluny La Sorbonne. **Open** times vary. No credit cards. **Map** p145 A3 34

Some 20 different films are screened in their original languages at this cheerful Latin Quarter venue every week – expect quality international arthouse flicks with the occasional *Matrix* option. Every Friday, fans of *The Rocky Horror Picture Show* turn up with drag, rice and water pistols – well worth a gawp.

Le Select p158

Montparnasse

Picasso, Soutine, Léger and other artists came to 'Mount Parnassus' in the early 1900s, driven from Montmartre by rising rents; they were joined by Chagall, Zadkin and other escapees from the Russian Revolution, and by Americans like Man Ray, Henry Miller, Ezra Pound and Gertrude Stein. Between the wars the neighbourhood symbolised modernity: studio buildings with large north-facing windows were built by avant-garde architects all over the district; artists, writers and thinkers drank and debated in the quarter's showy bars; naughty pastimes – like tango – flourished. Since then, Montparnasse has lost much of its soul. The Tour Montparnasse, the only skyscraper in central Paris, is the most visible of several 1970s redevelopment projects; at least there are fabulous views from the panoramic café on the 56th floor, and the tower is an inescapable landmark. There's a free ice rink next to it in winter months should a skate appeal.

Sights & museums

Les Catacombes

1 av Colonel Henri-Rol-Tanguy, 14th (01.43.22.47.63/www.catacombes.info). M° Denfert Rochereau. **Open** 9.30am-4pm Tue-Sun. **Admission** €5; free-€3.30 reductions. **Map** p155 C3 ❶

The only publicly accessible part of the 3,000-km network of subterranean passages that runs under the city. With public burial pits filling up in the era of the Revolutionary Terror, the bones of six million people were transferred to the catacombs (including those of Marat, Robespierre and their cronies). It's an extraordinary sight, and not one for the claustrophobic: you have to descend a narrow spiral staircase that takes you below ground to a mass of bones.

Cimetière du Montparnasse

3 bd Edgar-Quinet, 14th (01.44.10.86.50). M° Edgar Quinet or Raspail. **Open** *16 Mar-5 Nov* 8am-6pm Mon-Fri; 8.30am-6pm Sat; 9am-6pm Sun. *6 Nov-15 Mar* 8am-5.30pm Mon-Fri; 8.30am-5.30pm Sat; 9.30am-5.30pm Sun. **Admission** free.
Map p155 B2 ❷

This 7.2sq km (1,800-acre) cemetery was formed by commandeering three farms in 1824. In true Left Bank style, the Montparnasse cemetery has a wealth of literary names attached to it: Beckett, Baudelaire, Sartre, de Beauvoir and Maupassant all repose here, as do Serge Gainsbourg, Man Ray and actress Jean Seberg.

Fondation Cartier pour l'Art Contemporain

261 bd Raspail, 14th (01.42.18.56.72/ www.fondation.cartier.fr). M° Raspail or Denfert-Rochereau. **Open** noon-8pm Tue-Sun. **Admission** €6.50; free-€4.50 reductions. **Map** p155 C2 ❸

Jean Nouvel's glass-and-steel building, an exhibition centre with Cartier's offices above, is as much a work of art as the installations inside. Shows by contemporary artists and photographers often have wide-ranging themes, such as 'Birds' or 'Desert'.

Fondation Henri Cartier-Bresson

2 impasse Lebouis, 14th (01.56.80.27.00/www.henricartierbresson.org). M° Gaîté. **Open** 1-8.30pm Wed; 1-6.30pm Thur, Fri, Sun; 11am-6.45pm Sat. Closed 20 Dec-11 Jan & Aug. **Admission** €4; free-€3 reductions. No credit cards. **Map** p155 A2 ❹

Opened in 2003, this two-floor gallery is dedicated to the great photographer

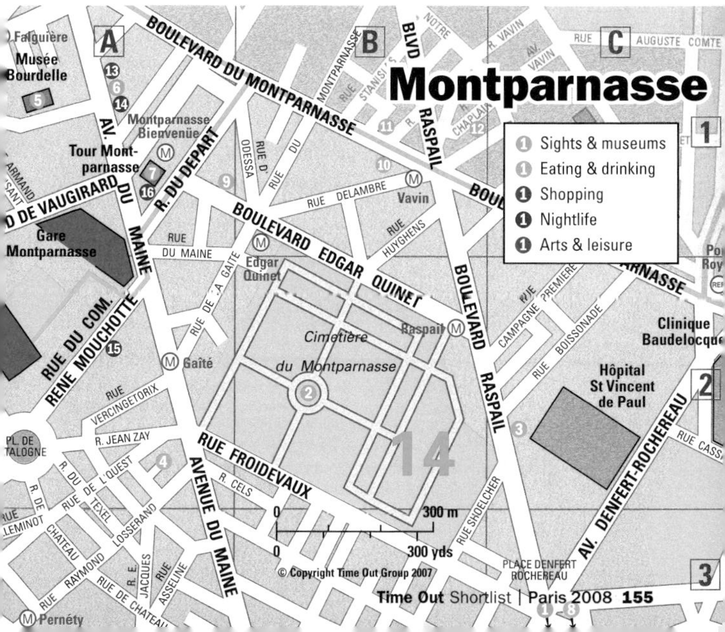

Henri Cartier-Bresson. Built in 1913, it consists of a tall, narrow atelier with a minutely catalogued archive open to researchers, and a lounge on the fourth floor screening films.The establishment hosts three annual arts shows a year in various disciplines.

Musée Bourdelle

16-18 rue Antoine-Bourdelle, 15th (01.49.54.73.73/www.paris.fr/musees/bourdelle). M° Montparnasse Bienvenüe or Falguière. **Open** 10am-6pm Tue-Sun. Closed public hols. **Admission** free. *Exhibitions* €4.50; €3 reductions. No credit cards. **Map** p155 A1 5

The sculptor Antoine Bourdelle, pupil of Rodin, produced monumental works like the Modernist friezes at the Théâtre des Champs-Elysées. Set around a small garden, the museum includes his apartment and studios. A 1950s extension tracks the evolution of his equestrian monument to General Alvear in Buenos Aires, and his masterful Hercules the Archer. A new wing houses bronzes.

Musée du Montparnasse

21 av du Maine, 15th (01.42.22.91.96/www.museedumontparnasse.net). M° Montparnasse Bienvenüe. **Open** 12.30-7pm Tue-Sun. **Admission** €5; free-€4 reductions. No credit cards. **Map** p155 A1 6

Set in one of the last surviving studio alleys, this museum was home to Marie Vassilieff, who opened her own academy and canteen to penniless Picasso, Cocteau and Matisse; Trotsky and Lenin were also guests. Shows focus on the area's past and present-day artists.

Tour Montparnasse

33 av du Maine, 15th (01.45.38.52.56/www.tourmontparnasse56.com). M° Montparnasse Bienvenüe. **Open** *Winter* 9.30am-10.30pm daily. *Summer* 9.30am-11.30pm daily. **Admission** €9; free-€6.50 reductions. **Map** p155 A1 7

Built in 1974 on the site of the old train station, this 209m steel-and-glass monster is shorter than the Eiffel Tower, and uglier. A fast lift whisks you to the 56th floor and fantastic panoramic views.

Eating & drinking

Apollo

3 pl Denfert-Rochereau, 14th (01.45.38.76.77/01.43.22.02.15). M° Denfert Rochereau. **Open** noon-3pm, 8pm-midnight daily. **€**. **Bistro**. **Map** p155 C3 8

This high-design restaurant in former RER offices brings a breath of novelty into a staid part of Paris. The decor fits nicely with the original design, but the menu is firmly in the 21st century. Modern takes on comfort food here include herring caviar and potatoes, *blanquette de coquilles St-Jacques*, and braised beef with carrots. The food is generally good and generously served.

La Cerisaie

NEW *70 bd Edgar Quinet, 14th (01.43.20.98.98). M° Edgar Quinet or Montparnasse Bienvenüe.* **Open** noon-2pm, 7.10pm Mon-Fri. Closed Aug & 1wk Dec. **€€**. **Brasserie**. **Map** p155 A1 9

Nothing about this tiny restaurant's red façade hints at the talent that lurks inside. With a simple starter of white asparagus served with preserved lemon and drizzled with bright green parsley oil, chef Cyril Lalanne proves his ability to choose and prepare the finest produce. On his daily blackboard menu you might find *bourride de maquereau*, or *cochon noir de Bigorre*, an ancient breed of pig that puts ordinary pork to shame.

La Coupole

102 bd du Montparnasse, 14th (01.43.20.14.20). M° Vavin. **Open** 8.30am-1am Mon-Thur, Sun; 8.30am-1.30am Fri, Sat. **€€**. **Brasserie**. **Map** p155 B1 10

La Coupole opened during the district's avant-garde heyday in 1927, and still has some of the old glamour. The people-watching is superb; the ranks of linen-clad tables, the slick waiters, art deco columns, mosaic floor and the sheer scale make coming here an event. The set menu offers so-so steaks, foie gras, fish and autumn game stews, but the real treat is the shellfish.

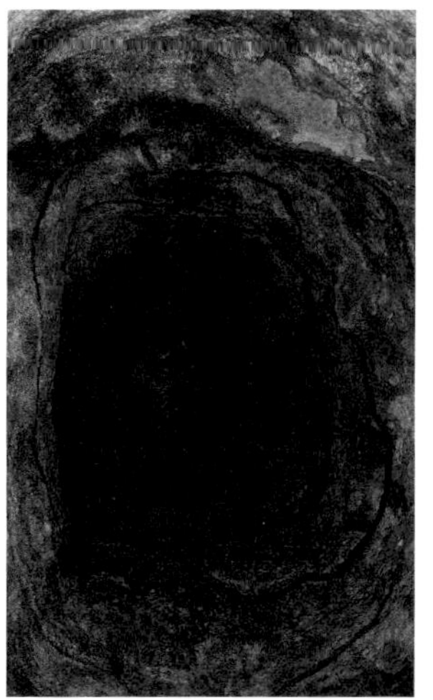

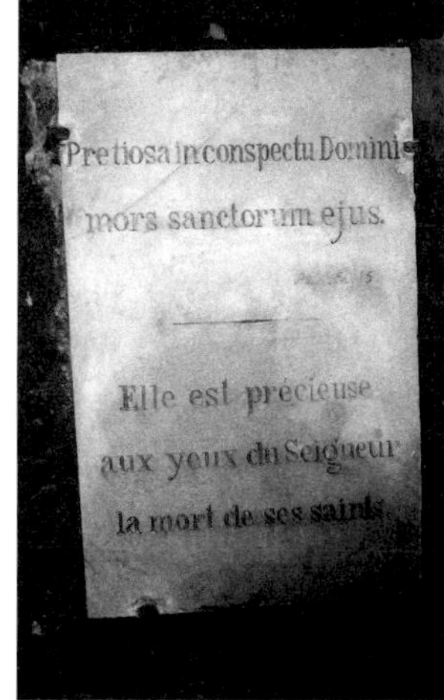

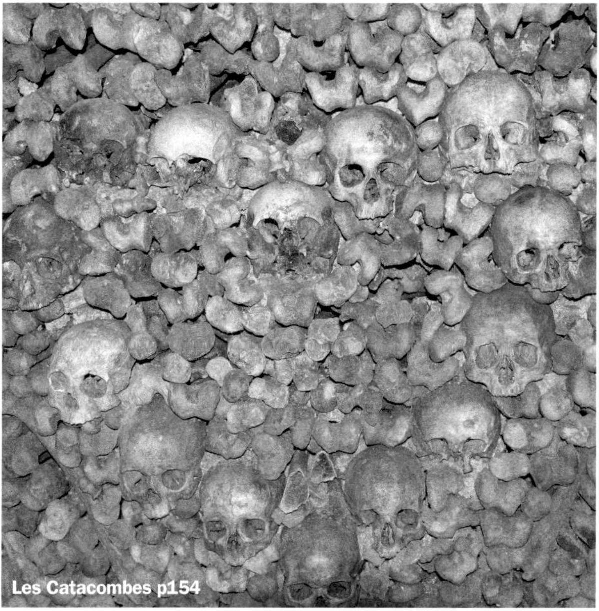

Les Catacombes p154

Le Select

99 bd de Montparnasse, 6th (01.42. 22.65.27). M° Vavin. **Open** 7am-2am Mon-Thur, Sun; 7am-4am Fri, Sat. **€€**. **Brasserie**. **Map** p155 B1 ⑪

For a decade between the wars, the junction of boulevards Raspail and Montparnasse was arts central, home to Man Ray, Cocteau and Lost Generation Yanks. Eight decades on, Le Select is the best of its inevitable tourist traps. Sure, its pricey menu is short on authenticity ('Cockney Brunch' of eggs, bacon and jam at €15), but happy hour from 7pm makes history affordable, and the cocktail and whisky list is extensive.

Wadja

10 rue de la Grande-Chaumière, 6th (01.46.33.02.02). M° Vavin. **Open** noon-2pm, 7.30-11pm Mon-Sat. **€€**. **Bistro**. **Map** p155 B1 ⑫

This creamy yellow bistro strikes a nice balance between simplicity and sophistication. À la carte, you might get foie gras sautéed with prunes, seasonal game or a classic *agneau de sept heures*; but there's also a *menu du jour* which, with a choice of two mains (one meat, one fish) with starter or dessert for just €14, is one of the best bargains in town. There are also some interesting wines.

La Cerisaie p156

Shopping

Kitchen Bazaar

11 av du Maine, 15th (01.42.22.91.17). M° Montparnasse Bienvenüe. **Open** 10am-7pm Mon-Sat. **Map** p155 A1 ⑬

KB stocks chrome gadgetry and modish kitchen fixtures aplenty. The sister shop Bath Bazaar, at No.6 on the other side of avenue du Maine (01.45.48.89.00), sells goodies for the bathroom.

Nightlife

Club Mix

24 rue de l'Arrivée, 15th (01.56.80.37. 37/www.mixclub.fr). M° Montparnasse Bienvenüe. **Open** 11pm-6am Wed-Sat; 5pm-1am Sun. **Map** p155 A1 ⑭

Club Mix has one of the city's biggest dancefloors and DJ booths. The music here is strictly house; the most popular event is the gay tea dance on Sundays.

Petit Journal Montparnasse

113 rue du Commandant-René-Mouchotte, 14th (01.43.21.56.70/ www.petitjournal-montparnasse.com). M° Gaité or Montparnasse Bienvenüe. **Open** 7am-2am Mon-Sat. *Concerts* from 10pm Mon-Sat. **Map** p155 A2 ⑮

This two-level jazz brasserie by the Tour Montparnasse showcases Latin sounds, R&B, soul and gospel. Dinner (€55-€85) starts at 8pm.

Le Redlight

34 rue du Départ, 15th (01.42.79. 94.53/www.leredlight.com). M° Edgar Quinet or Montparnasse Bienvenüe. **Open** midnight-11am Fri, Sat. **Map** p155 A1 ⑯

A house mecca with local and global DJs. BPM and Strictly House nights take place once a month on Fridays; Saturdays attract a well-groomed gay clientele. Admission includes one drink.

Parc de La Villette p162

Worth the Trip

West

Bois de Boulogne

16th. M° Porte Dauphine or Les Sablons.
The vast area of woodland that is the Bois de Boulogne was landscaped in the 1860s. It boasts the Jardin de Bagatelle, famous for its roses, daffodils and water lilies; two racecourses; a children's amusement park; an orangery; the Musée National des Arts et Traditions Populaires; and a number of terrace restaurants. Boats can be hired on the lakes. At night the Bois seethes with transsexuals and swingers of every stripe. Recently plans have been mooted to reduce the traffic and replant some of the scrubbier patches of woodland.

Musée Marmottan – Claude Monet

2 rue Louis-Boilly, 16th (01.44.96. 50.33/www.marmottan.com). M° La Muette. **Open** 10am-6pm Tue-Sun (last entry 5.30pm). **Admission** €8; free-€4.50 reductions.
Once a museum of the Empire period, this old hunting pavilion has become a famed holder of Impressionist art. Its Monet collection, the largest in the world, numbers 165 pieces, including the seminal *Impression Soleil Levant,* plus sketchbooks, palette and photos. A circular room was created for the superb series of water lily canvases. Upstairs are works by Renoir, Manet and Gauguin.
Event highlights 'Georges de Bellio', the artworks of a 19th-century collector (9 Oct 2007-3 Feb 2008).

East

Bois de Vincennes

12th. M° Porte Dorée.
Bois de Vincennes – the city's largest park – was created, like the Bois de

Fortress of magnitude

The Château de Vincennes reopens to the public.

After more than a decade with its heavy doors shut, the colossal keep at the Château de Vincennes (p161) reopened to the public in May 2007. Some 12 years of work have cleaned the exterior and restored the architecture and decoration inside. Visitors can now see the royal council chamber, the royal apartments, and artefacts and illuminated manuscripts from the time of Charles V. The upper floors and roof terrace of the 52-metre (170-foot) edifice, the largest fortified medieval structure in Europe, are only accessible on a guided group visit; ring for details.

The château is not exactly handsome: the massive complex is a forbidding mix of medieval and 17th-century military architecture. However, it's dripping with history; parts are older than the Louvre. At various times it was used as as a prison, and famous inmates have included Louis XIV's finance minister Nicolas Fouquet – banged up for building himself a palace at Vaux-le-Vicomte whose splendour rivalled the king's – and the writers Mirabeau, Diderot and the Marquis de Sade. The English architect John Vanbrugh was also incarcerated here in the late 17th century, and some scholars say his design for Blenheim Palace owes something to his time at Vincennes.

People weren't just banged up; some were banged into the next world. The Duc d'Enghien, author of a failed coup against Napoleon, met the firing squad in the grounds in 1804; Mata-Hari was shot here in 1917. But perhaps the oddest event at the Château is one that never came to pass. In 1964, Charles de Gaulle decided the Palais de l'Elysée wasn't grand enough to be the president's official residence, and set in motion plans to move it to Vincennes. His workload got the better of the scheme, but you have to ask: what was he thinking?

Boulogne, when forest was landscaped for Baron Haussmann. A fine place to escape city living, you'll find cycle paths, picnic areas, a Buddhist temple, a baseball field, Paris-themed crazy golf, a small farm and the ever-active Cartoucherie theatre complex here. There's also boating on offer on Lac Daumesnil, and regular concerts on summer weekends. On the park's northern edge, the Château de Vincennes (01.48.08.31.20), which is open to visitors, still houses an army garrison; see box p160.

Cité des Sciences et de l'Industrie

La Villette, 30 av Corentin-Cariou, 19th (01.40.05.70.00/www.cite-sciences.fr). M° Porte de la Villette. **Open** 10am-6pm Tue-Sat; 10am-7pm Sun. Closed public hols. **Admission** €7.50; free-€5.50 reductions.

The modern science museum at La Villette pulls in some five million visitors each year. The awaiting show whisks you through space, life, matter and communication, where scale models of satellites, planes and robots and interactive exhibits make for an exciting journey.

Disneyland Paris/ Walt Disney Studios

Marne-la-Vallée (08.25.30.60.30/UK 0870 503 0303/www.disneylandparis.com). RER A or TGV Marne-la-Vallée-Chessy. **Open** *Sept-mid July* 10am-8pm Mon-Fri; 9am-8pm Sat, Sun. *Mid July-Aug* 9am-11pm daily. **Admission** *Disneyland Park or Walt Disney Studio Park* €43; €35 3s-11s; free under-3s. *One-day Hopper for both parks* €53; €45 3s-11s; free under-3s. *Three-day Hopper* €115; €95 3s-11s; free under-3s.

The giant theme park to the east of the capital is Europe's most popular tourist attraction: millions come here every year. For Brits, there's a direct Eurostar service from London. Attractions include the white-knuckle rides of Adventureland and Frontierland, as well as the film-themed fun of the Walt Disney Studios; Disneyland Paris also comes into its own at Hallowe'en and Christmas, when there are parades. In 2008 the Twilight Zone Tower of Terror launches and is expected to become the top attraction in the resort.

Musée de la Musique

221 av Jean-Jaurès, 19th (01.44.84.44.84/www.cite-musique.fr). M° Porte

Bois de Vincennes p159

Disneyland Paris p161

de Pantin. **Open** noon-6pm Tue-Sat; 10am-6pm Sun. **Admission** €7; free-€5.60 reductions.

Alongside the concert hall, the innovative music museum houses a restored collection of instruments from the old Conservatoire, interactive computers and scale models of opera houses and concert halls. The musical commentary is a joy, playing the appropriate instrument as you approach each exhibit.

Event highlights 'Richard Wagner, Vision d'Artiste' (25 Oct 2007-20 Jan 2008).

Parc de La Villette

av Corentin-Cariou/av Jean-Jaurès, 19th (01.40.03.75.03/www.villette.com). M° Porte de La Villette or Porte de Pantin.

Formerly the city's main cattle market and abattoir, La Villette now contains the Cité des Sciences et de l'Industrie, the spherical La Géode IMAX cinema and the Argonaute submarine. Dotted with red pavilions and folies, the park is a feast, with lawns, playgrounds and ten themed gardens.

South

Bibliothèque Nationale de France François Mitterrand

quai François-Mauriac, 13th (01.53.79.59.59/www.bnf.fr). M° Bibliothèque François Mitterrand or Quai de la Gare. **Open** 2-7pm Mon; 9am-7pm Tue-Sat; 1-7pm Sun. **Admission** *1 day* €3.30; *2 weeks* €20.

The national library was the last and costliest of Mitterrand's *grands projets*. Its design, controversially, hides readers underground and stores the millions of books in four L-shaped glass towers. In the central void is a garden with 140 trees. The library is open to the public.

Parc André Citroën

rue Balard, rue St-Charles or quai Citroën, 15th. M° Javel. **Open** 8am-dusk Mon-Fri; 9am-dusk Sat, Sun, public hols.

This park is a postmodern version of a French formal garden by Gilles Clément and Alain Prévost. It has glasshouses, computerised fountains, waterfalls and

themed gardens. The tethered Eutelsat helium balloon takes visitors up for panoramic views in fair weather.

Piscine Josephine Baker

NEW *Port de la Gare, quai de la Gare, 13th (01.56.61.96.50). M° Bibliothèque François Mitterrand.* **Open** times vary. **Admission** €2.60; €1.50 reductions.
Paris's newest and coolest swimming pool opened in the summer of 2006, and was the focal point of the Left Bank part of the Paris-Plage jamboree. The pool is contained by a giant, purpose-built barge that floats on the Seine by the four towers of the Bibliothèque Nationale: it has a 500sq m (5000sq ft) sundeck, a café, a poolside area for 500 people and a sliding glass roof.

Versailles

Centuries of makeovers have made Versailles the most sumptuous château in the world. Architect Louis Le Vau first embellished the original building – a hunting lodge built during Louis XIII's reign – when Louis XIV saw Vaux-le-Vicomte, the impressive home of his finance minister, Nicolas Fouquet. The Sun King had Fouquet locked up, but gave work to his architect, his painter, Charles Le Brun, and his landscaper, André Le Nôtre, who laid out terraces, parterres, fountains and lush groves.

After Le Vau's death in 1670, Jules Hardouin-Mansart took over as principal architect, transforming Versailles into the château we know today, adding the two main wings, the Cour des Ministres and the Chapelle Royale. In 1682 Louis moved himself and his court in – and rarely set foot in Paris. In the 1770s, Louis XV had Jacques-Ange Gabriel add the Opéra Royal. With the fall of the monarchy in 1792, most of the furniture was lost, but the château was saved from demolition after 1830 by Louis-Philippe.

Versailles has hosted the official signings of many historic treaties – European recognition of the United States, the unification of Germany in 1871, the division of Europe after 1918 – and is still used by the French government for summits. In the gardens, the Grand Trianon accommodates heads of state.

The gardens are works of art in themselves. On summer weekends, the spectacular jets of water are set to music, a prelude to the firework displays of the Fêtes de Nuit. Beyond the gardens are the Grand Canal and the wooded parkland and sheep-filled pastures of the estate's park. Hidden here are the Grand Trianon, the Petit Trianon – and Marie Antoinette's play village. Outside are the Sun King's garden and stables, today housing the Académie du Spectacle Equestre.

Versailles is currently undergoing an overhaul. The first phase will run until 2010; the famous Hall of Mirrors reopened, looking fabulous, in spring 2007.

Parc André Citroën p162

Château de Versailles

78000 Versailles (01.30.83.76.20/ advance tickets 08.92.68.46.94/www. chateauversailles.fr). **Open** *Apr-Oct* 9am-6.30pm Tue-Sun. *Nov-Mar* 9am-5.30pm Tue-Sun. **Admission** €13.50; €10 after 4pm; free under-18s.

Allow a whole day to appreciate the sumptuous State Apartments and the Hall of Mirrors, the highlights of any visit. The Grand Appartement, where Louis XIV held court, houses six gilded salons. The Queen's Apartment includes the Queen's Bedroom, where royal births took place in full view of the court. Hardouin-Mansart's Hall of Mirrors is where a united Germany was proclaimed in 1871 and the Treaty of Versailles signed in 1919. It was here that the Sun King would hold extravagant receptions.

Domaine de Versailles

Gardens **Open** *Apr-Oct* 7am-dusk daily. *Nov-Mar* 8am-dusk daily. **Admission** *Winter* free. *Summer* €3; free-€1.50 reductions. *Grandes Eaux Musicales* (01.30.83.78.88). **Open** *Apr-June, Oct* Sun. *July-Sept* Sat, Sun. **Admission** €7; free-€5.50 reductions. *Park* **Open** dawn-dusk daily. **Admission** free.

The meticulously planned gardens consist of parterres, ponds, statues and a series of fountains. On weekend afternoons from spring to autumn, these great fountains are set in action to music for the 'Grandes Eaux Musicales' – and serve as a backdrop for the Fêtes de Nuit, reviving the splendour of the Sun King's celebrations with fireworks and music.

Grand Trianon/ Petit Trianon

Open *Apr-Oct* noon-6.30pm daily. *Nov-Mar* noon-5.30pm daily. **Admission** *Summer* €9; €5 after 3.30pm; free under-18s. *Winter* €5; free under-18s.

Louis XIV had Hardouin-Mansart build the pink marble Grand Trianon in the park, away from the court. Here Louis, his children's governess, and his secret second wife, Madame de Maintenon, could admire the intimate gardens from the colonnaded portico. It still retains the Empire decor of Napoléon, who stayed here with his second Empress, Marie-Louise. The Petit Trianon, built for Louis XV's mistress Madame de Pompadour, is a wonderful example of neoclassicism. Marie-Antoinette took this as her main residence, and had the gardens include an open-air theatre and her fairytale farm and dairy.

Getting there

By car

20km (12.5 miles) by the A13 or D10.

By train

Take the RER C5 (VICK or VERO trains) to Versailles-Rive Gauche or take a Transilien SNCF train from Gare St-Lazare to Versailles-Rive Droit.

Tourist information

Office de Tourisme

2bis av de Paris, 78000 Versailles (01.39.24.88.88/www.versailles-tourisme.com). **Open** 11am-5pm Mon, Sun; 9am-6pm Tue-Sat.

Essentials

L'Hôtel p178

Hotels

As with London and New York, the hotel marketplace is in ruddy health in Paris: hotels are opened, reopened, renovated and/or reinvented all the time. The biggest new arrivals are the **Hôtel Fouquet's Barrière Champs-Elysées**, a luxury four-star with spa, and, also by the Champs-Elysées, the **Hôtel Daniel** – only the second Relais & Châteaux hotel to set up in Paris. And then there's the wacky **Hôtel Amour**, which pushes the art in art hotel to the max.

Whatever your needs, there'll be a Paris hotel to fit the bill. We've found the best in each category, from marble-clad palaces to cosy hotels with bare-stone breakfast rooms. We've also got budget addresses where you needn't stay any longer than it takes for a shower and some shut-eye.

We've divided the hotels into four categories, according to the price for one night in a double room with shower/bath facilities: Deluxe €300+ **€€€€**; Expensive €200-€300 **€€€**; Moderate €100-€200 **€€**; Budget up to €100 **€**.

Timings and rates

Hotels are often booked solid during the major trade fairs (January, May, September), and it's extremely hard to find a quality pillow during fashion weeks (January, March, early July and October). At the quieter times of July and August, hotels can offer reasonable deals at short notice; phone ahead or check their websites to find out.

Same-day reservations can be arranged in person for a nominal commission fee at the **Office de Tourisme de Paris** (see p188).

Of the many discount websites www.parishotels.com guarantees the lowest prices online.

Champs-Elysées & Western Paris

Four Seasons George V

31 av George V, 8th (01.49.52.70.00/fax 01.49.52.70.10/www.fourseasons.com). M° George V or Alma Marceau. **€€€€**.

There's no denying that the George V is serious about luxury: chandeliers, marble and tapestries; almost over-attentive staff; glorious flower arrangements; divine bathrooms; and ludicrously comfortable beds in some of the largest bedrooms in Paris. The Versailles-inspired spa includes whirlpools, saunas and an impressive menu of treatments for an unabashedly metrosexual clientele; non-guests may reserve appointments in the week, and it's worth every euro.

Hôtel le A

4 rue d'Artois, 8th (01.42.56.99.99/fax 01.42.56.99.90/www.paris-hotel-a.com). M° St-Philippe-du-Roule or Franklin D Roosevelt. **€€€€**.

The black-and-white decor of this smart designer hotel is popular with models, artists and media types in the lounge bar area; splashes of colour come from conceptual artist Fabrice Hybert. The 26 rooms all have granite bathrooms, and the starched white furniture slipcovers, changed after each guest, make the smallish spaces seem larger than they are. The dimmer switches are a nice touch – as are the lift lights swiftly changing colour as you pass each floor.

Hôtel Daniel

NEW *8 rue Frédéric-Bastiat, 8th (01.42.56.17.00/fax 01.42.56.17.01/www.hoteldanielparis.com). M° St-Philippe-du-Roule or Franklin D Roosevelt.* **€€€€**.

The city's second Relais & Châteaux hotel (the first was the Hôtel de Vigny, see p169) is only a five-minute walk from the Champs-Elysées, but it feels

SHORTLIST

Best new
- Duo (p174)
- Hôtel Daniel (p167)
- Hôtel Fouquet's Barrière (p169)

Best bargains
- Grand Hôtel Jeanne d'Arc (p174)
- Hôtel Chopin (p170)
- Le Quartier République (p177)
- Regents Hôtel (p178)

Best concept
- Hôtel Amour (p173)
- Kube Rooms & Bar (p173)

Best luxury
- Four Seasons George V (p167)
- Hôtel de Crillon (p170)
- Le Meurice (p171)
- Hôtel Ritz (p171)

Best hotel bars
- Hôtel Plaza Athénée (p169)
- Kube Rooms & Bar (p173)
- Murano Urban Resort (p174)

Best bathrooms
- Hôtel le A (p167)
- Hôtel Edouard VII (p171)
- Hôtel de Vigny (p169)
- Le Montalembert (p177)

Best spas
- InterContinental Paris Le Grand (p170)
- Le Meurice (p171)
- Hôtel Fouquet's Barrière (p169)

Best alfresco breakfast
- Hôtel des Grandes Ecoles (p180)
- Hôtel des Marronniers (p178)
- Regents Hôtel (p178)

Illustrious guests
- L'Hôtel (p178)
- Hôtel Istria Saint Germain (p181)
- Hôtel Ritz (p171)

like a world apart. A romantic gem, it's decorated in chinoiserie and a palette of rich colours, with 26 rooms cosily appointed in toile de Jouy (the top floors have private balconies and great views) and an intricately hand-painted restaurant that feels like a courtyard.

Hôtel Fouquet's Barrière

NEW *46av George V, 8th (01.40.70.05.05/www.fouquets-barriere.com). M° George V.* €€€€.

The long-awaited hotel adjoining iconic Champs-Elysées brasserie Fouquet's occupies five buildings remodelled by the unlikely combination of decorator Jacques Garcia and architect Edouard François. At times it seems to confound luxury with scale: big rooms, gigantic wardrobes and vast quilted bedheads. Amusing touches include François's aluminium chestnut branches that stretch across the courtyard façade, and there's plenty of glitz; but the interiors lack Garcia's usual tongue-in-cheek touch. A restaurant in a glass-fronted rotunda provides modern fare centred around a featured product, and the massive basement spa includes a swimming pool and water treatments devised by Villa Thalgo.

Hôtel Fouquet's Barrière

Hôtel Plaza Athénée

25 av Montaigne, 8th (01.53.67.66.67/fax 01.53.67.66.66/www.plaza-athenee-paris.com). M° Alma Marceau. €€€€.

This palace is ideally sited for Chanel, Vuitton, Dior and other 8th boutiques. Material girls and boys will enjoy the high-tech room amenities such as remote-controlled air-con and video game access on the TV via infra-red keyboard, and mini hi-fi. A stylish bar has modern decor, a cool cocktail list and staff who know what service is.

Hôtel de Sers

41 av Pierre-1er-de-Serbie, 8th (01.53.23.75.75/fax 01.53.23.75.76/www.hoteldesers.com). M° George V or Alma Marceau. €€€€.

The dowdy old Hôtel Queen Elizabeth was completely gutted and reopened in 2004 as the Hôtel de Sers, with a highly ambitious mix of minimalist contemporary furnishings (often with deep red and mauve highlights, though, nothing too austere), plus a few pop art accessories and leftover 19th-century features such as the grand staircase.

Hôtel de Vigny

9-11 rue Balzac, 8th (01.42.99.80.80/fax 01.42.99.80.40/www.hoteldevigny.com). M° George V. €€€€.

The first Relais & Châteaux hotel in Paris has the feel of a plush townhouse: it's a discreet hotel that pulls in a low-key clientele. Its 37 rooms and suites have marble bathrooms and individual decor in tasteful striped or floral fabrics. You can enjoy dinner in the art deco Baretto restaurant, or a cup of tea in front of the library fireplace.

Le Sezz

W6 av Frémiet, 16th (01.56.75.26.26/fax 01.56.75.26.16/www.hotelsezz.com). M° Passy. €€€€.

Set in the upmarket 16th, sexy boutique hotel Le Sezz opened its doors in 2005 with some 27 suites all meticulously crafted by sought-after French

Hôtel Daniel p167

furniture designer Christophe Pillet. Daring decor includes black parquet flooring, rough-hewn stone walls, camp-style beds placed in the centre of each suite, and one-way glass in the stylish bathrooms.

Opéra to Les Halles

InterContinental Paris Le Grand

2 rue Scribe, 9th (01.40.07.32.32/ fax 01.42.66.12.51/www.paris-le-grand.intercontinental.com). M° Opéra. **€€€€**.

This 1862 landmark hotel is the chain's European flagship – but, given its size, perhaps 'mother ship' would be more appropriate: the hotel occupies the entire block (three wings, almost 500 rooms) next to the opera house. In addition to a stylish allure and technical convenience bestowed by a recent multi-million-euro refit – the work of illustrious decorator Pierre-Yves Rochon, who also did up the George V – the space under the vast *verrière* is one of the best oases in town. Spa and sea-water treatments, too.

Hôtel Brighton

218 rue de Rivoli, 1st (01.47.03.61.61/ fax 01.42.60.41.78/www.esprit-de-france.com). M° Tuileries. **€€**.

With several rooms overlooking the Tuileries garden, this hotel is very good value. The Brighton, all faux-marble and mosaic decor, was opened at the beginning of the 20th century as the Entente Cordiale got under way, and has recently been restored. Rooms are spacious; for a good view, make sure you book well in advance.

Hôtel Chopin

10 bd Montmartre, 9th (01.47.70.58.10/fax 01.42.47.00.70/www.hotelbretonnerie.com/chopin.htm). M° Grands Boulevards. **€**.

Nicely located in a historic, glass-roofed arcade, the Chopin's original 1846 façade adds to the old-fashioned appeal. The 36 quiet and functional bedrooms have salmon-coloured walls and green carpet. A low-cost favourite.

Hôtel de Crillon

10 pl de la Concorde, 8th (01.44.71.15.00/fax 01.44.71.15.02/www.crillon.com). M° Concorde. **€€€€**.

The height of neo-classical magnificence, the Crillon lives up to its *palais* reputation with decor strong on marble, mirrors and gold leaf. The Michelin-starred Les Ambassadeurs has an acclaimed chef, and the Winter Garden tearoom has a gorgeous terrace and live harp music. Classes given here by top floral designers show how to recreate those trendy flower arrangements seen throughout the hotel. A gym, business centre, bar and free parking add to the attraction for high-end guests.

Hôtel Edouard VII

39 av de l'Opéra, 2nd (01.42.61.56.90/ fax 01.42.61.47.73/www.edouard7 hotel.com). M° Opéra. **€€€€**.

Owned by the same family for five generations, this refined hotel includes artful touches such as Murano glass lights, smooth wooden features and contemporary sculptures around the entrance hall. The stylish bar and restaurant Angl'Opéra (presided over by resident star chef Gilles Choukroun) is decked out in dark mahogany and comfortable stripes. Some of the individually decorated bedrooms offer wonderful balcony views of the Garnier opera house.

Hôtel Madeleine Opéra

12 rue Greffulhe, 8th (01.47.42. 26.26/fax 01.47.42.89.76/www. hotel-madeleine-opera.com). M° Madeleine. **€**.

This bargain hotel is situated just north of the Eglise Madeleine, in the heart of the city's theatre and *grands magasins* districts. Its sunny lobby sits behind a 200-year-old façade that was once a shopfront. The 24 rooms are perhaps a touch basic, but are still pleasant enough, and breakfast is brought to your room every morning.

Hôtel Ritz

15 pl Vendôme, 1st (01.43.16.30.30/ fax 01.43.16.31.78/www.ritzparis.com). M° Concorde or Opéra. **€€€€**.

The grande dame of Paris hotels has proffered hospitality to Coco Chanel, the Duke of Windsor, and Dodi and Di. Today's guests have the choice of 162 bedrooms, of which 56 are suites, from the romantic Frédéric Chopin to the glitzy Impérial. There are plenty of corners in which to strike poses or quench a thirst, from Hemingway's elegant cigar bar and the plush Victorian champagne bar to the poolside one inspired by ancient Greece.

Le Meurice

228 rue de Rivoli, 1st (01.44.58.10.10/ fax 01.44.58.10.15/www.lemeurice. com). M° Tuileries. **€€€€**.

Having spruced up its extravagant Louis XVI decor and intricate mosaic tiled floors in a lengthy facelift, Le Meurice is looking absolutely splendid. All of its 160 rooms are done out in distinct historical styles; among the 36 suites (25 full and 11 junior), the Belle Etoile on the seventh floor provides 360-degree panoramic views of Paris from its terrace. You can relax by the Winter Garden to regular jazz performances; for more intensive intervention head over to the lavishly appointed spa with its *vinothérapie* treatments – or get grape products directly into your bloodstream at the high-ceilinged Bar Fontainebleau.

Résidence Hôtel des Trois Poussins

15 rue Clauzel, 9th (01.53.32.81.81/fax 01.53.32.81.82/www.les3poussins.com). M° St Georges. **€€**.

Just off the beaten track in a pleasant *quartier*, and within uphill walking distance of Montmartre, the Résidence offers hotel accommodation in the traditional manner, but also self-catering studios with small kitchenettes. The decor is equally traditional, with a strange preference for yellow.

Montmartre & Pigalle

Blanche Hôtel

69 rue Blanche, 9th (01.48.74.16.94/ fax 01.49.95.95.98). M° Blanche. **€**.

If you're prepared to forgo frills and don't mind the rather racy aspect of the neighbourhood, this is a good-value bet. The interior is far from palatial

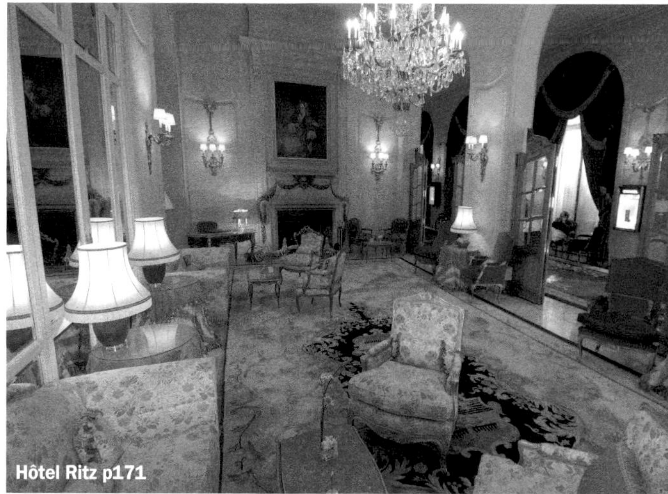
Hôtel Ritz p171

and features 1970s furniture, but the rooms are a pretty good size and there's a bar in the lobby.

Hôtel Amour

8 rue de Navarin, 9th (01.48.78. 31.80/fax 01.42.05.21.01/www.hotel amour.com). M° St Georges. **€€.**

Graffiti artist André and creative partner Lionel (the team behind nightclubs Le Baron, see p64, and Paris Paris, see p81) have created one of the most talked-about hotels for years. Each of its 20 rooms is unique, decorated according to the theme of love by a coterie of contemporary artists. Seven rooms contain installations, two others have a private bar and large terrace. Details are quirky, colourful and risqué, the crowd is beautiful and staff are charming.

Hôtel Roma Sacré-Coeur

101 rue Caulaincourt, 18th (01.42.62. 02.02/fax 01.42.54.34.92/www.hotel roma.fr). M° Lamarck Caulaincourt. **€€.**

This hotel on the trendier, north side of Montmartre, away from the postcard shops and coach parties, is still within walking distance (albeit uphill) of Sacré-Coeur. From the modest lobby, an Astroturf-covered staircase leads to the 57 rooms, simply decorated in pastels; the priciest ones enjoy views of the basilica. Air-conditioned rooms are also available for an extra €10 per day.

Kube Rooms & Bar

1-5 impasse Ruelle, 18th (01.42.05. 20.00/fax 01.42.05.21.01/www.kube hotel.com). M° La Chapelle. **€€€€.**

The younger sibling of the Murano is a more affordable design hotel, with a lounge atmosphere and the city's first ice bar. Once they get past security, visitors step into the courtyard of a 19th-century building. Within, a solitary glass cube houses the hotel's reception desk. Upstairs, the Ice Kube bar serves a range of vodkas in glasses that, like the furnishings, are carved from ice. Fortunately for serious drinkers, access to the hotel's 41 rooms – with cool details such as beds lit from underneath – is gained by fingerprint technology.

Royal Fromentin

11 rue Fromentin, 9th (01.48.74.85.93/ fax 01.42.81.02.33/www.hotelroyal fromentin.com). M° Pigalle. **€€.**

Wood panelling, art deco windows and a vintage glass lift echo the hotel's origins as a cabaret hall; its theatrical feel attracted Blondie and Nirvana. The 47 rooms, many overlooking Sacré-Coeur, have been renovated in French style, with bright fabrics.

The Marais & Eastern Paris

Duo

NEW *11 rue du Temple, 4th (01.42.72.72.22/fax 01.42.72.03.53/www.duoparis.com). M° Hôtel de Ville.* **€€.**

Formerly the Axial Beaubourg, this stylish boutique hotel has expanded (under the same management): it now occupies the Axial space and the building next door. It's decorated with white marble floors, mud-coloured walls, crushed-velvet sofas and exposed beams, and is just a few yards from the Centre Pompidou. Its bedrooms are not particularly large, but exude refinement and comfort. Great value.

Grand Hôtel Jeanne d'Arc

3 rue de Jarente, 4th (01.48.87.62.11/fax 01.48.87.37.31/www.hoteljeannedarc.com). M° St-Paul. **€.**

This hotel's strong point is its location on a quiet road near pretty place du Marché-Ste-Catherine. A recent refurbishment has made the reception area striking, and the huge mirror adds wow value and the illusion of extra space. The bedrooms are colourful (you like orange, right?) and, for the price, are all well sized, comfortable and clean.

Hôtel Beaumarchais

3 rue Oberkampf, 11th (01.53.36.86.86/fax 01.43.38.32.86/www.hotelbeaumarchais.com). M° Filles du Calvaire or Oberkampf. **€€.**

This contemporary hotel in the bar-starred Oberkampf area is also within walking distance of the Marais and Bastille. Its 31 bedrooms are brightly decorated (colourful walls, mosaics in the bathrooms, wavy headboards and Milan glass bedside lamps); breakfast is served on the garden patio in summer.

Hôtel Bourg Tibourg

19 rue du Bourg-Tibourg, 4th (01.42.78.47.39/fax 01.40.29.07.00/www.hotelbourgtibourg.com). M° Hôtel de Ville. **€€€.**

This is a jewel box of a boutique hotel. Aside from its enviable site in the heart of the Marais and its fashion-pack fans, miniature Bourg Tibourg is all about Jacques Garcia's neo-Gothic-cum-Byzantine decor. Scented candles, mosaic-tiled bathrooms, luxurious fabrics in rich colours and the cool contrast of crisp white linens create the perfect escape.

Hôtel du Petit Moulin

29 rue de Poitou, 3rd (01.42.74.10.10/fax 01.42.74.10.97/www.hoteldupetitmoulin.com). M° St-Sébastien Froissart. **€€€.**

Within striking distance of the Musée Picasso and the trendy shops on and around rue Charlot, this listed façade masks what was once the oldest boulangerie in Paris, restored as a boutique hotel by Nadia Murano and Denis Nourry. They recruited fashion designer Christian Lacroix for the decor, and the result is a riot of colour and trompe l'oeil effects. Each of its 17 exquisitely appointed rooms is unique, and three feature drawings from Lacroix's sketchbook.

Mercure Terminus Est

5 rue du Huit-Mai 1945, 10th (01.55.26.05.05/fax 01.55.26.05.00/www.mercure.com). M° Gare de l'Est. **€€.**

Conveniently located opposite the Gare de l'Est, this great railway hotel combines modern interior design with elements that evoke the classic age of steam: leather luggage handles on the wardrobes, retro bathroom fittings and a library in the lobby. The 200 rooms and public areas offer wireless internet.

Murano Urban Resort

13 bd du Temple, 3rd (01.42.71.20.00/fax 01.42.71.21.01/www.muranoresort.com). M° Filles du Calvaire or Oberkampf. **€€€€.**

Behind this unremarkable façade is a super-cool and luxurious hotel popular

Hôtel Amour p173

with the fashion set for its slick design and high-tech flourishes – like Bang & Olufsen sound systems and coloured-light co-ordinators that allow you to change the mood of your room. The bar has 140 varieties of vodka, which can bring the op-art fabrics in the lift to life and make the fingerprint room access a godsend. Nine suites, two with pools.

Le Quartier République, Le Marais

NEW *39 rue Jean-Pierre-Timbaud, 11th (01.48.06.64.97/www.lghhotels.com). M° Filles du Calvaire.* **€€**.
See box p179.

Seine & the Islands

Hôtel des Deux-Iles

59 rue St-Louis-en-l'Ile, 4th (01.43.26.13.35/fax 01.43.29.60.25/www.deuxiles-paris-hotel.com). M° Pont Marie. **€€**.
This peaceful 17th-century townhouse offers 17 soundproofed, air-conditioned rooms done out in faintly colonial style. Attractive features include a tiny courtyard off the lobby, and a vaulted stone breakfast room with fireplace. The Hôtel Lutèce, at No.65 (01.43.26.23.52), is under the same management.

Hôtel du Jeu de Paume

54 rue St-Louis-en-l'Ile, 4th (01.43.26.14.18/fax 01.40.46.02.76/www.jeudepaumehotel.com). M° Pont Marie. **€€€€**.
With a discreet courtyard entrance, original 17th-century beams, private garden and a unique timbered breakfast room that was once a real tennis court built under Louis XIII, this really is a charming hotel. It's now filled with an expertly slung-together array of modern and classical art. A dramatic glass lift and catwalks lead to the bedrooms.

7th & West

Grand Hôtel Lévêque

29 rue Cler, 7th (01.47.05.49.15/fax 01.45.50.49.36/www.hotel-leveque.com). M° Ecole Militaire. **€**.
Recently renovated complete with air-conditioning, the Lévêque is excellent value for its location on the market street rue Cler. A charming tiled entrance leads to 50 well-equipped rooms, all with sparkling bathrooms, except the basin-only singles.

Hôtel Duc de Saint-Simon

14 rue de St-Simon, 7th (01.44.39.20.20/fax 01.45.48.68.25/www.hotelducdesaintsimon.com). M° Rue du Bac. **€€€**.
A lovely courtyard leads the way into this popular hotel situated on the fringes of St-Germain-des-Prés. Of the 34 bedrooms, four have terraces over a closed-off leafy garden. It's perfect for lovers, though if you can do without a four-poster bed, there are more spacious rooms here than the Honeymoon Suite.

Hôtel Eiffel Rive Gauche

6 rue du Gros-Caillou, 7th (01.45.51.24.56/fax 01.45.51.11.77/www.hotel-eiffel.com). M° Ecole Militaire. **€**.
The Provençal decor and warm welcome make this a nice retreat. For the quintessential Paris view at a bargain price, ask for one of the upper floors: you can see the Eiffel Tower from nine of the 29 bedrooms. All of them feature Empire-style bedheads and modern bathrooms. There's also a tiny, tiled courtyard with a bridge.

Le Montalembert

3 rue de Montalembert, 7th (01.45.49.68.68/fax 01.45.49.69.49/www.montalembert.com). M° Rue du Bac or Solférino. **€€€€**.
This boutique hotel opened in 1989 and is a benchmark of quality. It has everything mode maniacs could ever wish for: bathrooms stuffed with Contemporel toiletries, a set of digital scales and 360° mirrors to check that silhouette. It's decorated in pale lilac, cinnamon and olive tones, and has wireless access and a modern vibe.

Le Walt

37 av de La Motte-Picquet, 7th (01.45.51.55.83/fax 01.47.05.77.59/www.inwoodhotel.com). M° Ecole Militaire. **€€€**.

ESSENTIALS

At this boutique hotel, walk the spotlit red carpet to your room, each decorated in chocolate tones, with wooden floors, walnut furniture and, above the bed, a giant painting. Many on the sixth floor have views of the Eiffel Tower. The restaurant, decorated in burgundy velour and caramel, with purple gossamer curtains, spills out into a little courtyard on warmer days.

St-Germain-des-Prés & Odéon

Le Clos Médicis

56 rue Monsieur-le-Prince, 6th (01.43.29.10.80/fax 01.43.54.26.90/www.closmedicis.com). M° Odéon. **€€**.

Designed more like a stylish, private townhouse than a hotel, Le Clos Médicis is located by the Luxembourg garden: perfect if you fancy a stroll among the trees. The decor is modern and chic, with rooms done out in taffeta curtains and chenille bedcoverings, and antique floor tiles in the bathrooms. The cosy lounge contains a working fireplace.

Grand Hôtel de l'Univers

6 rue Grégoire-de-Tours, 6th (01.43.29.37.00/fax 01.40.51.06.45/www.hotel-paris-univers.com). M° Odéon. **€€**.

Making the most of its 15th-century origins, this hotel has bare beams, high ceilings and antique furniture. Manuel Canovas fabrics lend a posh touch, but there are also practical features such as a laptop for rent. The same helpful team runs nearby Hôtel St-Germain-des-Prés (36 rue Bonaparte, 6th, 01.43.26.00.19, fax 01.40.46.83.63, www.hotel-paris-saint-germain.com), which can boast a medieval-themed room and the sweetest attic in Paris.

L'Hôtel

13 rue des Beaux-Arts, 6th (01.44.41.99.00/fax 01.43.25.64.81/www.l-hotel.com). M° St-Germain-des-Prés. **€€€€**.

Guests at the glam L'Hôtel are more likely to be models and film stars than the starving writers who frequented the place during Oscar Wilde's final days. Under Jacques Garcia's careful restoration, each room has its own special theme: Mistinguett's chambre retains its art deco mirror bed, and Oscar's deathbed room has, appropriately, been decorated with green peacock murals. Make sure you don't miss the cellar swimming pool and fumoir.

Hôtel du Globe

15 rue des Quatre-Vents, 6th (01.43.26.35.50/fax 01.46.33.62.69/www.hotel-du-globe.fr). M° Odéon. **€€**.

The Globe has retained much of its 17th-century character – and very pleasant it is, too. Gothic wrought-iron doors lead into florid corridors, and an unexplained suit of armour supervises guests from a post in the miniature salon. The rooms with baths are a bit bigger than those with showers and there is a four-poster bed to be had as well. All 14 rooms were completely renovated in 2004. Take care on the small, winding staircase.

Hôtel Lutetia

45 bd Raspail, 6th (01.49.54.46.46/fax 01.49.54.46.00/www.lutetia-paris.com). M° Sèvres Babylone. **€€€€**.

This historic Left Bank hotel is a masterpiece of art nouveau and art deco architecture dating from 1910. The 250 rooms, revamped in purple, gold and pearl grey, have a 1930s feel. Its plush jazz bar and lively brasserie also face the fashionable Le Bon Marché department store across the road.

Hôtel des Marronniers

21 rue Jacob, 6th (01.43.25.30.60/fax 01.40.46.83.56/www.paris-hotel-marronniers.com). M° St-Germain-des-Prés. **€€**.

Hidden in the heart of St-Germain through a leafy courtyard, this hotel offers peace and quiet. Afternoon tea is served in the lovely conservatory overlooking a garden at the back, where you'll find the chestnut trees that give the hotel its name. The 37 rooms are mostly reasonably sized.

Regents Hôtel

44 rue Madame, 6th (01.45.48.02.81/fax 01.45.44.85.73). M° St-Sulpice. **€**.

Chic on the cheap

Le Quartier République, Le Marais

Boutique hotels are all fine and dandy, but unless you're happy to spend at least €300 a night, all you are likely to see of them is their designer bar. So where can the city-break urbanite find a cool spot in which to cop some zeds without having to pay a fortune in hotel rates – or taxi fares? Where can they enjoy a late, hangover-friendly breakfast, a sauna, gym and a cocktail bar?

Thankfully, the LGH mini-chain (www.lghhotels.com) of hotels fills just that gap. The current roster of three venues (there's a fourth opening later in 2007, and one in Toulouse) all occupy sites in Paris's prime nightlife areas: Le Quartier République, Le Marais (see p177) is, despite the name, near the bar haven of Oberkampf; and Le Quartier Bastille, Le Faubourg is located exactly where its name suggests. As well as providing convenience to the discerning bar-hopper, all bear the low-key, minimalist hallmarks of designer Jean-Philippe Nuël, responsible for the Sofitel at La Défense and in Budapest.

This is particularly striking in the case of Le Quartier République, Le Marais, whose old building was given a floor-by-floor revamp in spring 2007. Still, remarkably, it's a two-star (you can nab one of six superior doubles for €105), and equipped with a modest gym; all in all, a welcome find close to the action.

If comfort (or late cocktails) are a greater priority, flagship hotel Le Général is your spot. It's practical, emininently chic and located just two steps from République; it also has a sauna, proper bar, recently trendified bathrooms and Gautier-style 'tattoo' art on the wall. Room service, including drinks 24/7, involves smoked fish carpaccio or duck breast. All branches provide tranquillity in the fashionably furnished rooms.

It's a treat to find a budget option with style, and this discreet hotel located in a quiet street is a lovely surprise. It has a courtyard garden, which is used for breakfast, and the reception rooms are decked out in sunny Provençal blue and yellow. Bedrooms are comfortable with modern bathrooms. Some of them have modest balconies too.

Latin Quarter

Les Degrés de Notre-Dame

10 rue des Grands-Degrés, 5th (01.55. 42.88.88/fax 01.40.46.95.34/www. lesdegreshotel.com). M° St-Michel. €€.

On a tiny street just across the river from Notre-Dame, this vintage hotel is a real gem. All of its ten rooms are bursting with character and boast features such as original paintings, antique furniture and exposed wooden beams (Nos.47 and 501 have great views of the cathedral to boot). Les Degrés also features an adorable restaurant and, a few streets away, two studio apartments that the owner tends to rent out to his preferred customers only.

Familia Hôtel

11 rue des Ecoles, 5th (01.43.54.55.27/ fax 01.43.29.61.77/www.hotel-paris-familia.com). M° Jussieu. €€.

Set on a bustling street in the Latin Quarter, this old-fashioned hotel has balconies hung with tumbling plants and walls draped with French tapestry replicas. The 30 rooms have lots of personalised touches such as sepia murals, cherry-wood furniture and stone walls; the communal areas were refurbished in 2005. The welcoming Gaucherons also own the Minerve (www.hotel-paris-minerve.com) next door, which offers the same splendid package. Both hotels are in demand, especially in high season: be sure to book well ahead.

The Five Hotel

NEW *3 rue Flatters, 5th (01.43.31. 74.21/www.thefivehotel.com). M° Gobelins or RER Port-Royal.* €€.

One of the refreshing breed of new moderately priced design hotels, the hotel where Marie Curie lived when she arrived in Paris is now a witty confection of glittery fibre optics, lacquer artworks, bead curtains and graphic bathroom tiles, plus unique odorama effects – choose one of five fragrances (sensual, tonic, etc) to be wafted around your room. There's even a scarily suspended bed – just the thing to rock you to sleep – in the suite.

Hôtel la Demeure

51 bd St-Marcel, 13th (01.43.37.81.25/ fax 01.45.87.05.03/www.hotel-paris-lademeure.com). M° Les Gobelins. €€.

This comfortable hotel on the edge of the Latin Quarter is run by a friendly father and son. The 43 air-conditioned rooms all have internet access; the suites have sliding doors to separate sleeping and living space. Wrap-around balustrades of the corner rooms offer lovely views of the city, and bathrooms feature either luxurious tubs or shower heads with elaborate massage possibilities.

Hôtel Esmeralda

4 rue St-Julien-le-Pauvre, 5th (01.43. 54.19.20/fax 01.40.51.00.68). M° St-Michel. €.

An offbeat, Bohemian piece of historic Paris, the Esmeralda has 19 floral rooms with antique furnishings and aged wallpaper, as well as the uneven floors and wonky staircase you would expect in a building that was built in 1640. Eight of the bedrooms overlook Notre-Dame.

Hôtel des Grandes Ecoles

75 rue du Cardinal-Lemoine, 5th (01.43.26.79.23/fax 01.43.25.28. 15/www.hotel-grandes-ecoles.com). M° Cardinal Lemoine. €€.

A breath of fresh air in the heart of the Latin Quarter, this country-style hotel has 51 old-fashioned rooms set around a garden where breakfast is served in the warmer months. The largest of the three buildings houses the reception area and a stylish dining room with a gilt mirror and piano.

Hôtel Bourg Tibourg p174

Hôtel Résidence Henri IV

50 rue des Bernardins, 5th (01.44.41.31.81/fax 01.46.33.93.22/www.residencehenri4.com). M° Maubert Mutualité. **€€.**

This belle époque-style hotel has eight rooms and five apartments, so all guests can be assured of the staff's full attention. It's well situated on a quiet cul-de-sac next to leafy square Paul-Langevin, a few minutes' walk from Notre-Dame. The four-person apartment rooms come with a handy mini-kitchen – although you may be reduced to eating on the beds in some of the smaller ones.

Hôtel de la Sorbonne

6 rue Victor-Cousin, 5th (01.43.54.58.08/fax 01.40.51.05.18/www.hotelsorbonne.com). M° Cluny La Sorbonne/RER Luxembourg. **€.**

This hotel between the Luxembourg garden and the Panthéon features wooden floors, beams and a fire in the salon. The 39 rooms are pale green or lavender, with cheerful geranium-filled window boxes. Bathrooms are small but clean; choose one with a shower rather than one with a gnome-sized tub.

Montparnasse

Hôtel Aviatic

105 rue de Vaugirard, 6th (01.53.63.25.50/fax 01.53.63.25.55/www.aviatic.fr). M° Duroc. **€€.**

This historic hotel has tons of character, from the Empire-style lounge and garden atrium to the bistro-style breakfast room. The polished floor in the lobby (watch your feet) and the hints of marble and brass lend impressive touches of glamour. The more costly Supérieure rooms have such extras as bathrobes and a modem connection.

Hôtel Istria Saint Germain

29 rue Campagne-Première, 14th (01.43.20.91.82/fax 01.43.22.48.45). M° Raspail. **€€.**

This is the place where the artistic royalty of Montparnasse's heyday – Man Ray, Marcel Duchamp, Louis Aragon – once lived. The Istria has been modernised since then, but it still has lots of charm with 26 simply furnished rooms, a cosy breakfast room and comfortable living area. Film fans take note: the tiled artists' studios next door featured in Godard's *A Bout de Souffle*.

Getting Around

Airports

Roissy-Charles-de-Gaulle

01.48.62.22.80/www.paris-cdg.com. About 30km (19 miles) north-east of Paris.

For most international flights. The two main terminals are some way apart; check which one you need for your flight back. The **RER B** line (08.92.35.35.39) is the quickest way to central Paris (40mins to Gare du Nord; 45mins to RER Châtelet-Les Halles; €7.75 single). A station gives direct access from Terminal 2; from Terminal 1 take the free shuttle. Trains run every 15mins, 5.24am-11.56pm daily.

Air France buses (08.92.35.08.20, www.cars.airfrance.fr; €12 single, €18 return) leave every 15mins, 5.45am-11pm daily, from both terminals, and stop at Porte Maillot and place Charles-de-Gaulle (35-50mins trip). Buses also run to Gare Montparnasse and Gare de Lyon (€12 single, €18 return) every 30mins (45-60mins trip), 7am-9pm daily; a bus between Roissy and Orly (€16) runs every 30mins, 6am-10.30pm Mon-Fri, 7am-10.30pm Sat, Sun.

RATP Roissybus (08.92.68.77.14; €8.40) runs every 15mins, 5.45am-11pm daily, between the airport and Opéra (at least 45mins); buy your tickets on the bus.

Paris Airports Service is a 24-hour door-to-door minibus service between airports and hotels, seven days a week. Roissy prices go from €24 for one to €12.40 each person for eight people, 6am-8pm (minimum €34, 5-6am, 8-10pm); you can reserve a place on 01.55.98.10.80, www.parisairportservice.com.

A **taxi** into central Paris from Roissy-Charles-de-Gaulle airport should take 30-60mins and cost €30-€50, plus €1 per luggage item.

Orly

01.49.75.15.15/www.paris-orly.com. About 18km (11 miles) south of Paris.

Orly-Sud terminal is international and Orly-Ouest domestic. **Orlyrail** (€5.65) runs to Pont de Rungis, for the RER C into central Paris. Trains run every 15mins, 6am-11pm daily; 50mins trip.

Air France buses (08.92.35.08.20, www.cars.airfrance.fr; €8 single, €12 return) leave both terminals every 15mins, 6am-11pm daily, and stop at Invalides and Montparnasse (30-45mins).

The **RATP Orlybus** (08.92.68.77.18) runs to Denfert-Rochereau every 15mins, 5.35am-11.05pm daily (30mins trip); buy tickets (€5.80) on the bus. High-speed **Orlyval** shuttle trains run every 7mins (6am-11pm daily) to RER B station Antony (shuttle and RER together is €9.05); allow 35mins for central Paris.

Orly prices for the Paris Airports Service (*see left*) are €22 for one and €8-€14 per passenger depending on the number. A **taxi** takes 20-40mins and costs €16-€26, plus €1 per luggage item.

Paris Beauvais

08.92.68.20.66/www.aeroportbeauvais.com. 70km (43 miles) north of Paris.

Budget hub. **Buses** (€13) to Porte Maillot leave 20mins after each arrival and 3hr 15mins before each departure. Tickets from Arrivals or 1 bd Pershing, 17th (01.58.05.08.45).

Arriving by car

Cars from the UK can use tunnel **Le Shuttle** (Folkestone-Calais, 35mins, 08.10.63.03.04, www.eurotunnel.com); **Hoverspeed** (Dover-Calais, Newhaven-Dieppe, 03.21.46.14.00, www.hoverspeed.com); or **Brittany Ferries** (08.25.82.88.28, www.brittanyferries.com), **P&O Stena** (01.55.69.82.28, www.po ferries.com) and **Sea France** (08. 25.04.40.45,www.seafrance.com).

Arriving by coach

International coaches arrive at **Gare Routière Internationale Paris-Galliéni** at Porte de Bagnolet, 20th. For tickets (in English) call Eurolines on 08.92.69.52.52 or (UK) 01582 404511, www.eurolines.fr.

Arriving by rail

The Eurostar from London Waterloo (01233 617575, www.eurostar.com) to Paris Gare du Nord (08.92.35.35. 39) takes 2hrs 25mins direct; allow slightly longer for trains stopping at Ashford and Lille. You must check in at least 30mins before departure.

Maps

Free maps of the métro, bus and RER systems are available at airports and métro stations.

Public transport

RATP (08.92.68.41.14, www.ratp.fr) runs the bus, métro and suburban tram routes, as well as lines A and B of the RER express railway, which connects with the métro inside Paris. State rail SNCF (08.92.35.35.35, www. sncf.com) runs RER lines C, D and E for the suburbs.

Fares & tickets

Paris and its suburbs are divided into eight concentric travel zones, with 1 and 2 covering the city centre. RATP tickets and passes are valid on the métro, bus and RER. Tickets and carnets can be bought at métro stations, tourist offices and tobacconists; single tickets can be bought on buses. Retain your ticket in case of spot checks; you'll also need it to exit from RER stations.

A ticket is €1.40, a carnet of ten €10.90. A Mobilis day pass is €5.50 for zones 1 and 2 and €18.70 for zones 1-8 (not including airports). A three-day Paris Visite pass for zones 1-3 is €18.25; a five-day pass is €26.65, with discounts on sights.

Métro & RER

The Paris **métro** is the best way of getting around. Trains run daily 5.30am-12.40am. Numbered lines have their direction named after the last stop. Follow the orange *Correspondance* signs to change lines. The five **RER** lines run 5.30am-1am daily across Paris and into commuterland. Métro tickets are valid for RER zones 1-2.

Buses

Buses run 6.30am-8.30pm, with some routes continuing until 12.30am, Mon-Sat; limited services operate on selected lines Sun and public holidays. You can use a métro ticket, a ticket bought from the driver (€1.40) or a travel pass. Tickets should be punched in the machine next to the driver; passes should be shown to the driver.

Night buses

The 18 **Noctambus** lines run from place du Châtelet to the suburbs (hourly 1.30am-5.35am Mon-Thur; half-hourly 1am-5.35am Fri, Sat); look out for the owl logo. A ticket is €2.70 and allows one change.

River transport

Batobus

08.25.05.01.01/www.batobus.com. Feb-Mar, Oct-Dec 10am-7pm daily; *Apr-Sept* 10am-10pm daily. *One-day pass* €11 (€5, €7).

River buses stop every 15-25mins at the Eiffel Tower, Musée d'Orsay,

St-Germain-des-Prés (quai Malaquais), Notre-Dame, Jardin des Plantes, Hôtel de Ville, the Louvre, Champs-Elysées (Pont Alexandre III). Tickets are available from Batobus stops, RATP and tourist offices.

Rail travel

Versailles and Disneyland Paris are served by the RER. Most locations out of the city are served by the SNCF railway; the TGV high-speed train has slashed journey times and is steadily being extended to all the main regions. Tickets can be bought at any SNCF station (not only the one from which you'll travel), SNCF shops and travel agents. If you reserve online or by phone, you can pay and pick up your tickets from the station or have them sent to your home. SNCF automatic machines (*billeterie automatique*) only work with French credit/debit cards. Buy tickets in advance to secure the cheaper fare. Before you board any train, stamp your ticket in the orange *composteur* machines on the platforms, or you might have to pay a hefty fine.

SNCF
08.92.35.35.39/www.sncf.com.
Open 7am-10pm daily.
The line can also be reached (inside France) by dialling 3635 and saying '*billet*' at the prompt.

Taxis

Taxis are hard to find at rush hour or early in the morning. Ranks are indicated with a blue sign. A white light on a taxi's roof means it's free; an orange one means it's busy. You also pay for the time it takes your radioed taxi to arrive. Payment by credit card – mention this when you order – is €15 minimum.

Airportaxis
01.48.40.17.17/www.airportaxis.com.
Alpha
01.45.85.85.85/www.alphataxis.fr.
G7
01.47.39.47.39/in English 01.41.27.66.99/www.taxis-g7.fr.
Taxis Bleus
01.49.36.24.24/08.25.16.24.24/ 08.91.70.10.10/www.taxis-bleus.com.

Driving

If you bring your car to France, you must bring its registration and insurance documents. An insurance green card, available from insurance companies and the AA and RAC in the UK, is not compulsory but is useful. Traffic information for Ile-de-France is given at 08.26.02.20.22, www. securite routiere.gouv.fr.

Breakdown services

The AA or RAC do not have reciprocal arrangements with an equivalent organisation in France, so it's advisable to take out additional breakdown insurance cover, for example with Europ Assistance (0870 737 5700, www.europ-assistance.co.uk). If you don't have insurance, you can use its service (01.41.85.85.85), but it will charge you the full cost. Other 24-hour breakdown services in Paris include: Action Auto Assistance (01.45.58.49.58); Dan Dépann Auto (01.40.06.06.53).

Parking

There are still a few free on-street parking areas in Paris, but they're often full. If you park illegally, your car may be clamped or towed away. Don't park in zones marked for deliveries (*livraisons*) or taxis. *Horodateurs*, pay-and-display machines, which take a special card (*carte de stationnement* at

€15 or €30, from tobacconists). Parking is often free at weekends, after 7pm in the evening and in August. Underground car parks cost €2.50 per hour, €20 for 24 hours. Some have lower rates after 6pm and offer season tickets. See www.parkingsdeparis.com.

Vehicle removal

If your car is impounded, contact the nearest police station. There are eight car pounds (*préfourrières*) in Paris; to find out where your car might be, contact 01.53.71.53.53, 08.91.01.22.22 or www.prefecture-police-paris.interieur.gouv.fr.

Car hire

To hire a car you must be 25 or over and have held a licence for at least a year. Some agencies accept drivers aged 21-24, but a day fee of €20-€25 is usual. Take your licence and passport. There are often good weekend offers. Weekly deals are better at bigger companies: around €300 a week for a small car with insurance and 1,750km included. Costlier hire companies allow the return of a car in other French cities and abroad. Cheaper ones may have a high charge for damage: read the small print before signing.

Ada
08.25.16.91.69/www.ada.fr.

Avis
08.20.05.05.05/www.avis.fr.

Budget
08.25.00.35.64/www.budget.fr.

Calandres
01.43.06.35.50/www.calandres.com.
Luxury cars are for those who've held a licence for at least five years.

EasyRentacar
www.easycar.com.

Europcar
08.25.82.55.13/www.europcar.fr.

Hertz
01.41.91.95.25/www.hertz.fr.

Rent-a-Car
08.91.70.02.00/www.rentacar.fr

Cycling

Since 1996, the Mairie de Paris has been promoting cycling in the city. There are now 353km (219 miles) of bike lanes. The Itinéraires Paris-Piétons-Vélos-Rollers – scenic strips of the city that are closed to cars on Sundays and holidays – have been consistently multiplied. The city website (www.paris.fr) can provide an up-to-date list of routes and a downloadable map of cycle lanes. A free *Paris à Vélo* map can also be picked up at any Mairie or from bike shops. Cyclists are also entitled to use certain bus lanes (especially the new ones, which are set off by a strip of kerb stones): look out for traffic signs with a bike symbol. If the thought of pedalling around alone in a city known for the verve of its drivers fazes you, consider joining a guided bike tour.

Cycle hire

Note that bike insurance may not cover theft: make sure you check before you sign.

Maison Roue Libre

1 passage Mondétour, 1st (08.10.44.15.34). M° Châtelet. Also Mar-Oct four RATP cyclobuses at Stalingrad, pl du Châtelet, porte d'Auteuil and parc Floral in the Bois de Vincennes (01.48.15.28.88/www.rouelibre.com). **Open** 9am-7pm daily.
Bike hire is €3 an hour, €9 a day, €14 a weekend. Helmets come free. Passport and €150 deposit required.
Other locations: 37 bd Bourdon, 4th (01.44.54.19.29).

Paris-Vélo

2 rue du Fer-à-Moulin, 5th (01.43.37.59.22/www.paris-velo-rent-a-bike.fr). M° Censier-Daubenton. **Open** 10am-7pm daily.
Mountain bikes and 21-speed models for hire. Five hours is €12, a weekend €30. Valid passport and €300 deposit are required.

Resources A-Z

Accident & emergency

Most of the following services operate 24 hours a day. In a medical emergency, you should call the Sapeurs-Pompiers, who have trained paramedics.

Ambulance (SAMU) **15**
Police **17**
Fire (Sapeurs-Pompiers) **18**
Emergency (from a mobile phone) **112**

Credit card loss

In case of credit card loss or theft, call one of the following 24hr services that have English-speaking staff.

American Express
01.47.77.70.00
Diners Club
01.49.06.17.50
MasterCard/Visa
08.36.69.08.80

Customs

Non-EU residents can claim a tax refund or *détaxe* (around 12%) on VAT if they spend over €175 in any one purchase and if they live outside the EU for more than six months in the year. At the shop make sure you ask for a *bordereau de vente à l'exportation.*

Dental emergencies

Look in the *Pages Jaunes* (www.pagesjaunes.fr) under *Dentistes*. For emergencies contact:

Hôpital de la Pitié-Salpêtrière
47-83 bd de l'Hôpital, 13th (01.42.16.00.00). M° Gare d'Austerlitz. **Open** 24hrs.
SOS Dentaire
87 bd Port-Royal, 13th (01.43.37.51.00). M° Les Gobelins/RER Port-Royal.
Urgences Dentaires de Paris
01.42.61.12.00/01.43.37.51.00. **Open** 8am-10pm Sun, hols.

Disabled

General information (in French) is available on the Secrétaire d'Etat aux Personnes Handicapées website: www.handicap.gouv.fr.

Electricity

France uses the standard 220-240V, 50-cycle AC system. Visitors with 240V British appliances need an adapter (*adaptateur*). US 110V appliances need an adapter and a transformer (*transformateur*).

Embassies & consulates

See also the *Pages Jaunes* under 'Ambassades et Consulats'.

Australian Embassy
4 rue Jean-Rey, 15th (01.40.59.33.00/ www.france.embassy.gov.au). M° Bir-Hakeim. **Open** *Consular services* 9.15am-noon, 2-4.30pm Mon-Fri. *Visas* 10am-noon Mon-Fri.
British Embassy
35 rue du Fbg-St-Honoré, 8th (01.44.51.32.81/www.amb-grandebretagne.fr). M° Concorde. Consular services 18bis rue d'Anjou, 8th. M° Concorde. **Open** 9.30am-12.30pm, 2.30-5pm Mon, Wed-Fri; 9.30am-4.30pm Tue. *Visas 16 rue d'Anjou, 8th (01.44.51.33.00).* **Open** 9am-noon Mon-Fri. *By phone* 2.30-5pm Mon-Fri.
British citizens wanting consular services (such as new passports) should ignore the long queue along rue d'Anjou for the visa department and walk straight in at No.18bis.
Canadian Embassy
35 av Montaigne, 8th (01.44.43.29.00/ www.amb-canada.fr). M° Franklin D Roosevelt. Consular

ESSENTIALS

services (01.44.43.29.02). **Open** 9am-noon, 2-4.30pm Mon-Fri. *Visas 37 av Montaigne (01.44.43.29.16).* **Open** 8.30-11am Mon-Fri.

Irish Embassy
12 av Foch, 16th. Consulate 4 rue Rude, 16th (01.44.17.67.00). M° Charles de Gaulle Etoile. **Open** *Consular/visas* 9.30am-noon Mon-Fri. *By phone* 9.30am-1pm, 2.30-5.30pm Mon-Fri.

New Zealand Embassy
7ter rue Léonard-de-Vinci, 16th (01.45.01.43.43/www.nzembassy.com/france). M° Victor Hugo. **Open** *Sept-June* 9am-1pm, 2pm-5.30pm Mon-Thur; 9am-1pm, 2-4pm Fri. *July, Aug* 9am-1pm, 2-4.30pm Mon-Thur; 9am-2pm Fri. *Visas* 9am-12.30pm Mon-Fri. Visas for travel to New Zealand can be applied for on the website www.immigration.govt.nz.

South African Embassy
59 quai d'Orsay, 7th (01.53.59.23.23/www.afriquesud.net). M° Invalides. **Open** *by appointment. By phone* 8.30am-5.15pm Mon-Fri. *Consulate and visas* 9am-noon Mon-Fri.

US Embassy
2 av Gabriel, 8th (01.43.12.22.22/www.amb-usa.fr). M° Concorde. Consulate and visas 2 rue St-Florentin, 1st (01.43.12.22.22). M° Concorde. **Open** *Consular services* 9am-12.30pm, 1-3pm Mon-Fri. *Visas 08.99.70.37.00.*

Internet

More and more public spaces are becoming Wi-Fi hotspots.

Cybor Cube
12 rue Daval, 11th (01 49.29.67.67/www.cybercube.fr). M° Bastille. **Open** 10am-10pm daily.

Milk
31 bd de Sébastopol, 1st (01.40.13.06.51/www.milkinternethall.com). M° Châtelet. **Open** 24 hrs daily.

Opening hours

Standard opening hours for shops are generally 9am/10am-7pm/8pm Mon-Sat. Some close on Mondays, some for lunch (usually between midday-2pm) and some in August.

Pharmacies

All French *pharmacies* sport a green neon cross. If closed, a pharmacy will have a sign indicating the nearest one open. Staff can provide basic medical services like disinfecting and bandaging wounds (for a small fee) and will indicate the nearest doctor on duty. These stay open late:

Dérhy/Pharmacie des Champs-Elysées
84 av des Champs-Elysées, 8th (01.45.62.02.41). M° George V. **Open** 24hrs daily.

Matignon
2 rue Jean-Mermoz, 8th (01.43.59.86.55). M° Franklin D Roosevelt. **Open** 8.30am-2am daily.

Pharmacie Européenne de la Place de Clichy
6 pl de Clichy, 9th (01.48.74.65.18). M° Place de Clichy. **Open** 24hrs daily.

Pharmacie des Halles
10 bd de Sébastopol, 4th (01.42.72.03.23). M° Châtelet. **Open** 9am-midnight Mon-Sat; 9am-10pm Sun.

Police

The French equivalent of 999/911 is **17** (**112** from a mobile), but don't expect a speedy response. If you're assaulted or robbed, report the incident as soon as possible. Make a statement (*procès verbal*) at the *point d'accueil* closest to the crime. To find it, contact the Préfecture Centrale (08.91.01.22.22) or www.prefecture.police.paris.interieur.gouv.fr. You'll need a statement for insurance purposes.

Post

Post offices (*bureaux de poste*) are open 8am-7pm Mon-Fri; 8am-noon Sat. All are listed in the phone book: under *Administration des PTT* in the *Pages Jaunes*; under *Poste* in the *Pages Blanches*. Most post offices have machines (in French and English) that weigh your letter, print out a stamp and give change, saving you from queuing. You can also buy stamps at a tobacconist.

Main Post Office
52 rue du Louvre, 1st (01.40.28.76.00). M° Les Halles or Louvre Rivoli. **Open** 24hrs daily.

Smoking

Smoking is banned in most public spaces. Restaurants are obliged to have a non-smoking area (*espace non-fumeurs*).

Telephones

All French phone numbers have ten digits. Paris and Ile-de-France numbers begin with 01; the rest of France is divided into four zones, 02 to 05. Mobile phone numbers start with 06. Numbers beginning with 08 can only be reached from inside France. The France country code is 33; leave off the first 0 at the start of the ten-digit number. Most public phones use *télécartes* (phonecards). Sold at post offices and tobacconists, they are €7.50 for 50 units and €15 for 120 units.

Tickets

For events tickets, go to a **Fnac** store (www.fnac.com). **Virgin** and **Ticketnet** have created an online ticket office, www.virginmega.fr.

Time

France is one hour ahead of GMT and uses the 24hr system.

Tipping

A service charge of ten to 15% is legally included in your bill at all restaurants, cafés and bars. It's polite to round up the final amount.

Tourist information

Espace du Tourisme d'Ile de France
Carrousel du Louvre, 99 rue de Rivoli, 1st (08.26.16.66.66/www.paris-ile-de-france.com). M° Pyramides. **Open** 8.30am-7pm Mon-Fri.
For Paris and the Ile-de-France.

Maison de la France
20 av de l'Opéra, 1st (01.42.96.70.00/www.franceguide.com). M° Opéra. **Open** 10am-6pm Mon-Fri; 10am-5pm Sat.
The state organisation for tourism in France: information galore.

Office de Tourisme et des Congrès de Paris
Carrousel du Louvre, 99 rue de Rivoli, 1st (08.92.68.30.00/www.parisinfo.com). M° Palais Royal Musée du Louvre. **Open** 9am-7pm daily.
Info on Paris and the suburbs; tickets.
Other locations *Gare de Lyon, 20 bd Diderot, 12th. Gare du Nord, 18 rue de Dunkerque, 10th. Montmartre, 21 pl du Tertre, 18th. Opéra, 11 rue Scribe, 9th. Pyramides, 25 rue des Pyramides, 1st. Tour Eiffel, Champ de Mars, 7th.*

Visas

European Union nationals do not need a visa to enter France, nor do US, Canadian, Australian or New Zealand citizens for stays of up to three months. Nationals of other countries should enquire at the nearest French Consulate before leaving home. If they are travelling to France from one of the countries included in the Schengen agreement (most of the EU, but not Britain or Ireland), the visa from that country should be sufficient.

What's on

Two small publications compete for consumers of Wednesday-to-Tuesday listings information: *L'Officiel des Spectacles* (€0.35) and *Pariscope* (€0.40).

Vocabulary

General expressions

good morning/hello *bonjour*; **good evening** *bonsoir*; **goodbye** *au revoir*; **hi** *salut*; **OK** *d'accord*; **yes** *oui*; **no** *non*; **how are you?** *comment allez-vous?*; **how's it going?** *comment ça va?/ça va?*; **sir/Mr** *monsieur* (M); **madam/Mrs** *madame* (Mme); **miss** *mademoiselle* (Mlle); **please** *s'il vous plaît*; **thank you** *merci*; **thank you very much** *merci beaucoup*; **sorry** *pardon*; **excuse me** *excusez-moi*; **do you speak English?** *parlez-vous anglais?*; **I don't speak French** *je ne parle pas français*; **I don't understand** *je ne comprends pas*; **speak more slowly, please** *parlez plus lentement, s'il vous plaît*; **good** *bon/bonne*; **bad** *mauvais/mauvaise*; **small** *petit/petite*; **big** *grand/grande*; **beautiful** *beau/belle*; **well** *bien*; **badly** *mal*; **a bit** *un peu*; **a lot** *beaucoup*; **very** *très*; **with** *avec*; **without** *sans*; **and** *et*; **or** *ou*; **because** *parce que*; **who?** *qui?*; **when?** *quand?*; **what?** *quoi?*; **which?** *quel?*; **where?** *où?*; **why?** *pourquoi?*; **how?** *comment?*; **at what time?** *à quelle heure?*; **forbidden** *interdit/défendu*; **out of order** *hors service* (HS)/*en panne*; **daily** *tous les jours* (tlj)

Getting around

where is the (nearest) métro? *où est le métro (le plus proche)?*; **when is the next train for...?** *c'est quand le prochain train pour...?*; **ticket** *un billet*; **station** *la gare*; **platform** *le quai*; **entrance** *entrée*; **exit** *sortie*; **left** *gauche*; **right** *droite*; **straight on** *tout droit*; **far** *loin*; **near** *pas loin/près d'ici*; **street map** *le plan*; **bank** *la banque*; **is there a bank near here?** *est-ce qu'il y a une banque près d'ici?*

Accommodation

do you have a room (for this evening/for two people)? *avez-vous une chambre (pour ce soir/pour deux personnes)?*; **full** *complet*; **room** *une chambre*; **bed** *un lit*; **double bed** *un grand lit*; **(a room with) twin beds** (*une chambre à*) *deux lits*; **with bath(room)/shower** *avec* (*salle de*) *bain/douche*; **breakfast** *le petit déjeuner*; **included** *compris*

At the restaurant

I'd like to book a table (for three/at 8pm) *je voudrais réserver une table (pour trois personnes/à vingt heures)*; **lunch** *le déjeuner*; **dinner** *le dîner*; **coffee** (espresso) *un café*; **white coffee** *un café au lait/café crème*; **tea** *du thé*; **wine** *du vin*; **beer** *la bière*; **mineral water** *eau minérale*; **fizzy** *gazeuse*; **still** *plate*; **tap water** *eau du robinet/une carafe d'eau*; **the bill, please** *l'addition, s'il vous plaît*

Numbers

0 *zéro*, **1** *un, une*; **2** *deux*; **3** *trois*; **4** *quatre*; **5** *cinq*; **6** *six*; **7** *sept*; **8** *huit*; **9** *neuf*; **10** *dix*; **11** *onze*; **12** *douze*; **13** *treize*; **14** *quatorze*; **15** *quinze*; **16** *seize*; **17** *dix-sept*; **18** *dix-huit*; **19** *dix-neuf*; **20** *vingt*; **21** *vingt-et-un*; **22** *vingt-deux*; **30** *trente*; **40** *quarante*; **50** *cinquante*; **60** *soixante*; **70** *soixante-dix*; **80** *quatre-vingts*; **90** *quatre-vingt-dix*; **100** *cent*; **1000** *mille*; **1,000,000** *un million*

Index

Sights & Areas

ESSENTIALS

Eating & Drinking

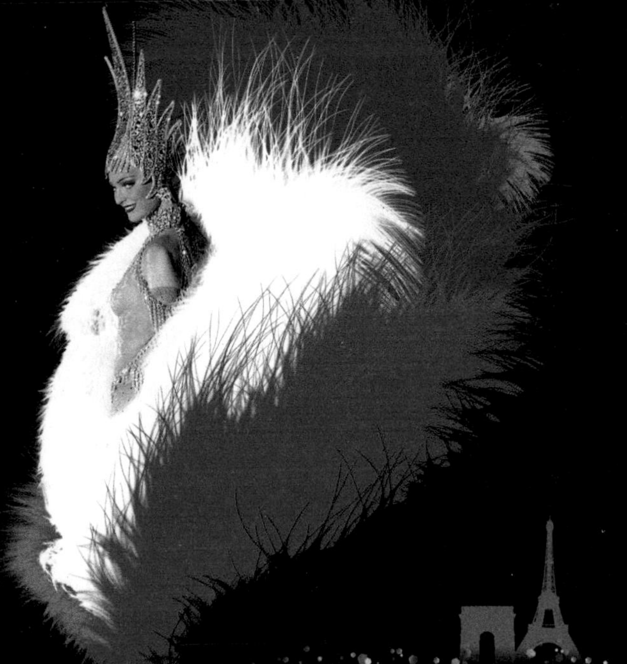